Reminiscing in Swingtime

JAPANESE AMERICANS IN AMERICAN POPULAR MUSIC: 1925-1960

George Yoshida

George Yoshida
Oct. 12, 1997

National Japanese American Historical Society

On the cover: Night Hawks. Sacramento, Calif. 1926. Left to right: Wesley Oyama, Richard Hamada, Clem Oyama, Henry Tanaka, Raymond Okumoto, Richard Okumoto, Smoky Kumamoto, Henry Onishi. Photo courtesy of Mary Fujihara.

Facing page: Nisei Music Makers. Chicago, Ill. 1944. Left to right: Tug Tamaru, George Yoshida, Tad Yamamoto. Roy Uno photo.

Copyright ©1997 National Japanese American Historical Society, Inc.

All rights reserved. No part of this book may be reproduced or utilized in any form or by any means without written permission in writing from the publisher. Inquiries should be addressed to: National Japanese American Historical Society, 1855 Folsom Street, San Francisco, CA 94103-4232 Phone: (415) 431-5007 Fax: (415) 431-0311 E-Mail: njahs@nikkeiheritage.org

The exhibition *Reminiscing in Swingtime, Japanese Americans in American Popular Music,* is funded in part by grants from the San Francisco Art Commission, Cultural Equity Program Fund, and the Civil Liberties Public Education Fund.

Published and distributed by
National Japanese American Historical Society
1855 Folsom Street
San Francisco, CA 94103-4232

Library of Congress Catalog Card Number: 97-69564
Yoshida, George
REMINISCING IN SWINGTIME, Japanese Americans in American Popular Music: 1925-1960
ISBN 1-881506-08-8

Book design: Andrew Fukutome, San Francisco
Editorial consultant: Chiori Santiago
First edition, September 1997
Printed in the United States of America

"You mean Grandpa George played a saxophone in a jazz band? I don't believe it...he's so-o old!"

—MARIAH MASAKO BUSBY, 1997

CONTENTS

* * *

ACKNOWLEDGMENTS • PREFACE • FOREWORD
INTRODUCTION: *It's Later Than We Think*

* * *

CHAPTER 1

THE ORIGINAL JAZZ SYNCOPATORS: *Pre-World War II Dance Bands* 3

THE SEATTLE SCENE 5
Nippon Kan 5 • Nisei Melodians 7 • Mikados of Swing 10

THE SAN FRANCISCO/OAKLAND SCENE 14
Teikoku Band 16 • Willie Ito and Nisei Bands 17 • Oakland Sons and Daughters Orchestra 23

THE SACRAMENTO SCENE 25
Richard's Original Syncopaters Orchestra (sic) 25

THE LOS ANGELES SCENE 30
Japanese Sandmen 30 • Club Harmony 31 • Melodians 31 • Sho Tokyans 34

CHAPTER 2

BATA-KUSAI JAZZ SINGERS: *Nisei Music Makers in Prewar Japan* 41

The Dawn of Jazz in Japan 43 • Claude Lapham 46 • Florida Dance Hall 47
Tekisei Ongaku 50 • Takaji Domoto 52 • Charlie Kikugawa 55 • Fumiko Kawabata 60
Betty Inada 67 • Taft Beppu 79 • Shinichiro Miyagawa 81 • Chizuko Miyagawa 84
Helen Sumida 87 • Raymond "Buckie" Shirakata 89 • Helen Honda 91 • Hisashi Moriyama 92
Tom Oshidari 99 • Sho Tokyans 101 • James Araki 112

CHAPTER 3

OF JIVE BOMBERS AND STARDUSTERS: *Dance Bands in "Assembly" Centers & Detention Camps* 119

"Buddhahead Blues" 120 • Santa Anita "Assembly" Center—Starlight Serenaders 129
Poston Detention Camp #1—Music Makers 131 • Poston Detention Camp #2—Camp #2 Band 137
Poston Detention Camp #3—Rhythmaires 140 • Minidoka Detention Camp—Harmonaires 142
Gila River Detention Camp, Canal Camp—Starlight Serenaders 143 • Gila River Detention Camp, Butte Camp—Music Makers 144 • Rohwer Detention Camp 148 • Jerome Detention Camp—Densoneers 149
Pomona "Assembly" Center—Pomonans 152 • Heart Mountain Detention Camp—George Igawa Orchestra 152 • Manzanar Detention Camp—Jive Bombers 163 • Merced "Assembly" Center—Stardusters 168 • Amache Detention Camp—Music Makers 170 • Tule Lake Detention Camp—Starlighters and Down Beats 174 • Tanforan "Assembly" Center—Tanforan Tooters 180
Topaz Detention Camp—Topaz Tooters 183, Jivesters 183, Savoy Four 186, Rhythm Kings 187

CHAPTER 4

GOIN' TO CHICAGO BLUES: *From War to Peacetime* 191

The Chicago Magnet 194 • Nisei Music Makers 199 • Hideo Kawano 203
Eager Beavers 205 • James Araki 207 • Paul Higaki 209 • Susumu Takao 221
Yoshio Tomita 223 • Harry Kitano 225 • Tadashi Yamamoto 229

CHAPTER 5

ESTABLISHING NEW ROOTS: *Postwar Music* 235

Paul Togawa 238 • George Takamoto 241 • Tetsu Bessho 243 • Sue Takimoto Okabe 245
Ethel Azama 248 • Elsie Itashiki 250 • Goro Suzuki 254 • Pat Suzuki 257

CHAPTER 6

REFLECTIONS ON THE BEAT: *Philosophical Statements* 267

George Yamasaki 269 • Kazu Maruoka 270 • Some Personal Statements 273 • A Pilgrimage to Topaz 280

* * *

NISEI DANCE BANDS AND BAND PERSONNEL 284
GLOSSARY 288 • INDEX 290 • SPONSORS 299

* * *

ACKNOWLEDGMENTS

Creating good prose is an art that requires a talent capable of selecting appropriate words and arranging them in a meaningful and aesthetically pleasing manner. It's very much like a masterful jazz soloist choosing just the right notes in an innovative, logical sequence to blow an exciting chorus of "Body and Soul." And when one doesn't have it to conceptualize and create reasonably well, and knows it, he seeks help. And so it is that I offer a cordial "thank-you" to a number of persons who graciously assisted in refining this document to be more accessible, easier to read, easier to understand:

Helen Yoshida, perceptive spouse/critic, accomplished the major clearing of clutter—removing a mess of superfluous words and untangling hopelessly tangled syntax.

Rosalyn Tonai, resourceful Executive Director of the National Japanese American Historical Society, actively and continuously supported my effort to record the fascinating story of Nisei music makers.

Chiori Santiago, (my) former sixth-grade pupil and now (my) turnabout teacher, injected logic, proper pacing and sequencing, and neat phrases which added spice to render this work palatable.

Mas Mambo, hip expatriate journalist/musician of Tokyo, provided precious Nisei jazz history notes—enriching this edition with rare stories of the past.

Richard Hadlock, compassionate teacher, melodic saxophonist and knowledgeable historian, added integrity to this project and bolstered my sagging confidence in the worth of this book.

Jin Konomi, ninety-four years young, produced artful, concise translations of impossible nuances in Japanese into proper English.

Finally, I plead guilty to the charge of "invasion of privacy" of my son Clay's household—wife Lynn, children Alan and Lane. My almost daily intrusion for four continuous years into the sanctity of their home—"cutting 'n' pasting" on their MacApple—must have been disconcerting at times. (All families need space to scream and holler.) But they made me feel welcome in their presence, always. For that I am truly grateful.

I treasure the many, many thoughtful interchanges of letters and phone calls with newly-discovered friends. The pleasure of connecting with good people I had not previously known was an unexpected dividend. I thank them for their kindness and support.

George Yoshida, 1997

PREFACE

This brief look into the parade of Nisei who played and sang popular American music for their own joy and for the pleasure of others has been a trip—an intense, enjoyable experience. There are many unnamed others who were equally a part of this special group of second-generation Japanese Americans. Nevertheless, I feel that the musicians included herein portray a representative group of pioneers in popular American music. Their anecdotes and stories are priceless. They provided the essential substance to make this account credible, entertaining and meaningful. I acknowledge their goodwill and the goodwill of others who assisted and encouraged me to gather and to record these remembrances of the past.

Furthermore, this document is a collection of accounts of individuals in a communal gathering—an expression through music of hope and joy in life. There is no intricate plot in these stories; no extended complications, no long-term problem-solving. For the great majority of the characters in this tale, making music was a finite experience in the totality of our life spans. The demands to "get on" in life were great, and music, despite its rewards, was not a stable, reliable source of material sustenance. We made our living doing other things, relegating the music to a smaller role in our lives. Perhaps, just because our experience in music was so brief, yet so memorable, it has grown in significance as the years have passed—rare objects attain great value over time. For the spiritual uplift in music; for that short period of creative output; and for just the pure enjoyment of it all, we Nisei music makers are thankful.

El Cerrito, California, 1997

FOREWORD

The National Japanese American Historical Society is proud to present this publication and the accompanying exhibition *Reminiscing in Swingtime, Japanese Americans in American Popular Music: 1925 to 1960*. These works memorialize the participation and contributions of Japanese Americans to the American music scene. In this examination of individuality and culture, we are pleased to honor the rarely acknowledged professional Nikkei musicians and make mention of the variety of amateur music enthusiasts.

The Nikkei Music History Project, under the direction of George Yoshida since 1991, was established to explore the diverse musical legacy passed on from the immigrant experience to the acculturation of the second generation. Their creative expressions bring to light the historical and social forces of the time.

Amid the desolation of camp life, Japanese Americans found hope in their own musical expressions behind barbed wire. Dance bands proliferated during the wartime incarceration of Japanese Americans. Performing the popular dance music of the era—the music of Tommy Dorsey, Duke Ellington, and Glen Miller—this flowering of expression behind barbed wire was a matter of survival for many; it was a natural movement in the acculturation of the Nisei—an affirmation of their identity as American youth.

The book and traveling exhibition embody the duality of forces influencing young Niseis at the time—to embrace their infatuation with popular American music, while struggling with the cultural expectations and their rooted Japanese heritage.

We thank George and all of you who have aided in our efforts to tell this important aspect of our cultural history.

Rosalyn Tonai
Executive Director
National Japanese American Historical Society

Not so long ago—say fifty years back—one could collect and keep all the important jazz books in a single orange crate. Today that crate might not accommodate just the books written about Louis Armstrong! It would seem that everything in jazz worth reporting must have been mined, refined and redefined by now.

Not quite so.

George Yoshida has brought forth a fascinating tale of American jazz and swing players whose lives remained unknown to most jazz fans and historians for the greater part of this century. In telling their stories this book teaches us valuable lessons in American history, as well as jazz history—lessons heretofore ignored in our textbooks.

Japanese Americans in California and elsewhere often dealt with the trauma and anger of World War II internment by attempting to push the experience right out of their memories. But the silent years have ended and George Yoshida, using his well-focused recollections of the '30s and '40s along with his gentle interviewing skills, sets the facts before us. The great photographs, nearly all reproduced for the first time, would themselves have made this an engaging, educational, very special book.

Reminiscing in Swingtime is clearly a work of one man's love for and dedication to his subjects. With its publication the author honors his many friends and colleagues (quite a few of them no longer living) who deserve wider recognition. He also honors the American music which has inspired all these singers and players since the '20s. We cannot fail to be touched by the faith in jazz and swing which bound all these performers to one another.

After reading these interviews, one can reasonably believe that big-band swing, jazz, dance and popular song played a vital role in the determination of an abused people to survive and thrive, in and out of the wartime detention camps.

It has been my pleasure to know George Yoshida as friend, neighbor, teacher, musician and historian for some thirty years. With this work he has gone well beyond local history to make a lasting, significant contribution to the annals of jazz and to the ongoing story of the Japanese American presence in America.

Thank you, George.

Richard B. Hadlock
Jazz writer, musician, host of *Annals of Jazz,* KCSM-FM
Berkeley, California, July 1997

INTRODUCTION

It's Later Than We Think

Miles is gone, Sarah is gone, Dizzy left us not too long ago. Charlie and Tamotsu split just last month. You're hip, you don't need surnames to know which Miles and Sarah and Dizzy I'm talking about; but Charlie and Tamotsu? They're the Kikugawa brothers who years ago worked their dad's Chinese restaurant on Post Street in the heart of Li'l Osaka, San Francisco's Japantown. Charlie and Tamotsu loved music; so much that Charlie gave up on the local scene and hopped a steamship in 1930 to play his traps in Japan. He never looked back.

    Charlie and Tamotsu were just two of the extraordinary Japanese American musicians I discovered in the course of researching for this book. The annals of jazz are filled with tales of great musicians, but "Orientals" blowing Herman, Dorsey and Basie? Yes, the Nisei, American-born children of Japanese immigrants, were born—not many of them, but enough—with *swing* in their bones. Theirs is a story of rare creative energy and high motivation.

    I wouldn't have learned of them if a couple of young cats, Mark Izu and Ken Yamada, had not come over to the house to interview me about my experiences as a member of the dance band in Poston, Arizona—one of ten detention camps for Japanese Americans forcibly removed from the West Coast during the onset of World War II. Most of their peers know little, if anything, about Nisei involvement in American music. They may be familiar with Hiroshima, the successful Japanese American fusion group, and assume it was the first to play popular music back in the 1970s. They'd be wrong. Their moms and dads made the scene years ago, playing jazz when it was a dirty word.

As much as my faulty memory would allow, I described to Mark and Ken the tedious routine of life in Poston and what music meant to me—first as a boy growing up in Seattle's Japanese American ghetto, and later as a jazz hipster stuck in a desert detention camp. Spurred by their intense interest in my musical past, I became curious about other camp dance bands and then about older Nisei who may have been engaged in popular American music.

At first, I thought that digging into the past would yield only meager information. To my surprise and delight, as I searched into the era of the Roaring '20s and the deep depression days of the '30s, a veritable treasure chest of precious stones was uncovered. Charlie and Tamotsu were two of the brighter ones. Unfortunately, both of them "marched in with the Saints" in 1993, but I can picture them wailin' happily on their traps all the way.

The point is that the primary sources for my investigation are rapidly disappearing. People who were an active part of the early music scene are gone or have become extremely debilitated. Pensively they repeat, "I just don't remember…it was such a long time ago." I feel now an urgency to put down on paper a bit of Nisei music history so that future generations will be informed, will acknowledge and, I hope, will admire the creative energy, irrepressible vitality and the spirituality of a relatively small cohort of sons and daughters of Japanese immigrants who experienced the joys of making popular American music—call it pop, swing or jazz.

George Yoshida

Rosebud Orchestra. San Francisco. 1927. Left to right: Willie Ito, Paul Kato, Charlie Kikugawa, Yuki Morikawa Saka, Henry Ishihara, George Mukai. Photo courtesy of Mari Kikugawa.

CHAPTER 1

The Original Jazz Syncopators

PRE-WORLD WAR II DANCE BANDS

"We all wanted to be blond and blue-eyed Americans, hated to be Japanese. We changed our Japanese names into American names. Were criticized for our short hairdos, but didn't care. Went to movies, were crazy about Clara Bow and Joan Crawford! Loved jazz...Red Nichols and the Five Pennies, Paul Whiteman 'The King of Jazz,' and clarinet-playing Ted Lewis, loved the vocals of Connie Boswell and Ruth Etting."

—LILY OYAMA SASAKI, SACRAMENTO, 1930

THE SEATTLE SCENE

NIPPON KAN (Japan Hall)

Back in 1932 in Seattle, I often walked to **Nippon Kan** with my mother to attend a concert of classical American music or to enjoy a Japanese movie—the kind in which a lone super-samurai with his razor-sharp sword knocks off a dozen clumsy, ugly baddies. We would leave our old flat on 12th and Main Street, walk uphill on the boardwalk on dusty, unpaved Main Street, past the old Buddhist Church with its ancient bent-cross logo adorning its entry and cross over to Washington Street with its row of whorehouses.

"Mama, what do they do in those places with women tapping on the windows?"

"Oh, they just drink and play cards," Mom would answer. My prepubescent innocence and curiosity thus satisfied, we'd walk a few more blocks, enter the noisy Nippon Kan and become one with the anxiously waiting audience.

I cite Nippon Kan because for three decades it was the center of educational and entertaining stage offerings for the prewar Japanese American community—truly a cultural cornerstone. The Issei sponsored scholarly lectures and political debates; Japanese plays; variety shows featuring traditional dance, music, and comedy; and pre-talkie Japanese movies with live *benshi* (narrators). In 1931 a scribe for The *Japanese American Courier* philosophized: "Nippon Kan may appear shabby in comparison to the modern beauty of the [Seattle] Civic Auditorium, yet it has served its purpose and will continue its usefulness until it gives way to a new building. To 'Little Tokyo,' Nippon Kan is a Carnegie Hall, but it has more value in that it has surrounding it at the present hour, tradition."

In time the children of the Issei matured and a new generation, the Nisei, added fresh color and variety to the Nippon Kan stage. To illustrate the vitality and diversity of this latter group, the following was excerpted from the January 1, 1931, *Japanese American Courier*:

> *Kelly Yamada—Although he is principally a saxophone player, many will remember his appearance as Little Eva, the peroxide blonde, in the Japanese Students Club entertainment not so long ago. Kelly shares the saxophone realm with George Okada, Shungi Kashiwagi, Hito Okada, Tad Yonago and Bill Mimbu, but Kelly's sax is perhaps the best known in this list of Nipponese Rudy Vallees.*

> *DAVE YAMAKA*—Appearing in "Loose Nuts" and "Musical Comedy," Dave is the first third of the Dave-Art-Welly [Shibata] vaudeville combination. He also sings solo parts in cantatas and plays the musical saw.
> *FUMIKO MORITA*—Excelling in both music and scholarship, Fumiko is a valedictorian as well as a good violinist. Recently she has been appearing quite frequently on Nisei programs and is usually accompanied by her sister Michiko, who plays the piano well.
> *KATSUMI NAKAYAMA*—Possessing a decided flair for burlesque, Kats has caused many an explosion of laughs through his comical stage cutups. His appearance as the aging waiter in the Buddhist entertainment and as the samurai in the Kengeki skit were among the highlights of the 1930 vaudeville year.
> *YURINO TAKAYOSHI*—It is said that Yurino, "the Ruth Chatterton of the Japanese Community," has never seen an entire Nippon Kan entertainment from before the footlights, since she is usually in them. She is very popular and effective as the heroine in Japanese tragedies and likes personally to enact these tragic roles that make people cry and cry and cry.
> *TOMEU TAKAYOSHI*—The community's golden-throated jazz singer needs no introduction and his popularity grows with each and every appearance. Last year Tomeu divided his singing time between Nippon Kan programs, downtown luncheons and weddings. He is usually accompanied by his sister Kimi, whose piano playing is a marvel.
> *MARY TAKAYOSHI*—Blues singer par excellence is this song-and-dance artist who appears with her brother Taiji in many of the bright skits which enliven community programs. She's the youngest of the T.T.T.'s (the Takahashi siblings).[1]

Nippon Kan deserves a biography of its own. The hall was built in 1909 by a Japanese investment company, then sold to Masajiro Furuya, a prominent Issei Seattle banker who became bankrupt during the depression in 1932. Nippon Kan reverted to its creditors who in turn contracted with the Tanaka family to manage the hall. The operation continued under their direction until the spring of 1942, when, after the Japanese attack on Pearl Harbor, the entire Seattle Japanese American community was forcibly interned by Executive Decree in the Puyallup Fair Grounds Assembly Center.

Due to the wholesale evacuation of the community, the neglected hall fell into shameful disrepair. In 1969, Ed and Betty Burke purchased the old cultural center and struggled to revive it over the next twelve years. Thanks to their tenacity and vision, and despite the apathy of both the Japanese American community and the city of Seattle in the postwar years, Nippon Kan was reborn in 1981. Today the hall is a beautifully restored site for stage performances and is available for rental use by the general public.

"The true owners of the hall, however, have always been [the Japanese community]," wrote the Burkes in 1983, "for the users of the hall are the ones who were and are the lifeblood of the theater. Their activities constitute the true history of the Nippon Kan."

THE NISEI MELODIANS

Churches, both Buddhist and Christian, were influential institutions in Japanese communities before World War II. In addition to religious instruction, churches provided opportunities for the socialization of the Nisei who were growing up in Japanese American ghettos isolated from the mainstream society. These churches were centers of assorted secular activities for immigrant parents and their American-born children. Japanese, the primary language of preschoolers, was gradually transformed into standard English; and their behavior, often to the distress of their elders, evolved into a freer, less disciplined lifestyle.

Some elders tolerated the youngsters' fascination with American ways, including that thing called swing, and Nisei musician **Kiyoshi Tomita**, born in 1910, credits Issei **Shisui Miyashita** as an influence behind the formation of the Nisei Melodians, a dance band organized in 1926 by a group of teenage members of the Seattle Japanese Baptist Church. Tomita was one of those teenagers.

Miyashita, an accomplished musician with credentials in music education, owned a modest music store on Jackson Street between Fifth and Sixth Avenues. He sold instruments, sheet music and gave lessons; Tomita bought his horn from Miyashita and was also an occasional pupil. At a 1936 Nippon Kan performance, Miyashita, dressed in a fine set of formal tails, conducted a sizable orchestra made up of members of the Seattle Symphony and led a choir of local Japanese voices. Miyashita also organized a young Issei band which played traditional band music, not jazz, at Kokugo Gakko (Japanese Language School) summer picnics.

Eventually, Miyashita gave up his unprofitable shop and opened a smallish recreation hall above some shops located at Broadway and Yesler Way. The room had a minimal stage, a pool table, and space for playing *shogi* (Japanese chess) and *go*, a game played with white and black markers on a checkered board. Said Tomita: "We didn't have much to do, so it became a hangout for us high school guys. Girls carefully avoided the place. Although Mr. Miyashita's musical preference was classical, he encouraged us to play our horns and to rehearse up there. We were the nucleus of the future Nisei Melodians.

"Although we were a bunch of amateurs, we had fun. We played for Nisei dances at the Collins Field House, the Queen Anne Field House and the Olympic Hotel. I remember playing tunes like 'Collegiate' and 'Sometime'…mostly fox-trots and waltzes, no dixieland. We didn't have band uniforms…wore white shirts with ties. Other than dances, we played several times for talent shows at Nippon Kan and even played for a Japanese Consulate-sponsored breakfast club function on a President Lines ship tied up at the waterfront pier."

Among others congregating in Miyashita's rec hall was **Kelly K. Yamada**, who was born in Seattle in 1911. His father operated a hardware store on Jackson Street between Maynard and Seventh Avenue. According to Yamada: "Kenny Heath, a wholesale salesman who serviced my father's store, played the saxophone. Somehow, I began taking sax lessons from him; he used to come every Saturday. I was eleven years old then. I took lessons for two years and eventually ended up playing in the Broadway High School orchestra (the first such orchestra at Broadway High). Outside of school I recall playing solos on my alto for worship services at the Baptist Church.

"In 1926 when I was fifteen years old, we formed the Nisei Melodians. We rehearsed at Sam Amano's house; they had a large room and a piano. Taft Beppu was the nominal leader…[he] waved the baton and also sang a bit. Tomé Takayoshi sang also; he had a good baritone voice. We bought stock arrangements—'My Blue Heaven,' 'St. Louis Blues,' 'Me and My Shadow'—and closed dances with 'Goodnight Sweetheart.' I really got excited when we picked up 'Alexander's Ragtime Band'—it had a nice swing to it! Incidentally, the other guys in the sax section made me play lead alto because I couldn't follow very well. We played only Nisei dances—many of them at the social hall located in the Rainier Heat and Light Building at Maynard and Jackson Streets. It was just a small place…held about fifteen or twenty couples. We didn't get paid for playing; we were glad just to have an audience."

Yamada stayed with the band for five years until 1931, when he was forced to drop out of the University of Washington, where he was studying aeronautical engineering. The Furuya Bank, which held his savings account, became insolvent and Yamada was unable to pay tuition fees. He reluctantly joined the U.S. Coast and Geodetic Survey Service and spent two years aboard ship as a captain's boy.

Fred "Mac" Kaneko, born in 1911, was another member of the gang of young Nisei who grew up in the Seattle Japanese Baptist Church. "There was a bunch of guys who hung out at the church. I remember we were all very close," he recalled. "We played basketball and all. One day someone, it might have been Taft Beppu, who was the chief instigator, decided to organize a dance band. I guess we were all sixteen or seventeen years old; most of us went to Broadway High. Someone asked me if I would like to join them; said they needed a trombone. I said to myself, 'Why not?' I hadn't played an instrument before, but thought I'd give it a shot. I asked my ol' man for a trombone, and he bought me one without hesitation."

Minoru Tsubota, a latecomer to the Melodians, joined the band around 1935. He was born in 1918 and grew up in Kent, a rural, berry-growing, truck-farming region in White River Valley between Seattle and Tacoma. Said Tsubota: "My father and mother both enjoyed Japanese music—*shamisen, odori* and *shibai* music. When I was around thirteen, my brother bought me a clarinet from one of the members of the disbanded White River Buddhist Church band, and I started playing in the Kent Junior High School band in 1933. The leader of the Melodians then was Albert Masuda of Ellensburg, Washington; he must have played the trumpet. Other members of the band were Shizuko Takakoshi Hoshide, piano; Shang Kashiwagi and Porgie Okada, saxes; Hats Takahashi, banjo; and Johnny Walker, a black drummer. I played the clarinet and tenor [saxophone]...wasn't much of a musician, but playing music with my friends was a great joy."

Tsubota remembered playing for Nisei dances at Washington Hall on Twelfth and Yesler Way: "Many of those dances were called 'taxi dances'; that is, the guys had to buy individual tickets for each dance. I suppose the sponsoring clubs made more money that way. The University Club (University of Washington), the JACL (Japanese American Citizens League), and church groups put on these dances; they also sponsored picnic dances at Lake Wilderness and Shadow Lake in the Kent-Auburn region. They were fun, too. Because I lived in Kent and had to drive into Seattle, I got a couple of dollars for gas money (gas was cheap then...ten or fifteen cents a gallon). I liked to dance. Since I was the youngest, fifteen or sixteen, the guys in the band would give me a break by letting me dance just one number before and one after the intermission."

Tsubota was drafted into the army in 1941 and was assigned to the 160th Regimental Band of the 40th Infantry Division at San Luis Obispo, California. The band consisted mostly of professional Los Angeles studio musicians who had joined the National Guard to avoid early conscription but were, to their dismay, activated sooner than they had expected. "Although my playing was way below the capabilities of the others, I enjoyed the experience very much," said Tsubota. He was later transferred to Camp Shelby, Mississippi, to become a member of the training cadre for the newly organized Japanese American 442nd Regimental Combat Team. About this time Tsubota sold his tenor sax and that spelled the end of his playing dance band music.

Other Nisei Melodians haven't played their instruments since World War II, but they continue to listen to "old time" jazz. Fred Kaneko reminisces about the days when Al Jolson was popular and the fox-trot was the dance of choice at the social hall over Arizumi's drug store on Yesler Way and Broadway. "Those were some very enjoyable times," he said. "I played the trombone also in the Broadway High School band for a while, but my career in music was short-lived. I never again picked up my trombone after the Nisei Melodians broke up."

Kelley Yamada admits: "Haven't touched my horn at all these past years…gosh, that was sixty-eight years ago! I still have my old sax…intended to resume playing in my retirement, but haven't picked up my horn. All the pads are dried out and cracked. Oh well, I had a great time playing with the Melodians."

THE MIKADOS OF SWING

"Seattle's Touring Mikados of Swing a Hit in California"
"Californians Wild About the Mikados; Members of the Northwest Nisei Jazz Band Widely Feted"
"Miks—One of the Finest Said California Writer"
"Seattle Band Scores Big Hit in San Jose"[2]

On June 12, 1941, fifteen high school youths carefully loaded five cars with instruments, uniforms and equipment. The **Mikados of Swing** of Seattle, on an adrenaline high, embarked on a grand barnstorming tour of eight cities in Oregon and California.

They'd started out as a kazoo band of eight boys who hummed tunes into simple toy instruments; they enjoyed mimicking the sounds of big bands. They graduated to playing standard instruments in a marching band organized by Mrs. Tajitsu of the Japanese Language School. They ignored Mrs. Tajitsu's strict orders to refrain from playing dance music and bought stock arrangements of current pop tunes—"In The Mood," "I'll Walk Alone," "Tuxedo Junction." A clunk of a piano was found for ten dollars, and rehearsals were held in a back room of the Owaki Bakery.

Koichi Hayashi Band, a.k.a. Mikados of Swing. Seattle. February 1940. Left to right, front row: Katsuro Yamamoto, Kaoru Kitayama, George Ogata, Satoshi Shiota, Art Hayashi, Yoshio Tomita. Back row: Joe Owaki, Teruo Kumagai, Masao Tomita, Henry Suzuki, Roy Yoshitomi. Photo courtesy of Yoshio Tomita.

A scribe for a Seattle Japanese American paper wrote in 1941:

'Twas an eventful night (ca. 1939) when Koichi Hayashi herded together a few saxes, trumpets, a drum and incidentally a few strong-lunged aspirants for a jam session in the then dingy basement of the old Buddhist Church. The corny, oft flat notes that prevailed through the winter night must have made the passersby shake their heads and frown. Practice, practice, and more practice. They offered their services to clubs and organizations for nothing. But the reception…it was almost heart-breaking. Talks of disbanding and giving up started, but the daydream that inspired the band persisted and practice, practice, and more practice was the agenda.

"During one of those early dances, a few in the crowd hissed and booed after a certain number," Koichi Hayashi remembered. "I went home disappointed and hurt." Dismayed but

J.A.F.L.
ANNUAL
Strawberry
Frolic

**Friday
June 13**
9:30 p. m. to 12:30

Koichi Hayashi's
**MIKADOS
of
SWING**

Ruby Stock Farm
GRESHAM, ORE.

Men 45¢

Dance ticket. 1941. Courtesy of Yoshio Tomita.

determined, the Mikados persevered. Then, in 1940 Tad Hirota of Oakland attended a Buddhist Church conference in Seattle and chanced to hear the Miks. Hirota was impressed. He conceived a California tour for the young musicians; the Young Buddhists Associations (YBA) of the respective cities would serve as hosts. The Mikados were scheduled to play for YBA dances in Gresham, Oregon, on June 13; Sacramento, California, on June 17; San Jose on June 20; San Francisco on June 22; Oakland on June 24; Santa Maria on June 27; Los Angeles on June 28; Fresno on June 29; then home to Seattle.

The "Mikados of Swing Send-off Dance" on June 7, 1941, the group's final appearance in Seattle before their departure on their California tour, was the occasion for **Florence "Chickie" Ishihara White's** début as a big band vocalist. The local Japanese American press covered the dance held in the Marine View Ballroom of the Seattle Chamber of Commerce Building with a story headlined, *TWO NISEI GIRLS TO SING WITH MIKADOS OF SWING:*

Singing with the Miks tonight will be Dorothy Nakamura, Seattle's talented and well-known songstress. Already familiar to Northwest Niseidom, her singing and lovely personality has won wide praise and attention. Songstress No. 2 is one of the most promising of Northwest singers—a thirteen-year-old miss, who, according to the orchestra's press agents, will positively "wow" the audience tonight.

Chickie was the thirteen-year-old miss. "Koichi Hayashi, the Miks' leader, offered me the chance to sing with the band," she remembered. "I accepted with some uncertainty—I wanted to sing, and yet I didn't. Being inexperienced, I was excited and terribly nervous at first. But after a bit, I began to get the feel of it. I sang 'My Sister and I' and 'These Are The Things I Love.' I probably should have sung one up-tempo tune. Well, anyway, I became convinced that I wanted to sing more and more. During this time, I took advantage of every opportunity to see movie musicals and especially vaudeville shows. As I watched, I imagined myself performing."

On June 24, Davis Hirahara, the Mikados' business manager, reported from Oakland:

"They scored their most decisive and major hit in 'Frisco Sunday night when they played before a capacity crowd. The boys on newspaper row were down to size up the kids. Pictures were taken right and left and the applause after every number was terrific. The kids were right in the groove and gave everything they had."

In a 1992 interview, Art Hayashi, former leader of the Mikados, described three incidents of the San Francisco dance. Carrying their instruments, band members arrived at the local Buddhist Church hall to find not only the arriving dance crowd, but also aggressive pickets from the Local #6 Musicians Union waving printed signs: "Don't Patronize Non-union Musicians!" To avoid a confrontation, the Mikados surreptitiously entered the church through the rear entrance. The dance proceeded without interruption.

Later that evening during an intermission, a Nisei teenager, carrying an instrument case, approached Hayashi. "Can I play trombone with you guys?" Never having experienced such a bold and direct request, and not having any idea as to the musical ability of this stranger, Hayashi, somewhat unnerved, replied with trepidation, "Well, why don't you take the Second Trombone chair?" The fifteen-year-old

"On the Road." Sacramento, Calif. 1941. Top to bottom, left to right: Kaoru Kitayama; Kaz Shitama; Joe Owaki, T.R. Goto, Yoichi Ito; George Ogata, Tosh Hori, Roy Yoshitomi, Sat Shiota, Masao Tomita; Teruo Kumagai. Photo courtesy of Yoshio Tomita.

youngster was **Paul Higaki**. Hayashi soon discovered he was good enough to take over the First Trombone chair. Paul pressured first Hayashi and then Paul's parents for permission to join the band for the balance of the tour. Hayashi assured Higaki's parents that he would take full responsibility for the welfare of the lad. Eight years later in 1949, their paths crossed again in Chicago. Higaki had moved on and up; he was the featured trombone soloist in Lionel Hampton's fabulous swing band!

Earlier on the day of the dance, Tad Hirota, the impresario who arranged the California performances, spoke to Hayashi about a singer from Oakland: "A friend of mine…can you use her?" Again, the bandleader had to make an instant decision in response to an unknown factor. He did not want to offend Hirota; he reluctantly agreed. The young vocalist was **Yasuko Tani**. To Hayashi's surprise and pleasure, Yasuko Tani sang in good voice and with style.

Yasuko Tani vividly remembered her début as a vocalist for the Mikados. She was twenty years old and a student at the University of California, Berkeley. As a youngster, Yasuko Tani had extensive experience in song and dance with Aunt Elise's Kiddies, a children's performance group sponsored by the *Oakland Tribune*. She later sang in elaborately staged musicals produced in the 1930s by members of the Oakland Methodist Episcopal Church and in Oakland Buddhist Church talent revues. Yasuko Tani was "thrilled and felt honored" to sing with the highly acclaimed dance band from Seattle. Heady with anticipation, she hurried out to purchase a gown for the special occasion. Tani recalls: "It was a beautiful white lace dress with a chiffon skirt. I think I rehearsed once with the band…sang 'Smoke Gets In Your Eyes', 'I'm In The Mood For Love', 'Deep Purple', and others. It was such a joy that night. I'll always remember it!"

The Mikados of Swing made their mark as the "Toast of the West Coast" and returned triumphantly to Seattle only to be confronted by an event that dramatically changed their lives—*Pearl Harbor!*

THE SAN FRANCISCO/OAKLAND SCENE

Before World War II, residents of Li'l Osaka, San Francisco's Japantown, enjoyed remarkable ethnic solidarity. They existed on an isolated island in a white ocean; theirs was a tiny plot inhabited by secure, neighborly folks communicating in polyglot English and Japanese. It was a time when congenial groups of young Americans with Asian faces walked to Japanese language schools after dismissal from "American school." Forced by their elders to learn how to read and

Teikoku Band. San Francisco. ca. 1915. Photo courtesy of Michi Kobi.

write strange characters, they'd complain: *"What a waste of time!"*

But there were compensations. Children eagerly anticipated school picnics in the summertime when the Red Team challenged the White Team to exciting relay races. They could hardly wait to gorge themselves on the picnic spread prepared lovingly by their patient mothers. When it was time for lunch, hungry kids unashamedly speared tasty teriyaki chicken legs and grabbed delicious rice balls with bits of sour red plum in the center and encased in sheets of toasted seaweed. With occasional bites of smelly, but oh-so-sweet, pickled *daikon* radish in its yellow splendor, life held no greater joy. All of this heavenly food would be washed down happily with ice-cold orange soda, its metal cap still intact, but with a tiny hole punctured with an ice pick—the luscious, fizzy liquid would last just a bit longer. It was a time of pleasurable innocence for Nisei children, insulated from the suspicious stares of the outside world.

THE TEIKOKU BAND

The **Teikoku Band** was one of the earliest to perform at community functions in San Francisco, but its origin, ca. 1915, remains a mystery. Michi Kobi of New York City is in possession of an original photograph of the band, given to her by an already aged Henry Kusama, who played the baritone horn in the ensemble. Unfortunately, Kusama could not remember the names of his fellow musicians, how frequently or where they played or where they had dispersed.

Kono Takeuchi. 1931. Photo courtesy of Frank Sotelo.

Members of the Teikoku Band were Issei, first-generation immigrants from Japan. Since the instrumentation of this band was basically brass and woodwinds and lacked strings, they must have played semiclassical and popular Western music: waltzes, marches and popular songs. It is highly probable that Japanese music was also in their repertoire. The Teikoku Band was not a dance band; nevertheless, its existence is of historical significance in that it was a forerunner of future Nisei dance bands—a role model for youngsters.

KONO TAKEUCHI, A.K.A. KONO-SAN

Active for several years in vaudeville in the late 1920s and into the '30s, **Kono Takeuchi**, a Nisei known onstage as "Kono-san," may have been the first professional Japanese American blues singer. It is purported that Sophie Tucker, the "Last of the Red Hot Mamas," and Kono-san were on friendly terms and that Tucker had taken Kono-san under her wing early in the latter's career. Promoted by a New York City booking agent, Kono-san traveled extensively throughout the States performing on the RKO stage circuit and also as a member of the Fanchon and Marco Troupe. Dressed in a kimono, playing a *shamisen,* a stringed instrument, she opened her vaudeville act singing a few Japanese tunes. This was followed by an almost instantaneous change—flinging off her kimono, now appearing in a glittering evening gown, she would break into a raucous rendition of "My Japanese Mama." The contrast must have been a dramatic shock and a great hit with American audiences. Kono Takeuchi was born in San Francisco and died in New York City.

Willie Ito. San Francisco. 1927. Photo courtesy of Nancy Takeshita.

WILLIE ITO

Within the confines of Li'l Osaka were Nisei who had become infatuated with the sounds of jazz. **Willie Ito, Sr.** was one. He was born in Hawaii, taken to Japan at an early age and returned to the U.S. mainland when he was thirteen years old. Old-timers described him as "a character"—energetic, highly motivated, a smooth ballroom dancer, a dapper dresser, a debonair fellow with a keen business sense. He was a clever craftsman. "He could do anything!" said Roy Abbey, a San Francisco friend.

Prior to World War II, he operated Willy's Sweet Shop at 1601 Post Street in Li'l Osaka, a modest soda fountain where one could order a tasty tuna sandwich and a cold chocolate shake. Willie was an excellent saxophone and clarinet player, a factor that attracted a crowd of Nisei musicians to Willy's place. The other bit of honey that drew Li'l Osaka habitués to the Sweet Shop was the back-room scene where *shi-go-ro,* a popular dice game, was played surreptitiously. Passersby were occasionally surprised

Berkeley YMWBA Orchestra. Berkeley, Calif. ca. 1927. Photo courtesy of Charles Kaneko. Left to right, front row: Takahashi, Dick Mansho, Masako Takahashi, Taihei Tsuda, Wataru Fujii, Mitsuye Matsuda, Martin Akiyama, Takeo Fujii, Okada. Back row: Shigeru Kosakura, Shigeru Nakamura, Hisashi Kaneko, Shigeo Kawakami, Miyamoto, Willie Ito, unknown, Masaki Toono, Charles Kaneko, Fukumoto. Inset: Hatsuko Muramoto Hoshi, Tomiko Harano Kosakura. Note—The swastika is an ancient symbol adopted by Buddhists to signify universal life. The emblem (with arms turning clockwise) on the bass drum is reversed in error.

to encounter sober-faced young men being loaded into the San Francisco Police paddy wagon for a trip to the city jail. If the passersby happened to be in the vicinity of the shop an hour or two later, an even greater surprise was in store—the return of these very same men with sheepish grins on their faces, ready to resume action at the gambling table. "Whitey," purportedly the son of the San Francisco mayor, was a familiar face at Willy's. It doesn't take much imagination to understand the politics of the quick dismissals these recalcitrants enjoyed.

Besides being a prodigious saxophone player, Ito was a capable, conscientious teacher. In 1927 he was asked to organize an orchestra for the Berkeley Young Men's and Women's Buddhist Association (YMWBA). He patiently recruited about twenty young Nisei and Kibei members. Being a part-time salesman for the Sherman & Clay music store, Ito helped them to finance the purchase of instruments. Shigeru Nakamura, a University of California student at that time, remembered paying thirty-five cents a week to Ito out of his $5.00 weekly houseboy salary towards the purchase of a clarinet.

Ito rehearsed a variety of semiclassical and popular tunes of the day with the YMWBA orchestra for performances at special church and community events. They also played for a few dances—very few, because church elders generally frowned upon social dancing. "Many youngsters had to sneak out to dance," according to Charles Kaneko, who played saxophone in the orchestra. Nakamura remembered vaguely playing a Berkeley Nisei Club dance in 1929 at the Berkeley Nihonjinkai Hall on Haste Street near Shattuck Avenue.

Of special interest to jazz fans of the '90s is the fact that the priest of the Berkeley Buddhist Temple, young Reverend Taisho Tana, unmarried then in 1927, strongly encouraged the organizing of an orchestra. **Akira Tana**, a son born years later, is today a highly acclaimed professional musician who has earned an international reputation for his superb jazz drumming. He has collaborated with Rufus Reid, an outstanding bass player, to produce TanaReid recordings featuring the nation's top jazz artists.

The success of the Berkeley YMWBA orchestra spurred the Oakland Buddhists to organize their own musical group. Ito agreed to provide the leadership and instruction. A fourteen-piece orchestra of eager young Nisei became the pride of the church. Among its members were Tony Yokomizo, fifteen years old, playing clarinet; Walter Okawa, trumpet; Tad Hirota and George Nobori, violins; Roy Akiyoshi, drums; and Maki Koyama, piano. Yokomizo remembered how proud he was when the orchestra performed in the celebration commemorating the 1927 opening of the new auditorium of the Oakland Buddhist Church.

Oakland YMWBA Orchestra. Oakland, Calif. ca. 1927. Photo courtesy of Tony Yokomizo. Left to right: John Kido, Giichi Yoshioka, Iwajiro Hosono, Nobuye Tani, Hajime Kawazoe, Tony Yokomizo, Maki Koyama, Tad Hirota, Mits Nakashima, Willie Ito, Roy Akiyoshi, Ikaru Mitoma, Fumi Masuda, Shigenobu Kuramoto, Fujio Okawa, Mary Nobori, Kengo Nakahara, Tadashi Tani, Rev. Masao Washioka, John Koyama.

The lure of popular music prompted a splinter group of the YMWBA orchestra to organize a jazz combo with Willie Ito's assistance. Augmented by outsiders such as John Yoshino of Alameda on trumpet, Charlie Kikugawa and "Shinglin" Omoto, both of San Francisco, on drums and guitar respectively, they played tunes such as "Stormy Weather" and "Star Dust"— not for dances, but for the joy of playing popular music in their informal jam sessions.

In the latter part of 1931, the following letter was published in the *Shin Sekai*, a San Francisco Japanese newspaper:

> FORUM AND AGAINST 'EM
> *Forum editor: Boy oh boy, I got the biggest laugh of the year when I read the New World English section, "A seven-piece Japanese dance orchestra is being imported from Salinas for the coming J.A.A.U. dance." What could be more humiliating? A small town like Salinas showing the big shots of S.F. how a dance orchestra can be successfully organized.*
>
> *What is the matter with Lil Osaka? Why can't Lil Osaka which is many times larger than Salinas boast of its own orchestra? No excuse, I think. I know for a fact that we are not lacking musicians. We have right here in our own back-yard a couple of swell trumpets in Sash Moriyama and Harry Yasuda, a nice trap drummer in Tomate Kikugawa, for saxophone we have Willie Ito, Shig Shigio, Teddy Yasukawa and Tosh Suzuki. Now I'm sure that if these fellows get together and practice, we could soon be boasting of our own crack dance unit.*

> *Piano players are plenty here in Frisco, no need mentioning the names of some of the girls who are real good in jazz technique. I'm not taking a crack at the musicians but I think we ought to have one orchestra. We did have one before you know, and why can't we now? Come on fellows, let's start up the band!*
>
> *(Signed) A Moosician*

Taking the challenge from the "Moosician," Willie Ito organized a jazz band which rehearsed at Sho Wa Lo, the Chinese restaurant on Post Street operated by the Kikugawa family. The community newspaper announced:

> *2ND GENERATION ORCHESTRA HAS FIRST PRACTICE*
>
> *The first practice of the newly organized second generation orchestra of this city was held on Wednesday night in the dance room of the Sho Wa Lo. Following are the members: trumpet, Akira Omoto; clarinets, M. Suzuki and Tom Matsuda; saxophones, Ted Yasukawa and Joe Morisuye; trombone, Willy Ito; piano, Tsuneo Fukushima; drums, Tamotsu Kikugawa. Under the leadership of Willy Ito, the practice opened with "Good Evening," "My Ideal," and several other popular pieces, and proved to be considerably a success. The practices will be held every Wednesday evening, and anyone with an instrument, even though a beginner, is welcome to join and make this orchestra a musical organization which will be recognized. Those who wish to join, please communicate with Willy's Sweet Shop on 1601-A Post Street.*

The Willy's Sweet Shop Cats. San Francisco. ca. 1930. Left to right: Charlie Kikugawa, Teddy Kozuma, Raymond Okumoto, Henry Onishi, unknown, Shigeru Omoto, Richard Okumoto. Photo courtesy of Mary Fujihara.

Tamotsu "Tomate" Kikugawa, drummer for this band, noted: "Started practice like a million $, but ended like thirty cents in about a month."

Sometime later, Kikugawa traveled south to play drums for the Sho Tokyans, a Los Angeles dance band. Joe Sakai, bass viol player in the same band, recalls: "Tomate was a great drummer. He played drums with a very steady beat!" Kikugawa learned dance band drumming from his brother, Charlie, and also enjoyed a reputation as a vocalist. On July 4, 1932, he sang "Lullaby of the Leaves" in a talent show at the Warfield Theater in San Francisco. Audience response was so overwhelming the theater management booked him for repeat performances for several upcoming shows. Kikugawa admired many different orchestral styles of the late '30s—the sweet and the hot—from Jan Garber and Guy Lombardo to Artie Shaw and Tommy Dorsey. Some popular tunes in Kikugawa's vocal repertoire were "Lazy Bones," "I'll String Along With You," "Walking My Baby Back Home" and "Always."

Undaunted by the failure of Ito's first band, another group, including several survivors from the '32 band, attempted to organize a dance band in 1934. The local press announced:

SF JAZZ BAND PLANS DEBUT—Six-Piece Orchestra Seeks Banjoist. Li'l Osaka will soon have something to croon about with the announcement of the latest addition to our community—a Japanese jazz orchestra. With Pasa Suzuki "poop-poop-adooping" as versatile crooner, a six-piece orchestra will soon make its debut; but when, it was not reported, but the fact is that there is an orchestra and judging from the number of rehearsals going on, the musicians are up to a grand debut soon. The members of the new orchestra includes Tamotsu Kikugawa, trap; Harry Yasuda, trumpet; Dick Motoyoshi, Ted Yasukawa, Toshi Suzuki, saxophones and Yuki Morikawa, piano. Just now, to complete the outfit, the orchestra is looking high and low for an expert banjoist. Anybody interested in this kind of hobby is invited to drop over and join—providing he can play a banjo. In other words, they're looking for a banjo player. Their headquarters is at 1512 Geary Street and holds rehearsals every Monday and Thursday.

It is not known whether or not an expert banjo player was located. Presumably, rehearsals were held and the new Li'l Osaka Jazz Band had its début.

The OSDS Orchestra. Oakland, Calif. 1926. Left to right: Hachiro Yuasa, Etsuji Utsumi, Setsu Kitamura Akaba, Noboru Idé, Mary Ikeda. Photo courtesy of Mary Ann Utsumi.

THE OAKLAND SONS AND DAUGHTERS ORCHESTRA
Oakland, California

The Oakland Sons and Daughters Society (OSDS) was the grandiose name of a social club organized by Issei parents for their Nisei offspring. The actual origin of the organization and the orchestra, however, is obscure. Surviving members, now in their eighties, have difficulty recalling what took place back in 1926 when the band was in existence. A photograph found by chance in an old Yawata family album is one of the few remaining pieces of evidence. In the carefully posed image, five youthful musicians are seated somberly on a simple stage decorated with strips of crepe paper.

Hachiro Yuasa played the alto saxophone in the band; Etsuji Utsumi, the banjo; Setsu

Kitamura Akaba, the violin; Noboru "Nabby" Idé, the drums and Mary Ikeda, the piano. In a 1994 phone interview, Yuasa, a retired architect, recalled with some hesitation: "I started playing the saxophone in Lincoln Grammar School, which had classes up to the eighth grade. I played cello parts with my E-flat alto sax. Our OSDS group...maybe, we played a dance or two. I think Etchie was the leader."

"We used to rehearse at the OSDS hall on Ninth and Franklin," **Etchie Utsumi** confirmed. "We played tunes like 'Moonlight and Roses' and 'Yes, Sir, That's My Baby.' I wasn't much of a musician. I first learned a few simple chords, mostly self-taught. I took up the banjo because it was a popular fad in those days. Eddie Peabody was the banjo king then. Nabby Idé, a funny, loose guy, was the clown in our group. He was not a schooled drummer, but he had a special knack for playing the drums.

"I think we gave up playing as a group after a year—baseball and basketball took precedence. But I like music so I listened to the big-band music of Paul Whiteman and, later, enjoyed Benny Goodman and Glenn Miller...and vocals by Perry Como, Bing Crosby and Dean Martin. Also, I used to go hear live music played in vaudeville shows at the T & D Theater on Eleventh and Franklin Streets."

During a telephone interview in 1994, **Setsu Kitamura Akaba,** the violinist, protested that she could not recall a thing about her experience in the Sons and Daughters Orchestra. "It was such a long time ago...don't remember if we played for dances or anything like that. I only know that when I was in grammar school my father bought me a violin and told me to take lessons. Certainly not my idea. The wife of the Oakland Methodist Episcopal Church minister taught me a few elementary exercises to practice. Didn't play in a school orchestra...just banged away at home. That's about all I remember about playing a violin."

"**Mary Ikeda** was everyone's piano teacher in those days in Oakland," says Amy Morizono Eto of the band's pianist. When Mary was a child, her parents bought her a toy piano. In no time she picked out "America" with one finger. Music and the piano became a major focus in her life; in 1931, at age eighteen, she graduated Mills College with a degree in music. Ikeda was in great demand to perform in Japanese community events. In the Talent Night on August 27, 1933, sponsored by the Japanese American Citizens League at the Buddhist Temple Hall in Alameda, she was the accompanist for Yasuko Tani, who danced two selections: "It Was So Beautiful" and "To A Wild Rose." She also played solo piano: "Fantasia in C" by Mozart.

Ikeda again accompanied Tani at the Nisei Concert presented by the Northern California Young Peoples Christian Conference on March 20, 1937.³ Now eighty-four years old, she lives in New York City, retired from a career as accompanist for ballet and modern dance classes. "I play only classical music," Ikeda insists. "I would have denied playing popular music had I not seen that photograph of the Oakland Sons and Daughters ensemble. I am at a complete loss trying to remember our orchestra. Actually, I am really shocked at myself for not remembering."

THE SACRAMENTO SCENE

RICHARD'S ORIGINAL SYNCOPATERS ORCHESTRA, A.K.A. MIKADOS, A.K.A. NIGHT HAWKS

One of the earliest Nisei dance bands was organized under the leadership of **Richard Okumoto** in Sacramento, California, circa 1926. Okumoto, a native of Hawaii, named his first group **Richard's Original Syncopaters Orchestra (sic)**.⁴ The band consisted mostly of high-school students. In time the original Original Syncopaters was augmented by other musicians, and the name of the orchestra was changed first to Mikados and then to Night Hawks. They played for Nisei dances and functions in Sacramento, Florin and other rural communities in the Sacramento River Valley. One of their more regular gigs took place at Sacramento's M Street Cafe, a Japanese-operated Chinese restaurant with a postage-stamp dance floor. It was a popular gathering place for the Sacramento Nisei in-crowd.

Richard Okumoto, Night Hawks. Sacramento, Calif. 1926.
Photo courtesy of Mary Fujihara.

As the Night Hawks, the musicians often were invited to play for private parties in the spacious home of George Iki, a prominent doctor. In June at the close of the school year, Nisei high school grads and their dates in their formal gowns and new suits would converge for their Senior Prom at the Oak Park Clubhouse and dance to the music of the Night Hawks.

CHAPTER ONE   25

Raymond Okumoto, Night Hawks. Sacramento, Calif. 1926. Photo courtesy of Mary Fujihara.

Richard Hamada, Night Hawks. Sacramento, Calif. 1926. Photo courtesy of Mary Fujihara.

Henry "Pete" Tanaka, Night Hawks. Sacramento, Calif. 1926. Photo courtesy of Mary Fujihara.

Henry Onishi, Night Hawks. Sacramento, Calif. 1926. Photo courtesy of Mary Fujihara.

Elizabeth Kozono Murata. Sacramento, Calif. 1929. Photo courtesy of Elizabeth Kozono Murata.

The Night Hawks included Richard Hamada, tuba; Wesley Oyama, trombone; Clem Oyama, trumpet; Henry "Pete" Tanaka, drums; Henry Onishi, tenor sax; Raymond Okumoto, banjo; Smoky Kumamoto, piano and Richard Okumoto, leader, saxophone and clarinet. At eighty-three years, Hamada's appetite for music had not waned. Despite a stroke that immobilized his left arm, he continued to play a snare drum-cymbal set with his one good hand. He was a member of a trio which performed for Friday afternoon dances at a senior center in Auburn. "I love music; it makes me feel good…so happy," he told me. "I can play twenty-four hours [without stopping]!"

Elizabeth Kozono Murata, also of Sacramento, was one of the few women to play a horn in a Nisei jazz band. She loved popular music and learned to play the C-melody saxophone in 1930 from Richard Okumoto. Lily Oyama Sasaki, a close friend, remembered: "Elizabeth moved into a little shack on her dad's ranch near her home so she could practice in privacy away from the rest of the family. Naturally, all the Issei and even Nisei thought playing a *blowing* instrument [like the saxophone] was so *unladylike*!"

"As soon as I could, I was playing in Richard's band," Murata recalled in 1991. "I also learned to play his alto and soprano saxophones. In those days there were many programs to keep the band busy. For two years I lived in San Francisco and attended Girls High School, where I joined the school orchestra. On different occasions I played my sax at the old Pine Methodist Church. Some of my favorite tunes were 'Me and My Shadow,' 'What'll I Do?' 'Blue Skies,' 'Dinah' and 'Alice Blue Gown.' I enjoyed listening to the music of Paul Whiteman, Ted Lewis, and Red Nichols and the Five Pennies." Murata played saxophone for about eight years. After she married in 1938, she gave her horn away. In 1994, at eighty-three years, she enjoyed playing piano for her own pleasure. She admires the piano stylings of Duke Ellington and Count Basie. "Music has given me *great* happiness and joy," she says. "As for my playing the sax years ago—my friends today never dreamed that I played such an instrument."

Bill Nikaido was born in Walnut Grove, California, in 1912. He graduated from Sacramento High School and went to Sacramento Junior College for a few semesters. He was the only Japanese in the high-school glee club and the a cappella choir at junior college. Nikaido recalls singing with the Mikados: "I really had fun with the guys in the band. I especially remember 'Shadow Waltz'—'In the shadows let me come and sing to you'…something like that. I've forgotten the words, but it was my favorite. We played a New Year's Eve dance and a few Christmas holiday dances in the vacant room next to the main dining section of Mr. Okabe's M

Street Cafe, but not too many dances. Our Issei parents were pretty strict in those days and wouldn't allow most of us teenagers to attend dances or even just to dance. They thought it was shameful. We also went to Walnut Grove to play a dance or two at the Japanese Hall there. I think the dancers had to pay about $1.50 per couple for admission. I didn't get paid for doing the band vocals, but didn't mind 'cause I enjoyed the experience so much."

THE LOS ANGELES SCENE

CHARLES IZUMI AND THE JAPANESE SANDMEN

In Los Angeles in the 1930s, Issei and Nisei listeners tuned in to the broadcast of traditional Japanese music featured every Monday night on community radio station KGER. On July 17, 1933, at 7:40 pm, listeners must have been surprised when the show departed from its routine to début the Japanese Sandmen, a ten-member dance band led by Charles Izumi. "Japanese Sandman" was their theme song. Listener response was so favorable the Sandmen became a regular feature of the show. Izumi played the piano; on trumpets were Mitsuya Yamaguchi and Hajimu Masuda; on saxes, George Abe and Susumu Chikami; George Kitahara was on banjo; Tsuneo Tajima on the sousaphone and Joe Fullert on the guitar. Joe Shimada played drums and alternated with Mariko Takasu on vocals. The *Rafu Shimpo* reported: "Mits Yamaguchi, whose trumpet playing is one of the features of the organization, kept the group up to a high standard and his performance merited much praise."

Mitsuya "Mits" Yamaguchi at the time was enrolled in the University of California at Los Angeles (UCLA) School of Medicine. In a telephone interview in 1995, Yamaguchi, who is still practicing medicine in Los Angeles's Li'l Tokyo, remembered: "We played music arrangements 'as played by' the Casa Loma Orchestra and other popular bands of the day. I remember vaguely playing a UCLA Japanese sorority dance. I had fun copying Clyde McCoy's version of the 'Sugar Blues'…you know, with the Harmon mute in the horn. Benny Goodman's orchestra was my favorite swing band. Later my favorite trumpeters were Ziggy Elman and Harry James."

Contemporary reports offer a sense of the repertoire and delivery of the Japanese Sandmen, as well as some of the popular acts of the day. The theme of the August 2, 1933, radio broadcast was "Old Timers Night." According to the *Rafu Shimpo*:

It was an evening of surprises with the presentation of numbers replete with the reminiscent flavor of years "only yesterday." The broadcast was marked by the début of Flora Matsuno, versatile Li'l Tokyo miss, who assumed the role of a torch singer in "Happy Days and Lonely Nights" with all the fervor of a Helen Morgan or a Libby Holman. Miss Matsuno truly lived up to advance notices. Two other favorites, "Buddy" Matsumoto and Melba Yonemura, were well received. Miss Matsumoto in "Have You Ever Been Lonely?" and Miss Yonemura singing "Paradise" were bright spots on the broadcast. Male vocals were by Joe E. Koike on "Home" and Joe Shimada sang "The Old Village Choir."

August 21, 1933, was "Japan Night" at T.C. Talley's Criterion Theater in Los Angeles. Several Japanese motion picture stars, including some Nisei actors who had secured occasional bit parts in American movies, were invited. Nellie Oliver, the venerable organizer/advisor of the all-Nisei Olivers Club, was also an honored guest. *The Kid From Spain,* starring Eddie Cantor, was the feature movie. On stage for the first time was Chuck Izumi and the Japanese Sandmen. On the program were: "Lying in the Hay," by the orchestra; "Twelfth Street Rag," a banjo solo by George Kitahara; "I've Got To Pass [Your House]," a vocal by Melba Yonemura; "Cinderella's Wedding Dance," by Keora Kono; a Hawaiian hula and songs by "Buddy" Matsumoto; and "Black-eyed Susan Brown," a final orchestra selection.

The August 29th broadcast was described in the *Rafu Shimpo* as "a delightful broadcast over KGER. Buddy Matsumoto went on the ether with 'Lonely Bluebird' assisted by Mits Yamaguchi and Joe Koike on the cornet and guitar respectively. Joe Shimada gave a vocal impression of 'Under a Blanket of Blue' with Koike as accompanist. 'Black-eyed Susan Brown' and 'Lying in the Hay' also received many favorable comments. Melba Yonemura, regular vocalist with Manny Harom's Orchestra and who had performed at the Roxie Theater in New York City, sang with Izumi's 12-piece orchestra."

THE CLUB HARMONY ORCHESTRA, A.K.A. THE MELODIANS

An abbreviated announcement appeared in the October 21, 1933, edition of *Rafu Shimpo*. It stated that a Harmony Club was being organized for the purpose of developing drama, vocal and instrumental groups. The call for interested persons brought forth positive results in a few months. On February 25, 1934, the paper announced an upcoming informal spring dance sponsored by **Club Harmony** on March 9, with proceeds earmarked for musical instruments and a public address system. Talented Nisei artists had been lined up for a floor show: the Takahashi sisters in a vocal and tap duo; a waltz presentation by Chitosé Townsend and Harry Yoshizaki; a banjo solo by George Kitahara; a Hawaiian dance by 'Buddy' Matsumoto; and a tap dance by Amy Tomita. Tickets cost 75 cents per couple. Even though it was an informal dance, the boys were asked to refrain from wearing cords.

Akira Ohno assumed leadership of the Club Harmony band. Several members of the ensemble belonged to the Anchovies, the Japanese Christian Church boys club. Pop music over the airwaves had seduced their ears. They especially enjoyed the sweet sounds of Guy Lombardo and Jan Garber; other favorites were Eddie Duchin and, later, Woody Herman, Benny Goodman and Tommy Dorsey.

"Guess we got serious about starting a dance band sometime in the early '30s," said Ohno. "It's hard to remember exactly who or when each of us started playing in the band, but George Saito, Mits Aiso and Mas Manbo played alto saxophones. George Abe, who was in the UCLA marching band, played tenor sax with us. I remember all the guys wanted Selmer saxophones. I suppose it's because many pros played a Selmer. George Sasaki of Brawley, who was also attending UCLA, played trombone. The rhythm section had Mary Kato on piano and George Kitahara played banjo with us for a while. He was a pro banjo player…used to perform on the Orpheum stage in L.A. Joe Shimada was our drummer. Joe Sakai played the ukulele and the viola, but we didn't want a lousy 'Jack Benny violin' in our band, so we urged him to get a bass 'cause the fingering wouldn't be so different."[5]

Masao Manbo, an L.A. expatriate now living in Tokyo, remembered those free-wheeling jam sessions. "In the early days, I used to take my horn over to Mits Aiso's home on the eastern fringe of Hollywood to play with him and George Saito. I still remember the funny crack Mits made. On radio, there was a popular group called The Happy Chappies and Mits used to say in response, 'We're the Happy Jappies.'"

In a 1994 letter Manbo offered a more detailed reminiscence: "I'll give you some dope on myself. I was born on December 28, 1912, in Riverside, California, and lived across the street from the Mission Inn, where (I read somewhere), years later, President Richard Nixon took Pat as his bride. When I was about ten, my folks took me and my older brother to Hiroshima for a two-year stay. And, thereafter, until I left with the Sho Tokyans for Japan in mid-1937, I was a Hollywood resident. I started playing the C-melody sax at Hollywood High. I played [class] B football for three years beginning in 1929 and did some running [track]. I then attended Los Angeles Junior College for two years.

"At home, for the fun of it, I played the sax while my brother Bill played the banjo. I thought that Benny Goodman was great, also Coleman Hawkins. And remember 'Stardust'?—it used to be an all-time favorite. I first joined a band formed in 1931 or '32 by Aki Ohno, a westside Los Angeles fellow who strummed the steel guitar in a manner inspired by one of his heroes—Alvino Rey, later the leader of a popular dance band. I think we called ourselves the **Los Angeles Melodaires**; I know we kept changing names. Our band was made up of guys from different parts of L.A. Mary Kato was our pianist. George Igawa, Sus Chikami and I played the tenor sax [while] doubling on clarinet. On some slow pieces, Chikami tooted the baritone and George and I played tenors. It sounded great, I thought. While the band might have been quite short of being first rate, I like to think that it wasn't too bad either. We played at some Christian churches; and, I think, as Sho Tokyans, when George Igawa took over, played for the first Los Angeles Nisei Week Talent Show (circa 1934). The show took place at Yamato Hall. I also remember playing a street dance in Little Tokyo, probably during that same Nisei Week."

Joe Sakai recalled his early association with Hajimu Masuda, the trumpeter of Ohno's first band: "Yeah, I remember Hy…he was born in Los Angeles; his father was a gardener. In the late '20s the Masuda family moved to Venice. They grew celery there. Hy went to Venice High; played baseball, shortstop or second base. He was pretty good. He was also a self-taught musician…played the trumpet in high school. Hy's trumpet hero was Clyde McCoy…remember McCoy's 'Wang, Wang Blues'? A few of us used to get together and jam at the Japanese Christian Church at Twentieth and San Pedro Streets in L.A. We liked Ben Pollack, Jimmy and Tommy Dorsey and the Benny Goodman band."

Months later, the August 15, 1935, *Rafu Shimpo* reported a standing-room-only Nisei Week Fashion Show at the Nishi Honganji Hall in Los Angeles. Fifty-one women and men modeled fashionable clothing designed, produced and sold by local Japanese sewing schools and clothing stores. "The hit of the men's fashions was Clem Oyama, wearing what the best-dressed man wore in the 1890s. His comical antics drew many laughs. The Melodians, a talented group of musicians, played music during the entire show." Another feature of the evening was the play, "Juliet and Romeo" [sic], presented by the Li'l Tokyo Players under the direction of Lois Izumida.

The second annual 1935 Nisei Week closed with a dance at the International Institute, where the Melodians provided the music for two hundred celebrants. A "Broom Dance" in which dancers periodically passed a broom from one couple to the next was held. The couple in possession of the broom when the last note of this dance sounded was charged with performing a solo exhibition dance. The "winners" were Tsuyuko Matsumura, who received a box of chocolates, and Shig Aratani, who received a bouquet of celery.

The Sho Tokyans. Los Angeles, Calif. 1937. Left to right, front row: Joe Sakai, Sachi Amano, Chiye Tawa, Ernest Arima. Back row: Tadashi Kamayatsu, Susumu Chikami, George Igawa, Masao Manbo, Akira Ohno. Photo courtesy of Akira Ohno.

THE SHO TOKYANS

George Igawa, a son of a farmer, was born on April 20, 1908, in Fowler, California. He grew up under the guidance of a strong-willed father. It was a no-nonsense life, with spare moments spent tending to chores required of young farm boys. When he was eighteen, Igawa was left alone to fend for himself when his father, leaving a few precious dollars for Igawa's subsistence, sailed for Japan to visit relatives. Igawa stayed in a dormitory, somewhat lost in his solitary state, until one evening he heard over the radio a lovely melody which struck a chord in his latent musical consciousness. The song was "Among My Souvenirs." He thought to himself, "How beautiful…it would be nice if I could play music like that!" Impetuously, he purchased a C-melody saxophone with a hundred dollars of the money his father had left for room and board—knowing full well that his father would never have approved of his newly acquired extravagance.

About that time, he received a letter from a friend: "Igawa, don't stick around Fresno…there's nothing there for you. Come on down to Los Angeles. There are jobs here and friends you can meet." Igawa went with his new horn and started work as a gardener while taking lessons and playing saxophone duets with Mas Manbo; they were joined later by Susumu Chikami. They purchased music arrangements, rehearsed diligently and enjoyed the camaraderie that grew from their common penchant for popular music.

"The members of our band kept changing," said Ohno, "but we tried to have at least three saxes, a couple of trumpets and a trombone plus a rhythm section. Sus Chikami and George Igawa on tenor saxes, and Ernie Arima and Hy Masuda on trumpets came on board later. As the guys came and went, we also changed the name of our band. We called ourselves Club Harmony Orchestra for a while, and later, Los Angeles Melodians. Eventually, we developed into a relatively stable group. When George Igawa assumed leadership of the band, we became, finally, the Sho Tokyans" [the Japanese derivative of "Little Tokyo," Los Angeles's Japantown].

Sachi Amano, the pianist for the Sho Tokyans for three years, was born in Seattle, Washington, in November 1912. At eight years she was introduced to piano lessons. "I just hated to practice! In fact, my teacher was satisfied with my weekly lesson reviews, but when she was told by my mother that I didn't practice at all at home, I remember my teacher actually crying! What I really liked was to play popular American music; my lessons fell by the wayside. During my teen years I fully developed my ear with some assistance from classes in music theory and harmony at Broadway High School.

"Fortunately for me, my older brother Sam led a dance band of seven or eight musicians which played for Nisei dances in the '20s. Since I had a good ear for chords, Sam, a drummer, wanted me to play piano, but my mom said, *'No!'* A staunch Baptist, she associated popular music with dance halls—loose women, fast men, sex and drunkenness. 'Sachi will not play in your band, Sam! What will the church members say if she did? We'll all be disgraced… *haji.*' So I practiced with the band, but couldn't play any dances.

"In the meantime, I had purchased many copies of popular sheet music—'Always,' 'Linger Awhile,' 'I'll String Along With You,'—a stack over an inch high. I came home from school

Chiye Tawa. Los Angeles. 1938. Photo courtesy of Lily Sasaki.

one day and discovered to my chagrin that they were missing from the top of the piano where I kept them—my mother had burned the 'sinful' music! I remember painfully staring at the smoldering remnants of my sheet music in the fireplace. What a blow it was; I was furious! Took a long time to get over that incident."

The Amano family moved from Seattle to Los Angeles in the late 1920s on the eve of the Depression. "Sometime later around 1933, George Igawa organized a dance band and I was invited to play piano," she recalled. "Again, Mom said, 'No.' But after much arguing and cajoling, I was able to convince Mom that it was all right, that we were in a strange city with no critical church members to be concerned about. She reluctantly relented. And besides, there were four other girls in the band—**Chiye Tawa**, who sang solo (she sang the blues very well—she sang with soul!), and the three who made up a vocal trio—Clara and Louise Suski and Kimi Sakai."

Tadashi "Tib" Kamayatsu became a member of the Sho Tokyans around 1936. He was an alumnus of the Oliver Club of Los Angeles, which had its beginnings in 1915. Miss Nellie Oliver, a grammar-school teacher at Hewett Street School, wished to enrich the lives of young Nisei boys in the Little Tokyo area. For this purpose she rented a hall in a two-story frame building located on Hewett Street, north of First Street. Early club activities centered on sports, mostly baseball and basketball, but under Miss Oliver's direction a cultural program that included drama, tap dancing and music instruction was initiated. Sam Seno, who lived in Boyle Heights in East Los Angeles, was invited to be a charter member of this downtown club because of his interest in choral music.

In a 1991 interview with Joyce Nako, Seno recalled: "Among the Oliver boys was my good friend Tib Kamayatsu. Tib was just naturally musical. He started by learning how to play the ukulele, and then he got into the banjo which was really popular in those days. Tib then became a very good guitarist; I used to play the clarinet. He would accompany me and we used to go around [performing]. We were invited a couple of times to broadcast over radio station KRKD, a small operation which used to do advertising [in the Japanese community]. Since the clarinet sounded kinda like a *shakuhachi,* a Japanese bamboo woodwind instrument in the lower register, and Tib could make the guitar kinda sound like a *koto,* we used to play [tunes] like *'Kojo No Tsuki,'* and other old [Japanese] standards in those days.

"Since I lived in Boyle Heights and Tib lived in Little Tokyo, I used to go to the Oliver Club House only on weekends. On the second floor was an old, rickety piano. There was a fellow, Dave [Sato], who lived in Boyle Heights, too, and played the piano. Dave, Tib and I used to get together and jam around. When couples heard the music, they would come up and dance to our music."

Lily Oyama Sasaki clearly remembered Dave Saito and his piano playing. "Dave lived next door to us. He loved music and played by ear, so he was really good at popular music. I still remember his playing 'Stars Fell On Alabama,' one of my favorite tunes. Dave also liked to write original pop tunes. One of the songs he composed was 'You Are My Song Of Love.' My sister Mary helped Dave write the lyrics. I don't know if that tune ever became a commercial hit…I don't think so."

The Sho Tokyans made their début at the Yamato Hall during the 1936 Nisei Week Festival Talent Show sponsored by the Los Angeles Japanese American Citizens League. Their many rehearsal hours and natural exuberance paid off in public acclaim. Dancers liked the Sho Tokyans, who gradually secured more and more bookings from Nisei clubs in southern California.

Mas Manbo remembered: "George Igawa got an Issei fellow skilled in carpentry to make music stands out of plywood for the band. Then we got my sister-in-law Mary to make drapes for the stands out of shiny, maroon-colored material. On days when we had engagements, I would load the music stands and drapes in the back of my Ford roadster along with my instruments and proceed to pick up Igawa and Chiye Tawa. I lived in Hollywood near Warner Brothers Studio. George lived close by. Chiye had a [domestic] job at Judge Albert Lee Stephens's home located near Beverly Hills. The judge had sons attending Hollywood High while I was enrolled there. I knew them so I was welcome inside the house while waiting for Chiye to get ready."

The Sho Tokyans usually saved a portion of their dance receipts to finance a fantasy trip to play dance halls in Japan. Igawa's father had passed away while visiting in Japan, and Igawa had gone there to attend the funeral. He chanced to visit a dance hall in Tokyo and was surprised at the poor quality of the music. He said to himself, "We play much better than this orchestra. I wonder if we can come over to play in Japan?" The idea of traveling to Japan with the Sho Tokyans became a compelling dream.

In the '36 Nisei Week Talent Show, Naoyuki Okami, a Japanese native who was studying Hawaiian steel guitar in Los Angeles, performed on the same program as the Sho Tokyans. Okami became acquainted with the members of the band and their casual backstage conversations developed into a serious discussion about the possibility of the Sho Tokyans working in Japan. Okami assured them that playing dance halls in Japan was not just a daydream and that he would work on it when he returned to Tokyo.

Weeks later the Sho Tokyans received striking news. Okami had secured a six-month contract for them to play dance halls in the suburbs of Tokyo—the Chante Claire in Warabi and the Ballet Tabarin in Kawaguchi. Soon after, in preparation for their overseas gig, the Sho Tokyans left Los Angeles on a fund-raising tour of northern California—to Santa Maria, Stockton, Sacramento and San Francisco.[6] "I fail to recall whether Sachi or Chiye Tawa, our vocalist, made the complete tour," said Manbo. "Tommy [Tamotsu] Kikugawa, our drummer, did not show up until our last stop in San Francisco because of his job at the fish market in L.A. Hicky Noma, an enterprising fellow who acted as our manager, beat the drums in Tommy's absence."

On the Road to Northern California. 1937. Left to right: Tib Kamayatsu, Joe Sakai, Susumu Chikami, Masao Manbo, Ernie Arima. Photo courtesy of Masao Manbo.

Pianist Sachi Amano did go on that tour during the summer of 1937. "Didn't get paid a cent for playing—most of the money went toward travel expenses and purchasing music arrangements," she said. "But those were great times! When the band secured in the latter part of 1937 a contract to play a dance hall in Japan, I didn't go. My dad said, 'OK', but mom said, 'No' and that was that. Sadly, it marked the end of my playing piano in a dance band." Amano was replaced by Lauro Planton, and in July of 1937 a reorganized Sho Tokyans sailed on the Tatsuta Maru from Los Angeles for Yokohama to embark on a series of exotic experiences in a very foreign country, the unfamiliar homeland of their parents.

---

1 In 1934-35 Mary Takayoshi secured contracts to sing and dance at a "handsome price" in shows and broadcasts at several venues—the Warfield Theater in San Francisco; the Paramount Theater in Seattle; club and radio engagements in Los Angeles and Butte, Montana.

2 Headlines from Japanese American newspapers.

3 Other performances included vocal solos by lyric soprano Ruby Yoshino; an appearance of Florence Takayama, a concert pianist; selections by violinist Kazue Tawara; two selections, including "The Flight of the Bumble Bee" by Tom Tsuji, who played the xylophone, accompanied by Takeru Iijima on the piano and four selections by the JACL chorus directed by H. Lindsay.

4 Many early dance bands, black and white, used "syncopators" as part of the band name. They avoided using "jazz" because in certain circles it was a slang expression synonymous with sexual intercourse.

5 Sakai subsequently became a full-time professional bass player, joined Los Angeles Local #47 Musicians Union and worked with Bill Boyd and his Gentlemen of Rhythm at the Hermosa Beach Biltmore Hotel from 1933 through 1936.

6 The Stockton dance was sponsored by the Stockton Esquires and took place on June 17, 1937, at the Moose Hall. The dance was scheduled to start at 9:00 pm and end at 1:00 am.

Nikkatsu film *Uramachi no Kokyogaku*. Tokyo, Japan. 1935. Left to right: Kyoji Sugi, Fumiko Kawabata, Isamu Kosugi. Photo courtesy of Masahisa Segawa.

CHAPTER 2

Bata-Kusai[7] Jazz Singers
NISEI MUSIC MAKERS IN PREWAR JAPAN

"*I was the only* one who wanted to lead a musician's life. The main reason for the others not wanting to become a pro was the discrimination in the strong musicians union. Since we were American citizens, we could join the union, but there'd be no jobs for us because our faces were Oriental. I met a Japanese trumpet player who worked on a transpacific liner. He invited me and a few others to go to Japan…said there'd be jobs for us. I jumped at the idea."

—CHARLIE KIKUGAWA, SAN FRANCISCO, 1930

THE DAWN OF JAZZ IN JAPAN

The economic depression of the 1930s in the United States prompted many Nisei, whose job-seeking efforts were exacerbated by racial discrimination, to look to Japan for employment opportunities. It was common knowledge that even with university degrees most Japanese Americans could not gain access to the mainstream professional and business world in the United States. Opportunities for many young Nisei were limited to menial jobs in San Francisco Chinatown art and curio shops operated by Japanese American entrepreneurs, hustling in wholesale produce houses on Western Avenue in Seattle or hawking fruits and vegetables in the hundreds of open-air stands in Southern California.

Many adventuresome Nisei did heed the cry, "Go west, young man!"—for them, that meant way, way, over-the-Pacific west. Fortified with American attitudes and demeanor and masked by their Japanese faces, they embarked upon an uncertain voyage to make it in the Far East. In 1935 the *Rafu Shimpo*, a Los Angeles vernacular press, reported that in 1933, according to Japanese Foreign Ministry sources, forty thousand Nisei from Hawaii, the U.S. mainland and Canada were working, going to school or visiting Japan.

Among these citizens were Nisei musicians who were frustrated in their goal to find a niche in the U.S. entertainment world. Aware of Japanese urbanites' vigorous appetite for American cultural fads, Nisei music makers, often encouraged by Japanese dance band members who worked the transpacific passenger liners, bought tickets for lengthy ocean voyages. In 1930 drummer Charlie Kikugawa sailed from San Francisco for Yokohama with three other Nisei hopefuls; other vocalists and instrumentalists followed from Seattle and from Los Angeles.

Conditions in Japan provided fertile ground for the reception and success of Japanese American musicians in the early 1930s. Japanese sophisticates eagerly sought jazz. Steamships carried recordings and sheet music to Japan from West Coast ports. Some tunes that were tops in popularity were "My Blue Heaven," "Blue Skies," "Lady of Spain," "Dinah" and "Margie." As public acceptance of jazz blossomed, Japanese musicians began first to replicate the sounds of American dance bands, then to create their own brand of jazz.

Ryoichi Hattori, an established composer and arranger, was a pioneer who arranged popular Japanese songs and traditional folk tunes into the jazz idiom by employing American dance band instrumentation, Western harmony, jazz syncopation and improvised solos. Hattori's jazz arrangements may be heard on early Japanese Columbia records, circa 1928; e.g., *"Kapporé,"* a geisha dance song; *"Toryansé,"* a children's song; *"Oedo Nihonbashi,"* an old folk song—all familiar tunes beloved by the Japanese. Hattori eventually became a prolific composer of popular tunes which reportedly exceeded three thousand!

Ryoichi Hattori Show with the Hyotan Orchestra. Morning Star School, San Francisco. 1950. Ryoichi Hattori, front row, center, with Shizuko Kasagi, to his right. Photo courtesy of Johnny Taniguchi.

In 1950 Hattori was invited to the States to perform his hit tunes for the San Francisco Japanese community. He brought a troupe of native Japanese singers, comediennes and a movie actress. The Hyotan Orchestra, made up of local Nikkei musicians and conducted by Hattori, accompanied the vocalists. The show took place at the Morning Star School Auditorium. As predicted, "Tokyo Boogie-woogie," sung by Shizuko Kasagi, created great excitement among the receptive audience. Kasagi was a young, high-energy singer who appeared in Japanese stage reviews and recorded extensively for Columbia of Japan. Her association with Hattori as her musical arranger established an extremely successful team which produced a multitude of best-selling pop songs.[8]

The collective effort of native Japanese musicians to duplicate jazz was no simple task. A music critic in the August 8, 1934, *Jiji Shinpo,* a Japanese publication, wrote in his review of the latest recordings produced by Columbia Records of Japan:

> *Among the four jazz records just recently released is one by the Japanese Betty Boop. She is a rank amateur who has little going for her. "Blue Melody" and "Jazz Aura" sung by Tadaharu Nakano with the Columbia Rhythm Boys is a performance which has no pep; it is uninspired and just so-so. The musical concept of the Rhythm Boys is a sound one, but unless they receive some direction, they will never be any good. Even their so-called hit, 'Dinah,' as jazz, is like stale beer… beer that has lost its kick.*

In contrast, this same reviewer praised the promise of Seattle Nisei vocalist Taft Beppu in his début recording of "St. Louis Blues": "I can't fault his performance; Taft Beppu surpasses all present-day jazz singers!"

A word of caution about the usage of "jazz" in Japan in the '30s to characterize the dance music of Japanese orchestras and the vocals of Nisei and native Japanese singers. Their interpretations, naturally, did not reach the level of classic jazz sounds of American swing bands or the incredible vocals of Billie Holiday and Sarah Vaughan. "Jazz" was a convenient, attractive label, for want of a more accurate term, in reference to popular American music in Japan. Actually, early pop singers in Japan sang *kayo kyoku,* a form of Japanese popular song which developed in the '20s and '30s by the fusion of Western and Japanese musical elements. Postwar native singers in time developed into valid jazz singers.

The most successful native Japanese jazz pioneer was Dick Miné, who is credited with introducing American popular music to the masses with his hit 1934 recording of "Dinah," sung in Japanese lyrics written by him and accompanied by Fumio Nanri and his Hot Peppers. Despite Miné's success, native singers were at a disadvantage in their attempts to vocalize as American singers did. Jazz evolution was driven by African American culture, and the Japanese, of course, had not been exposed to that experience. On the other hand, Nisei had American "ears" for syncopation, Western harmony and jazz singing styles. They were also facile in the English language and its pronunciation, enunciation and phrasing. Nisei singers inevitably sounded "jazzier" than their Japanese cousins. With these advantages, they sailed with some confidence and reasonable hope for career fulfillment to what was for them the unknown homeland of their Issei parents?

As it turned out, several Nisei did achieve star status. Among them were Fumiko Kawabata, Betty Inada, Chizuko Miyagawa, Helen Sumida, Helen Honda, Rickey Miyagawa,

Taft Beppu, Charlie Kikugawa and Hisashi Moriyama. The Columbia Records album, *Jazz Songs of Japan,* a collection of five historical LP records reproduced from original 78 rpm records of the period from 1928 through 1943, includes a side entitled, *Jazz Singers—Top Ladies.* Among the three women featured in eight songs are two Nisei, Miyagawa and Inada, and the third, **Midge Williams**, an African American, who played an influential role as the prototype jazz singer at the beginning of the Japanese swing era. Williams, as a vocalist, traveled subsequently with Louis Armstrong and his orchestra and made recordings in 1936 with Teddy Wilson and other top jazz personalities such as Cozy Cole, Bunny Berigan and Joe Marsala.

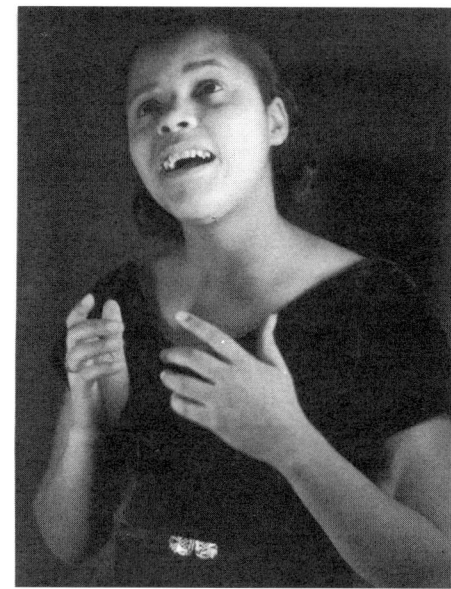

Midge Williams. Tokyo. 1934. Betty Inada collection.

In the 1934 recordings on *Top Ladies,* Williams sings "Lazy Bones," "Dinah" and "St. Louis Blues"—the first chorus of each song in Japanese and the final chorus in English.[10] The album also features sixteen songs by Fumiko Kawabata of Los Angeles. The side *Jazz Singers—Top Guys,* includes vocals by three Nisei: Miyagawa, Beppu and Moriyama and two Japanese natives: Nakano and Matsudaira. These recordings exemplify the prominence of Nisei in the development and popularization of jazz in Japan.

CLAUDE LAPHAM

Of historical interest is the presence at this time in Japan of **Claude Lapham**, an American composer and arranger who gained prominence among Japanese musicians. Lapham, a versatile musician, was called to Japan from New York City by Columbia Records for the purpose of moving Japanese jazz closer to U.S. standards. He had been a staff member of the Frank Skinner Company, an established New York City publisher of stock arrangements for dance bands. In Japan Lapham was assigned to write orchestral arrangements for jazz singers, including those mentioned above, and dance music for Columbia Records of Japan. The tunes he orchestrated were drawn heavily from American pop sources, but he also utilized native tunes.

On July 1, 1933, the world premiere of Lapham's *Sakura,* the first grand opera in Japanese featuring Miyoshi Sugi Machi in the title role, took place at the Hollywood Bowl in Los Angeles.

The local press responded with mixed reviews of this unique musical presentation, which boasted "a cast of 2,000 and an audience of 20,000." A news reporter wrote: "The plot is slight and ends in abundant tragedy for hero, villain and heroine. The music was composed by Claude Lapham and the libretto, by Yaemitsu Sugimachi. The international cast of principals sang Japanese words to music moderne, Nipponese and Puccinesque, with Japanese Kabuki dancers performing inscrutably against a background of gorgeously contrasted costumes and settings."

Jin Konomi, while a reporter for the Los Angeles *Rafu Shimpo,* interviewed Lapham following the musical extravaganza. He observed that Lapham was wearing a handsome black *montsuki,* a silk jacket imprinted with a traditional Japanese family crest. The interview disclosed that Lapham was a devoted Japanophile—"loved living in Japan, loved the Japanese lifestyle, the Japanese people, Japanese food and even contemplated marrying a Japanese woman."

In 1948 Lapham produced and directed *Nisei Hollywood Romance,* a musical revue which introduced four leading Nisei in the operatic field: Mitzi Ohye, Frank Watanuki, Kathy Yoshizawa and Ralph Nagai in featured roles. This show opened on October 31 at the International Studio Theater in Hollywood.

THE FLORIDA [DANCE HALL]

The development of jazz in Japan owes its impetus to the existence and appeal of dance halls which provided employment for dance bands and the opportunity for their maturation. "Foreign musicians began making their way into Japan after dance halls sprouted up in the country in the 1920s," wrote Mas Manbo, expatriate Nisei musician/journalist. "Japan became a little melting pot of jazz in the prewar period when it had as many as fifty dance halls."

Unlike ballrooms in the United States, Japanese dance halls in the '30s were generally establishments which were patronized by men, both single and married, who paid for the privilege of dancing with hostesses in the employ of the hall—recreation purely for the benefit of men. Wives rarely, if ever, accompanied their husbands to dance halls. The standard tariff in Tokyo was: noon to 3:00 pm, 5 *sen* per dance; 3:00-6:00 pm, 10 *sen* per dance; 6:00-11:00 pm, 20 *sen* per dance, with Florida charging 22 *sen* per dance. The division in the ticket revenue between the hall and its hostesses was generally 60 percent to the employers and 40 percent for the ladies.[11]

The following excerpt from *The History of Japanese Jazz and Pop Music, Japan Victor Record Company,* provides some insight into the scene at one well-known hall:

"The beginning of the Jazz Age in Japan was marked by the colorful boom in dance halls that began in 1931 and lasted for several years until the halls were shuttered by military decree on October 31, 1940. Each dance hall vied with others to create its own distinctive atmosphere by exclusively contracting jazz and tango bands. As a result the quality of dance music of the period advanced phenomenally. Of all these dance halls, head and shoulders above the rest by its elegant management and novel programming, was the Florida at Tameiké in Akasaka Ward. With the biggest floor space of all, the hall in Tokyo opened in August, 1929. The celebrated manager Matataro Tsuda's ideas and enterprise made it the refined gathering place for leading personages from all segments of Tokyo society.

"In the fall of 1930, the Florida brought from the United States the Wayne Coleman Band as the featured nighttime band; in 1932 it invited the Moulin Rouge Band from France. The genuine tango rhythms brought to Japan for the first time by the Moulin Rouge became the Florida's main draw. The Al King Band from New York was later invited and performed for two years at the Florida. It couldn't compare with Count Basie or Duke Ellington's band, but it had the characteristic Negro rhythm and showmanship and it was the talk of the town. In 1937 manager Tsuda took note of the popularity of the rhumba and brought in a five-member rhumba band from Cuba, thus introducing genuine Latin music. Tsuda was always at the forefront of the New Age.

"During this period quite a few singers were launched on their careers from the Florida stage. Noriko Awaya, Queen of the Blues, and Dick Miné débuted here and went to go on to their later greatness. The Florida reached the zenith of its popularity around 1935. Bandsmen, singers and dancers who congregated nightly in Akasaka were the epitome of the prewar culture of modern Japan.

"The dance hall was now in its heyday with many jazz and tango bands vying with one another. The singers who sang along with the bands also were expected to carry the ambience of genuine articles. As for audiences, they had become more sophisticated, having been exposed to dance records imported from Europe and America. Into Japan's vocal scene now appeared singers who impressed audiences as being *bata kusai*—Nisei singers who started to invade Japan in droves beginning around 1932.

"At the top of the new crop was Fumiko Kawabata, who immediately captivated the fans with her coquettish face and the acrobatic tap in which she took full advantage of her beautifully proportioned body. Betty Inada, a close friend of Kawabata, came to Japan in 1933. She is best known because she stayed on until after the war, appearing at the Florida and in other stage shows, and made long tours as a team with Dick Miné. Helen Sumida came to Japan in 1934 at age seventeen and immediately contracted with Victor and recorded some sixteen titles before returning to America in 1937.

"Besides the above, there were the Miyagawa duo, Rickey and his sister Harumi, who came to Japan in 1933 and Dolly Fujioka, who came in 1937 with a Nisei band. There were others. Their contributions to Japan's show business in song and dance deserve a new evaluation today. Their forte was that being American-born, their vocals were *bata-kusai* and they could sing both in Japanese and English. This pattern was also in vogue at one period after World War II, and no doubt there are many former fans today who recall it with nostalgia."

Dance Hall, Charlie Kikugawa & Orchestra. Yokohama, Japan. ca. 1931. Photo courtesy of Mari Kikugawa.

TEKISEI ONGAKU
Music of Enemy Origin

The right-wing political arm of the government eventually impacted the vitality of the burgeoning jazz in Japan. Japanese capitalism had reached an impasse in the early 1930s. Military leaders of the country advocated the acquisition of new territories to augment Japan's meager arable land area and to provide the raw materials needed to further their goals of increased industrialization. In September 1931, the Japanese army invaded Manchuria and in March 1932 instituted a pro-Japanese puppet state. This action was taken with the hope of establishing a crucial buffer state between Japan and the Soviet Union. It certainly would ensure access to Manchuria's valuable natural resources and provide additional living space for Japan's overabundant population. Programs to colonize Manchuria materialized; Japanese farmers in poor mountain villages were enticed by the slogan: "Go to Manchukuo—Own a thousand acres of farmland."

The first group of settlers left Japan in 1932. One thousand Japanese families were sent in 1937, initiating a projected twenty-year plan which anticipated a million more colonists (actually, by the end of the war, somewhat more than 320,000 Japanese had migrated to Manchuria). Japanese immigration came to an abrupt end on August 9, 1945, when Soviet forces crossed the Amur River into Manchuria.

On February 26, 1936, dissatisfied with the passive nature of the parliamentary government then in power, radicals in the Japanese Army, led by junior officers, mounted an insurrection and assassinated liberal statesmen Admiral Makoto Saito, Jyotaro Watanabe, Korekiyo Takahashi and Kantaro Suzuki. Other key heads of government—Prime Minister Keisuke Okada, Count Nobuaki Makino and Prince Kinmochi Saionji—survived. The young militants who perpetrated the killings were apprehended, court-martialed and sentenced to death. Despite the execution of the offenders, true governing power shifted to the hands of military authorities. Their goal was to organize the Japanese economy to prepare for a large-scale military invasion of China for the purpose of exploiting its abundant resources.

Though the coup d'état engineered by the young militants did not accomplish its perpetrators' goals, it contributed to the burgeoning strength of the right-wingers who soon overwhelmed antiwar liberals. It was not long before thousands of additional troops were transported overseas to the Chinese mainland. In 1937, while military exercises were conducted by the Japanese in the vicinity of the Marco Polo Bridge near Peking (Beijing), the Japanese claimed that Chinese soldiers fired upon the Japanese garrison and killed one of its troops. This was simply a pretext for sending more armed forces to mount a full-scale war against China. Soon thereafter Shanghai was taken and occupied by Japanese troops. In 1938 a euphemistic catchword designed to arouse the Japanese nation to support and to justify the aggressive policy of the military government was propagated: *Dai toa kyoei ken* (Greater East Asia Co-Prosperity Sphere).

With the Japanese attack on the U.S. Naval Base at Pearl Harbor, Hawaii, on December 7, 1941, World War II broke out in its full fury. In Japan, anti-British and anti-American propaganda activities evolved into hysterical, extreme measures on the part of super-patriotic Japanese military authorities. Restaurants and business enterprises with English names were required to take Japanese names. English names in children's textbooks were brushed over with black ink. No English language songs were allowed; Christian churches were forced to disband their choirs.

In January 1943, the Ministry of the Interior and the Ministry of Information conferred to issue regulations controlling "music of enemy origin" with the following introduction: "Banish Decadent Music—It is surprising to find that under wartime conditions when Japan is fighting for its life, the decadent music of America and England is being popularized. More than a year after war has been declared, we still find outrageous jazz records being played in bars and cafes."

About a thousand titles, generally jazz recordings, were deemed inappropriate and a "request" was made that they not be played. The importation of English-language music records and sheet music was forbidden. All American and English music scores published in America or Japan, whether they were jazz or not, were to be destroyed. Jazz dance bands were banned; furthermore, trumpet and trombone players were prohibited from using mutes in their horns—"the true sound of instruments should not be distorted." Since Hawaiian music was also considered to be *tekisei ongaku,* the use of the steel guitar and ukulele was prohibited—"their effeminate slur and glissando weakens young people's spirit."

By the end of 1940, doors of all dance halls were padlocked by governmental decree—"You will not listen to enemy music; you will not dance to enemy music!" Prior to their closure, a military policeman was stationed in each to monitor the behavior of dancing couples. When it was deemed that a man danced too closely with his partner, the "guilty" person would be summoned discreetly to an obscure corner and be given a tidy whack on the side of his head—just a warning to behave himself "like a Japanese gentleman should!"

Meanwhile, local food supplies and other daily necessities for the civilian population ran increasingly short due to the insatiable demands of overseas troops and to wartime conditions which restricted the import of sorely needed foodstuffs. As warfare overseas raged and the tide of war gradually changed to favor the Americans and their Allies, the critical lack of food caused severe malnutrition among civilians. The rigid austerity of the war effort and the daily U.S. B-29 incendiary bombings gave rise to an extended, crippling psychological and physical numbing in an increasingly emaciated general populace.

Tazuko Usuki White was a six-year-old child when the *kenpei* (Japanese military police) and the district warden came, as forewarned, to the Beniya to confiscate her mother's collection of over two hundred phonograph records. Mrs. Usuki was the proprietress of a *kissaten* (coffee house) with an adjoining *stando-bah* (corruption of "stand bar") in the city of Otaru, Hokkaido. Patrons had been accustomed to listen leisurely to classical and popular Western music as they sipped a demitasse and enjoyed a bit of French pastry. Whiskey and Russian vodka with an assortment of simple snacks were available at the bar.

On the evening before the military authorities were to remove her record collection, Mrs. Usuki invited her friends and her shop employees to a farewell party—to gather for the last time to listen to music they loved. It was a warm, intimate evening. Caught in the euphoria brought on by music, drinks and friendly interaction, no one was aware of the intrusion of a thief. During the evening, someone quietly entered and stole every pair of boots neatly lined up inside the shop's front entry. The party which began so lightheartedly ended on a sour note!

On the next day, at the appointed time, authorities came to perform their "patriotic" duty. Phonograph records were boxed to be taken away on a truck. In Tazuko's memory remains one favorite record among all of those confiscated that day—"Lady of Spain," a vocal selection. As the truck drove away from the Beniya, Mrs. Usuki wept.

The Beniya bar, in time, had to close down—sources of whiskey and vodka became more and more scarce and then disappeared. The same fate awaited the *kissaten*. Coffee beans, which were imported, gradually became scarce to a point where they were no longer available. Furthermore, people were ordered not to drink coffee because "drinking coffee was *not* Japanese."

Between the rise and fall of dance halls and lavish stage productions, Nisei musicians made a living singing and playing their particular brand of jazz.

TAKAJI "KAJI" DOMOTO
Pioneer trumpeter from Oakland, California

Takaji Domoto, a trumpeter who organized a dixieland jazz combo in Tokyo in the mid-'20s, was a pioneer of Nisei jazz in Japan, according to *California Origins of the Jazz Boom in Occupied*

Japan, 1945-1952, a paper by Sidney Brown, Professor of History, University of Oklahoma. Domoto was born in Los Angeles in 1904 and graduated from Fremont High School, Oakland, in 1921. His father, an Issei, headed the North American Mercantile Company based in San Francisco, a successful import-export firm which was the first to import canned king crab meat from Hokkaido, Japan. His mother, an attractive, poised woman who spoke fluent English, was educated in a Christian mission school in Japan and later attended Mills College in Oakland. She was a woman of elevated social graces who held any music other than classical in disdain. Educational expectations were firmly entrenched in Domoto family values—daughters Yukiko and Yoshiko attended Wellesley College and Vassar College; Takaji attended Amherst College.

Cousin Toichi Domoto remembered: "Kaji was a natural-born musician who had good ears; he could play almost any instrument. He could listen to a jazz recording and play the identical tune on the piano without a music score. When Kaji was young, he would listen intently to his sister Yukiko practicing the piano. When she finished playing the final notes of her lesson, he would sit at the piano and accurately repeat what he had just heard—causing his sister to weep in frustration. He was that good.

"I think Kaji first started to play the trumpet in grade school. I used to hear him practice in the Fremont High School gym; he was leading a jazz band which he had organized."

In the mid-'20s Mr. Domoto transferred his base of operations to Tokyo, which became the new home for the entire Domoto family. During their transpacific voyage, Takaji played his trumpet in the ship's salon orchestra. The Japanese musicians recognized his talent and asked him to remain on the job. Unfortunately for Takaji, his mother nixed the attractive offer—no son of hers would play in a dance orchestra.

Sidney Brown learned that in 1925 Takaji enrolled in Keio University, where he formed a jazz band, the **Red and Blue Stompers Jazzband**. (Red and blue were the school colors.) The Stompers enjoyed a short-lived success playing for dance parties at legations and the Foreign Ministry; they even recorded several popular American jazz tunes. Unfortunately, Takaji was in time expelled from Keio for performing "immoral music." The Stompers were defunct. Still, Domoto is recognized by Koichi Uchida, a Japanese jazz historian, as a founder of jazz in Japan. With his reputation as a trumpeter intact, Domoto was employed in 1929 by H. White, president of Japan Columbia, to organize a Columbia Jazz Band. He assembled the best musicians available and remained on the fringe of the Japanese jazz world for many years.

Although he was an American citizen, Domoto elected to remain in Japan. Cousin

George Mukai, Rosebud Orchestra. San Francisco. 1930. Photo courtesy of Nancy Takeshita.

Paul Kato, Rosebud Orchestra. San Francisco. 1930. Photo courtesy of Nancy Takeshita.

Toichi explained: "Kaji preferred the Japanese lifestyle because in Japan men enjoyed their status as *danna sama* (privileged masters); women were assigned the role of submissive servants." During wartime he acted as an interpreter for a Japanese Army unit which guarded a POW camp. After the war Takaji joined a U.S. Army officer, a former prison inmate, in an emotional reunion here in the States. The officer was grateful to Takaji for contraband food Takaji regularly hid in the toilet for him and others during their incarceration in the prison camp. Covertly securing food for the POWs by bartering his personal belongings in exchange for scanty farm products, Takaji would order the Americans, 'Go clean the shit-house!'—Takaji's code message for 'I've hidden some foodstuffs for you.'"

CHARLIE KIKUGAWA
Expatriate from San Francisco

Charlie Kikugawa, born in San Francisco in 1907, was the oldest of four brothers. Three of them eventually became dance band drummers. Charlie started in junior high and continued playing drums in the high-school orchestra. While in high school, he joined with his white teenage friends to form a dance band that "played for peanuts at private dance parties, weddings, etc." Later, Charlie became the day manager of Sho Wa Lo, his dad's Chinese restaurant on Post Street. He opened the restaurant in the morning and closed it from 1:30 to 4:30 pm, during which time he would go to Willy's Sweet Shop "to jerk sodas."

Charlie Kikugawa. San Francisco. 1930. Photo courtesy of Nancy Takeshita.

In 1991 Kikugawa sent a letter from Japan describing his early San Francisco days: "After a few years [at nineteen-years-old], I formed the Rosebud Orchestra with some Nisei friends of mine. We decided on the name 'Rosebud' because we all hoped that someday the rosebud will bloom into a beautiful big rose." Members of the band were: Willie Ito, alto and soprano saxophones; Paul Kato, tenor sax and clarinet; Yuki Morikawa, piano; Henry Ishihara, trumpet and violin; and George Mukai, banjo. Bandleader Kikugawa played drums and sang.

"They were all fairly good players, but didn't intend to make music their career,"

Roy Jazz Band. Tokyo, ca. 1931. Four Nisei from San Francisco. Right to left, front row: Richard Okumoto, Shigeru Omoto. Back row: Charlie Kikugawa, Teddy Kozuma. Photo courtesy of Mary Fujihara.

Kikugawa continued. "I was the only one who wanted to lead a musician's life. The main reason for the others not wanting to become a pro was the discrimination in the strong Musicians Union. Since we were American citizens, we could join the union, but there'd be no jobs for us because our faces were Oriental.

"In 1929 I met Roy Koseki, a Japanese trumpet player, at the Ogawa Hotel; I think it was on California Street just above Grant Avenue. He was playing at a private dance with his ship's orchestra. In those days most of the big passenger liners plying between Japan and the States provided an orchestra for first-class passengers. Koseki invited me and a few others to go to Japan...said there'd be jobs for us. I jumped at the idea. I rounded up three musicians and came to Japan in 1930. Me, at age twenty-three.

"Here are their names: l. Teddy Kozuma, banjo; a cousin of Willy's (Ito) from Hawaii. Kozuma played on the Orpheum vaudeville circuit as a solo banjoist. He played in Japan, but went back to Los Angeles before the war. 2. Richard Okumoto, alto sax from Sacramento. After playing in Japan for a few years, he became a member of a ship's orchestra. He became sick while docked in San Francisco, so he returned to Sacramento, where he later died. 3. Shigeru "Shinglin" Omoto, guitar, lived on Bush between Buchanan and Webster, across the street from Kinmon Gakuen. He was doing quite well in Japan, but died of illness before the war."

The December 16, 1937, issue of the San Francisco *Nichi Bei Shinbun* (Japanese American News) reported Omoto's death in Mukden during his tour of Manchuria. He had been a member of a Japanese troupe of fifteen musicians and fifteen chorus girls contracted to perform for two years at the Broadway, a dance hall in Mukden. Prior to his last engagement, Omoto had been an orchestra leader at the Florida in Tokyo and also recorded with Polydor Record Company during his stay with the Takarazuka Theater.

Kikugawa continued: "Roy Koseki said that there would be a job ready for us. Well, it was a different story when we got here. Roy started looking for jobs after we got here. First we went on the road with a Tokyo comedy troupe. After coming back to Tokyo, we played theaters, putting on stage shows between movies. These jobs were few and far apart, so we decided to split and started to look for jobs individually. Luckily, we four Nisei found jobs quite easily. In Yokohama I found a job in a dance hall that was run by my father's friend who was from the States. The customers there were almost all non-Japanese, so the boss was really happy to have me in the band—I could speak with the customers freely in English to get their requests. About a quarter of the non-Japanese were locals and the others were mostly from the ships in port.

Some liners had an orchestra on board and the musicians used to come and bring us music, drum heads, sax reeds, etc. They were really a good bunch."

Edgar Pope, a University of Washington student of ethnomusicology, interviewed Charlie Kikugawa in Saitama, Japan, on August 14, 1992. Kikugawa, at 85 years, had a bagful of stories to tell about his musical career in Japan. The following are a few of the biographical incidents he disclosed.

Blue Knights, Charlie Kikugawa, leader. Yokohama, Japan. ca. 1932. Photo courtesy of Mari Kikugawa.

After his entry into Japanese dance music work, Kikugawa in time became the leader of his own band, the Blue Knights, at the Pacific, a dance hall in Yokohama. This elegant hall was graced by dance hostesses who were the first in Japan to be dressed in white satin gowns. The band, which included several outstanding Japanese jazz musicians such as Fumio Nanri, Nobu Matsumoto and Susumu Kudo, was composed of three saxes, a trumpet, a trombone and a four-man rhythm section.

About the time of Kikugawa's stay at the Pacific, Japan was embarked on expanding its economic and political boundaries. For the purpose of maintaining public morale and to support the war effort, the Japanese government had instituted a harsh austerity program. Suppression of Western music assumed bizarre forms. Straitlaced military authorities limited the number of saxophones, "instruments of the enemy," to a ratio of one saxophone to five other instruments in an orchestra. Musicians on the bandstand were not permitted to move in time with the music—no swaying, no overt movements. They were forbidden to wear their customary band uniforms. Instead, even for public performances, they were directed to wear drab khaki outfits—jackets with high military collars and cotton puttees wrapped around each leg from knee to ankle. Women were all expected to wear the unattractive *mompé*—simple, baggy pantaloons with cuffs drawn around the ankles.

Noriko Awaya, Queen of the Blues. Tokyo. ca. 1939. Photo courtesy of Kathy Neville.

When Kikugawa's contract at the Pacific was concluded, he was invited by Noriko Awaya and Hideo Oyama to join their tango band as their drummer. This was a stroke of good fortune for Kikugawa because the Argentine tango, not being of American origin, received the stamp of approval of the military police—the tango was not *tekisei ongaku,* so tango bands enjoyed a freedom denied other musicians. Kikugawa admitted that he was financially better off with Awaya than when he played in a standard dance band. Moreover, Noriko Awaya was such a prominent entertainer that she claimed privileges not afforded to others. She refused to wear a *mompé*—she demurred; after all, she was the Queen of the Blues! Awaya's tango band traveled and dined relatively in high style as they entertained civilians and military personnel in Japan and overseas in Manchuria and Korea. The only distraction they had to endure was having to comply with a governmental decree requiring the occasional playing of patriotic music and military marches.

When Japan's surrender ended the war, opportunities for jazz musicians flourished again. Thousands of American and Allied occupation personnel sought recreation in the larger urban areas of Japan; bars, cabarets and dance halls proliferated. Kikugawa sang, played drums and led his own fifteen-piece big band at the KMC Dance Hall in Kobe. He appeared on television and worked later as the master of ceremonies introducing a variety of acts at the Johnson Air Force

Base Non-commissioned Officers Club. Kikugawa worked the same club, six shows a week, for eleven consecutive years.

Aside from a visit or two to San Francisco, Kikugawa was an expatriate who never returned to the United States. He remained active in music well into his seventies; he sang with Jimmy Harada and the Old Boys, a six-piece dixieland band. In 1981 Kikugawa recorded with the Old Boys for Japan Victor (VCK-22170); he sang "All Of Me" and "It's A Sin To Tell A Lie" with style and youthful energy belying his seventy-four years. In his later years he taught English in a language school in Saitama and occasionally found employment dubbing Japanese into English for animated films. With his white goatee, Kikugawa resembled Colonel Sanders of Kentucky Fried Chicken. When he appeared in public, he would attract hordes of happy children who would gleefully shout, "It's Colonel Sanders…it's Colonel Sanders!"

Charlie Kikugawa, San Francisco Nisei musician, died in May, 1993, at age eighty-five in Saitama, Japan.

FUMIKO ALICE KAWABATA
Sojourner from Los Angeles

In 1934 a Japanese newspaper reported (translated): "Fumiko Kawabata, a Nisei jazz singer and eccentric dancer, is in her ascendancy. She [came] to Tokyo a year ago and prepared the way for wave after wave of other American-borns to Japan. As a result there are now here in Tokyo more than ten Nisei singers."

Fumiko Kawabata, née Fumiye Tachibana, was born in 1916 in Honolulu,

Fumiko Kawabata. Tokyo. 1935. Photo courtesy of Masahisa Segawa.

Hawaii. When she was three, the Kawabatas moved to Los Angeles, where she attended Maryknoll School. She started dancing at twelve years, underwent rigorous training in tap dance at the Ramsdell Studio, and soon became a teenage sensation when she made her début at the Orpheum Theater in Los Angeles. For some time she danced with "Fanchon and Marco Ideas," and then went on an RKO tour which opened at the Palace Theater in New York City. In 1929, at fourteen, she was dancing at the Roxie Theater in New York. While Japanese girls on the American stage generally performed in tumbling acts, Kawabata uniquely filled a double role of dancing and singing. Wherever she went, she won glowing press comments. Betty Inada, a Sacramento Nisei who followed Kawabata to Japan, recalled in a 1992 interview that Fumiko sang and danced high kicks with her feathery ostrich plumes in the RKO vaudeville circuit. As opposed to classical ballet, her earlier forte, Kawabata had turned to jazz dancing to become an instant hit. After a season on Broadway, Kawabata sailed for Japan in the fall of 1932.

Rose McKee wrote from Tokyo in a 1935 column:

Ticket for a stage show featuring Fumiko Kawabata, the "amber-colored Josephine Baker," a world-class dancer and outstanding singer. Morinaga Chocolate Co., sponsor. Shimonoseki, Japan. October 16, 1935. Photo courtesy of Masahisa Segawa.

SECOND GENERATION GIRLS INTRODUCING AMERICAN DANCE

There are four American-born Japanese girls now in Tokyo who are competing against one another in the entertainment field. Each in her own pleasant manner is smiling herself into the hearts of the Japanese. One does it with high kicks, another with the Hawaiian hula, another with a torch song or two, one with the good old accordion.

They trip along blossom-embroidered paths, but their road has not been easy, to hear them tell it. The girls are Miss Fumiko Kawabata, Miss Betty Inada, Miss Helen Honda and Miss Helen Sumida. Pioneer of them all is tall, pretty eighteen-year-old Fumiko Kawabata, who suggests the finery of a Paris hat box—looks just about as if she had been made to order.

The funny thing about it is that Miss Kawabata came to Japan to hide. Having made her first stage appearance at twelve, she decided that it was about time she forgot the stage for a little serious study. In fact, she had broken a contract to come here. But her fame had traveled before her and when she arrived, she was sought after for appearances on the local stages. She discovered that the Japanese did and did not want American dancing. They wanted her to appear all right and they wanted to see "jazz dancing," but they came knowing it was vulgar and they left muttering.

So Miss Kawabata's job was that of a pioneer. She had to teach her audiences what to appreciate, to show them that jazz was not necessarily vulgar. She had to educate a mass ear for Western music and a mass eye for Western dancing. To a less interested person, the task would have been pronounced futile, but this young girl stuck to it.

Sixteen-year-old Fumiko Kawabata arrived in Yokohama on the Asama Maru on October 30, 1932. She first sang on a noontime entertainment broadcast on radio station JOAK (now NHK) on February 10, 1933. On February 26 she débuted as a dancer and jazz singer at the Tokyo Gekijo and charmed her way into the hearts of the urban sophisticates of Tokyo. Kawabata's spectacular and showy dancing featured her touching the back of her head with her toes; she was extremely facile and light-footed in tap dance. As an experienced singer of show tunes, she specialized in torch songs. Widespread publicity ads for her stage reviews shouted: "FUMIKO KAWABATA: SINGS LIKE MARLENE DIETRICH! DANCES LIKE JOSEPHINE BAKER!" Her records proved to be best-sellers, and in no time she had recorded over twenty jazz songs. Singing in both Japanese and English, she established a style unique to Japanese audiences; she decidedly added exotic color to the Japanese jazz age.

In an LP album tracing the development of jazz in Japan, Columbia devotes an entire record to "Nisei Jazz Singer" Kawabata's early '30s 78 rpm recordings—sixteen American-origin tunes—"Lover, Come Back To Me," "Side By Side," "East Side, West Side," "Let Me Call You Sweetheart," to name a few. The following are excerpted translations of Japanese reviews of three of her early recordings:

"Sweet Jennie Lee," a tune written in 1930 by W. Donaldson, composer of "My Blue Heaven," was recorded on October 14, 1933. Kawabata was accompanied by the Columbia Jazz Band in a swingy arrangement written by Thomas Missman. Pleasant solos were by

Shin Matsumoto on tenor and Masuo Obata on trumpet.

"Side By Side" was first introduced in the States by Paul Whiteman in 1927. Several other orchestras helped popularize this tune. This recording on January 9, 1934, is a duet with Barton Crane—a joyous combination of rousing vocals with a smart arrangement by Missman.[12]

"Who?" is from the 1925 Broadway musical "Sunny," a big hit written by Jerome Kern and Oscar Hammerstein II. Kawabata sings "Who?" up-tempo at a fast clip with a pleasant swingy feeling. What makes this recording very special is Ryoichi Hattori's terrific arrangement, somewhat reminiscent of the Casa Loma Orchestra.[13] Masuo Obata on trumpet and Fujio Tsuruta on trombone contribute much to this record with their jazz solos. Recorded on January 9, 1934.

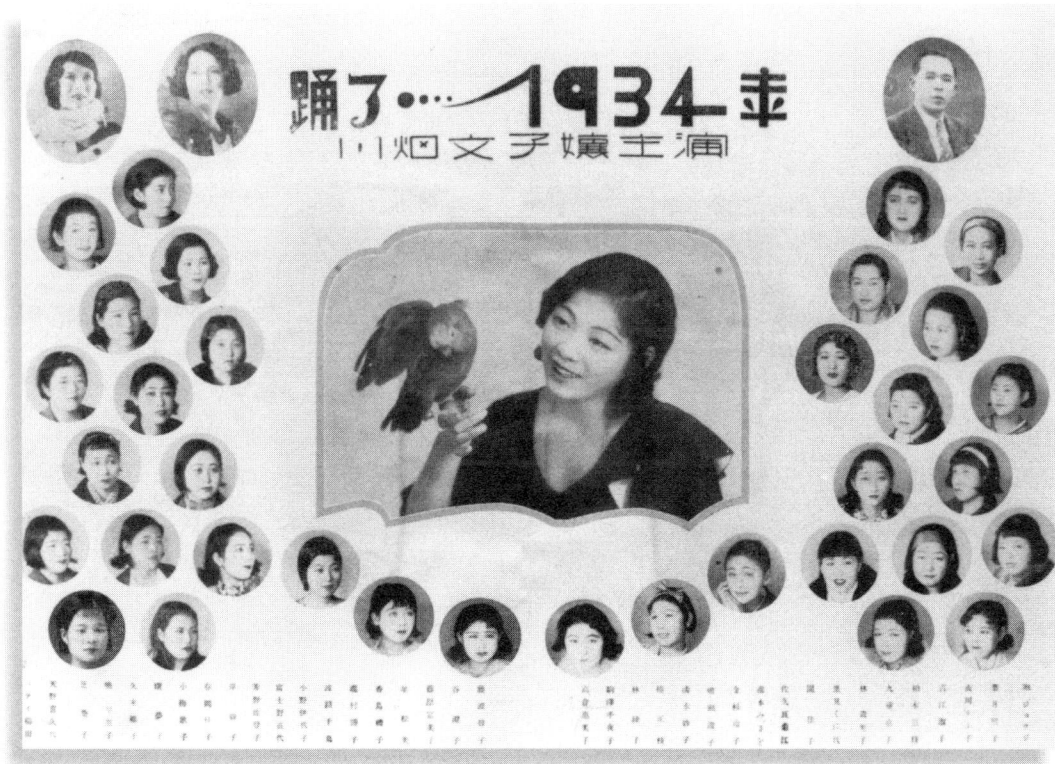

Advertisement for "Odori, 1934" ("Dance, 1934") Fumiko Kawabata, producer. Nichigeki Theater, Tokyo. 1934. Photo courtesy of Masahisa Segawa.

After two years with Columbia, Kawabata switched to Teichiku Records in 1934. Under the direction of Dick Miné, she recorded in just a few months many more songs. In the fall of 1933, Kawabata was given complete charge of a company of dancers and produced her own musical revue. She created dance numbers and routines, directed the entire show and even invented the musical scores for the tuneful sequences. The January 21, 1934, issue of the San Francisco *New World Daily News* reported:

FORMER L.A. DANCER IN THEATRE OPENER
Tokyo—The plaudits of five thousand theatregoers of Tokyo were lavished on the performance of Fumi Kawabata, former Los Angeles Nisei dancer in her headline act in the Orient's most pretentious theatre, Nippon Gekijo, at the gala opening held here last December. Forty-three chorus girls danced in the stage presentation of 'Odori 1934.' Bessie (Betty) Inada, Sacramento dancer, was featured among the supporting cast; all of which indicates the popularity of second generation talents.

The San Francisco *New World Daily News*, July 3, 1934, disclosed:

Fumiko Kawabata. Film still from "Uramachi no Kokyogaku." Tokyo. 1935. Photo courtesy of Masahisa Segawa.

FUMI KAWABATA IN JAPAN MOVIE
Tokyo—Fumi Kawabata is in the movies now. The prominent Nikkatsu Film Company has signed up the former Los Angeles Nisei to appear in a cinema soon together with none other than the "Clark Gable" of Japan, Denmei Suzuki. Creating a sensation on the vaudeville stage with her Americanized tap dancing and also her warbling, the little Angeleno lass who went to school here at the Maryknoll institution of book larnin' will just be recording another of her hits. The feature film will be directed by the

"DeMille" of Japan, director impresario Yutaka Abé and will be labeled as a Nikkatsu "super-spectacle." The contract for the film career of Fumi Kawabata calls for a handsome remuneration for the petite star and was signed only recently. The production will go into being at the Kyoto studio of the Nikkatsu soon.

"Waka Fufu Shiken Bekkyo" ("Trial Separation of a Young Couple") was the title of this Nikkatsu production in which Kawabata played a leading role. In one scene she is seen strumming a ukulele while leaning against a palm tree and singing "By the Waterfall" from the U.S. movie *Footlight Parade*.

In February, 1935, Kawabata appeared in Tokyo on the Shinjuku Theater stage in hilarious skits with **Sessue Hayakawa** and Ryoichi Tsujino in a thirty-minute repartee of gags in the American style. Subsequently, the March 11, 1935, Los Angeles *Rafu Shimpo* reported: "Tsuruga (Japan). Fumiko Kawabata, former Los Angeles Nisei and now the darling of the Ginza as a toe dancer, blues and jazz singer par excellence, will comfort the Japanese soldiers in Manchukuo in their trials and tribulations in the blistering cold in the wilds of that new country when she leaves at 7:00 tomorrow night for Manchu (Occupied Manchuria) on the Manchu Maru."

In the spring of 1935, Kawabata returned home to Los Angeles on the Asama Maru after an absence of three years. Just prior to her return, she had starred in *"Uramachi no Kokyogaku"* ("Back Street Symphony"), another Nikkatsu super-special, all-talkie production for which she was awarded first honors for outstanding performance. This movie was shown for a week in April at the Fuji Theater in Los Angeles and Kawabata appeared in person each night to address the audience.

Fumiko Kawabata. Tokyo. 1933. Betty Inada collection.

The August 11, 1935, Los Angeles *Rafu Shimpo* published a Bean Takeda interview:

> *Fumiko Kawabata, who aspires to be a dancing teacher, is modest and natural with an extremely pleasant personality. This young idol of thousands spoke of her meteoric stage success in much the same manner as a happy, enthusiastic child would be in describing a backyard amateur success. She disclosed that stage revues in Japan are patterned after the French, which is altogether different from the United States. Kawabata had plans to study dancing for a year before going to New York to fulfill a contract with the RKO stage circuit. Her mother denied that her daughter was engaged to be married to Konichi Nakaoka, slayer of Premier Hara in 1921. Nakaoka had earlier made a marriage proposal to Kawabata.*

In August 1935, on Japan Day at the amphitheater of the California Pacific International Exposition in San Diego, Kawabata sang "Johnnie," a Marlene Dietrich song, and danced for an audience of 15,000 including 7,000 Japanese Americans. "Fumi Kawabata, pride of Li'l Tokyo was 'tops' in every way. Her interpretive dancing manifested ability and talent," reported the L.A. *Rafu Shimpo*.

Poster for Fumiko Kawabata Show. Hibiya, Nichigeki Theater, Tokyo. May 31, 1938. Photo courtesy of Masahisa Segawa.

Kawabata, by now a significant star in the budding Japanese jazz scene, who served as a bridge for aspiring Nisei, returned to Japan before the outbreak of World War II. In May 1939, she married and withdrew from performing. During the war years, she reputedly lived with her two children and her husband's family in Hokkaido.

Despite her successes in Japan, Kawabata returned to California in 1948. She co-chaired the Japanese American Citizens League Queen Contest of the 1948 Nisei Week celebration and was also seen conferring with dancers during rehearsals of the Nisei Week Variety Show. In

December of the same year, Kawabata, together with Sue Takimoto Okabe, was in charge of costumes and make-up for a gigantic Koyasan YBA Variety Revue of traditional Japanese and Western music. This program was a benefit for the Tuberculosis Society and consisted of a collection of outstanding Nisei talent in song and dance, including the Futaba Band for Japanese music, the Hawaiian Surfriders and Tets Bessho's dance band for pop and swing music.

It has been alleged that Kawabata may be living currently in San Francisco. The 1989-90 San Francisco phone book listed a "Kawabata, F." without an address. A phone call in 1994 was fruitless; the phone number had been reassigned to a stranger. Fumiko Kawabata's current status is a mystery. Very few Nikkei, if any, are cognizant of Kawabata's achievements as an acclaimed entertainer in Japan. Her successes in show business, her creative energy, her many talents and her adventuresome courage deserve acknowledgment and acclaim.

Betty Inada. Tokyo. 1934. Photo courtesy of Mary Fujihara.

BETTY FUMIKO INADA

Sojourner from Sacramento, California

Betty Inada at eighty-years is a charming, attractive woman. She subtly radiates an unusual inner glow and energy—call it sex appeal. She lives with husband Cecil Silva in an unpretentious apartment—a crowded living room, a tiny kitchen and a bedroom—in Los Angeles's bustling Koreatown.

My entrée into Inada's life was a glamorous 5" x 7" photograph of her, professionally posed, with her personal signature in the lower right-hand corner: "To Raymond, For a happy future. Bette Inada, March 13, 1934."[14] I uncovered this precious photograph when scanning snapshots in an album belonging to Raymond Okumoto, banjo player in Richard's Original Syncopaters, the early Sacramento dance band.

Betty, approaching twenty-one then, had embarked impetuously on an adventure to Japan; she had been at a crossroads in her aspiration to become a professional vocalist. Affiliation with Fanchon & Marco, a vaudeville dance troupe, proved to be less than adequate for her needs. For Inada, who wanted to sing, calls were few and far between. It seems jugglers and acrobats in exotic costumes were stereotypical "Oriental" acts that were in vogue and in public demand.

Fumiko Kawabata of Los Angeles, with her singing and high dancing kicks, enjoyed relative success on the RKO circuit. However, by 1934, she had abandoned stateside theaters and was singing in Tokyo. Betty, spurred by Fumiko's success, implored her parents for permission to go to Japan to try her luck. After much dogged persistence on the part of Betty, Mr. Inada finally acquiesced with trepidation. He and his wife were comforted somewhat by the knowledge that the Kawabatas in Japan would assume responsibility for Betty and that **Toyo Miyatake**, a Los Angeles photographer, and Mrs. Miyatake would accompany her on the lengthy ship's voyage across the Pacific.

Fumi Kawabata and Betty Inada. Tokyo. 1934. Betty Inada collection.

One may wonder what motivates people to venture haphazardly into potentially grave predicaments—to trade the security of their home for an unpredictable, often disappointing, world. A glance into Inada's environment in her adolescence provides some clues to her inner spirit. Recollections of Betty by Sadie, her sister younger by six years, provide hints about Betty's disposition of spunk and boldness: *"Neisan* (elder sister) was born in Sacramento on November 10, 1913. My parents named her 'Fumiko.' Sometime later she became 'Bessie'…dad probably gave her that name. She hated it, so she changed it during high-school days to 'Betty.' Speaking of names, most of us had Japanese names, but often our grammar-school teachers had difficulty pronouncing them, so they either gave us American names or we chose one for ourselves. My parents called me 'Sadako'…I changed it to 'Sadie.'

"Neisan was very popular in high school…she had lots of boy friends. Even though I was much younger, mom often used to make me chaperon her to dances. Betty didn't like that at all. Early in life *neisan* had an independent mind of her own…headstrong. Mom told me that whenever *neisan* disobeyed or acted up, mom would chase her around the house with a broom… and I remember telling Betty: 'Mind mom for your own good!' Of course, my saying that didn't

do any good. My mother is now one hundred years old…played the *shamisen* and performed Japanese dances until she was ninety-five years. And my father liked to jitterbug with my little sister who took Japanese *odori* and tap dance lessons. I think Betty was dad's favorite…in his eyes she could do no wrong. That's why he let Betty go to Japan when she did."

World War I had opened up opportunities for women to move into work and duties which had been exclusive to men—women's liberation received a tremendous boost. It was an era of change, of exciting innovations in attitude and in lifestyle. With the cessation of the deadly war and its terrible consequences, it was time for healing and looking forward to a bright new future.

Prohibition of making, transporting and selling liquor was legislated in 1920 and then repealed in 1933—booze was flowing again. Women's skirts were shortened and worn daringly above the knees; women's hair was cut short. Eric Gill, English designer/artist penned the following quatrain:

If skirts should get shorter
Said the flapper with a sob,
There'll be two more cheeks to powder
And one more place to bob.

Betty Inada in a Tokyo stage review. ca. 1934. Betty Inada collection.

Betty Inada. Shibuya Shochiku Theater, Tokyo. 1940. Betty Inada collection.

The infectious, sizzling sounds of black jazz artists such as Louis Armstrong and Sidney Bechet encroached into the musical consciousness of white America, which had been dancing to sedate dance bands. Many white musicians—Benny Goodman, the Dorsey brothers, Gene Krupa, et al.—listened intently and became ardent converts as jazz worked its way up the Mississippi River from New Orleans to Chicago. Concurrently, in their Midwest isolation, Kansas City musicians—Bennie Moten, Count Basie, Jay McShann, Ben Webster, et al.—contributed significantly to the exciting new music form with their own unique flavor of jazz. Dance styles became highly energized. New steps quickly came into vogue one after the other—the Black Bottom, the Charleston, the Big Apple and the Lindy Hop.

The lifestyle of the Roaring '20s carried over into the '30s and infected even the placid Japanese community of sleepy Sacramento with Betty Inada smack-dab in the middle of it. **Lily Oyama Sasaki** remembers conservative Nisei girls with long, rich black hair held back by a simple metal clasp, eyeing Betty and her flapper pals, who wore their hair short, enhanced by celluloid barrettes covered with bright red and green stones. And *lipstick!* And short skirts with "rolled down hose, I'm one of those…" Lily remembers another song whose lyrics were in part: "I'm a rolling stone, I roll my own [stockings], Just an inch below my dimpled knees…"

Lily continues: "We Nisei all wanted to be blond and blue-eyed Americans; hated to be Japanese. **Michio Ito**, an internationally known Japanese exponent of modern Western dance, criticized us young Nisei for our short hairdos—thought we should be proud of our long, black hair. But we didn't care. We changed our Japanese names into American names. Went to movies, were crazy about Clara Bow and Joan Crawford! Loved jazz…listened to the exciting sounds of Red Nichols and his Five Pennies, Paul Whiteman, 'The King of Jazz,' and clarinet-playing Ted Lewis. Loved the vocal styles of Connie Boswell and Ruth Etting. Hawaiian music, also, was in."

Betty Inada and Michio Ito. Los Angeles. 1934. Toyo Miyatake photo. Photo courtesy of Masahisa Segawa.

Betty, extremely bored in the Sacramento Japanese ghetto, embraced the exciting new lifestyle. She became a conspicuous flapper in high heels, indulging occasionally in a furtive cigarette or two—a member of the jazzy set. Raising many an eyebrow, she and her like-minded friends aroused consternation among the community fuddy-duddies, both young and old. Being forward and unconventional, fired with an ambition to make it as a professional vocalist, she, not surprisingly, left dusty Sacramento on June 9, 1933, for Japan.

Betty had a difficult time finding entrée into the entertainment business when she arrived in Tokyo. Unable to speak fluent Japanese and working in a profession of relatively low status, she did not receive much respect—"I was treated like a *kawara kojiki*." (a beggar who lives in a dried-out river bed.)

Another unexpected barrier that Betty had to face was the lack of microphones in large halls. (The technology of efficient microphones was not advanced enough to permit their use by vocalists.) Megaphones (remember Rudy Vallee?) were used to project singers' voices into the audience over the accompaniment of orchestras. Betty did not use a megaphone. She explained: "They cramped my style…they were awkward. They hid my face…I hated them. What I did was to shout my songs. That strained my voice, but I had no choice. I didn't want to use a megaphone." Fortunately, microphone technology did improve in a few years. Betty was able to sing in her natural voice once again after a period of abuse—luckily, her vocal cords had not suffered damage.

Singers of popular songs were hired by recording studios, theaters and dance halls; night clubs featuring music were not in existence when Inada first arrived in Japan. Betty's break came when she signed a recording contract with Columbia Records of Japan. One of her earliest records was Kate Smith's popular anthem, "When the Moon Comes Over the Mountain," sung in Japanese. Betty was billed as a "jazz singer," but she, as well as other Nisei singers, was not a true jazz singer in the American sense. She sang *kayo kyoku*, a relatively commonplace form of Japanese popular songs in the '30s.

The following notes describing Inada's 1934 Columbia recordings provide a sampling of reviews of her work:

> *1. 'Happy Days Are Here Again.' A masterpiece hit as sung by Rudy Vallee and Charles King as the theme song of MGM's 1930 movie, 'I'm Always Chasing Rainbows,' is a melodious song. Though not well known in Japan, it is still heard in America. The arrangement by Takeo Niki is bouncy, and with the addition of strings is reminiscent of the Hollywood picture. Betty sings with a light, bright touch. The clarinet obbligato in the latter half of the record is sweet.*

2. *'Should I?' This tune today is popularly performed by dixieland bands. It was originally composed as the theme song of MGM's 1930 'Lord Byron of Broadway'. Niki's arrangement of this tune is strongly flavored in jazz. The outstanding trumpet solo is by Mitsuyuki Obata; the tenor sax, by Shin Matsumoto; and the piano, by Tatsuo Kato. Betty projects a great deal of energy when singing this fast-tempo arrangement.*

According to Japanese writer Jin Hayashi (translated):

Betty Inada was the Number One swing singer; her dance specialties were the hula and tap. Although her complexion was somewhat dark, she was charming. She had a bright disposition and was liked by all. She was on good terms with the Florida's mama [owner] and, therefore, this special relationship meant frequent appearances at the Florida. The bright cobalt colored skydome ceiling of the Florida was imbedded with hundreds of tiny lights, creating a

Betty Inada in stage review. Tokyo. ca. 1934. Betty Inada collection.

romantic illusion overhead of stars in the southern sky. Although most Japanese at the time thought that the hula was very immodest and sexy, a shiri furi dansu [butt shaking dance], I still remember that in this setting Inada's hula was terrific.

Kiyonao Okami, a native Japanese who now lives in Great Britain, adds in a letter:

When the Columbia Record Company held their annual All-Star Cast Show at one of the well-known theaters in Tokyo, we [Hilo Hawaiians] did our bit as one of the exclusive artists of that company. Betty Inada danced a hula accompanied by our music. Believe it or not, when she finished dancing and returned backstage, the Tokyo Metropolitan Police Vice Squad was waiting to arrest her. After much negotiation and explanation about traditional Hawaiian dancing which is nothing obscene, the arresting officers reluctantly released her...oh, my aching back!

Betty Inada and the Hilo Collegians. Tokyo. 1934. Front row, left to right: Shinichi Hirazawa, Naoyuki Okami, Kiyonao Okami, Betty Inada. Back row: Osamu Tominaga, Shigenori Obara. Betty Inada collection.

Betty Inada had a relaxed style of singing; she sang the popular ballads of the day with great appeal in Japanese and English. The Columbia Recording Orchestra accompanied her. Inada records sold well. At the Florida she shared the vocal billing with **Noriko Awaya**, the Queen of the Blues, a singer of Japanese-style blues and the vocalist for the alternate tango band. In addition, live shows on the theater stage, alternating with movies, provided many opportunities to perform. The following illustrates a typical program which featured a movie and the *atorakushon* ("attraction": stage review) at a Tokyo theater. The film: *It Happened One Night*, starring Claudette Colbert and Clark Gable. The stage presentation, titled "The Jazz Review," featured Teichiku recording star Dick Miné, Betty Inada of Japan Columbia, Helen Honda of Polydor Records and the Moana Glee Club. The program opened with Inada singing "Maleii Mele," followed by Dick Miné's "Black Pupil" (sic) ("Dark Eyes"?), then "My Little Grass Shack In Hawaii" sung by Helen Honda. Other selections were "Blue Hawaii," "Don't Sing Aloha," "Akaka Falls," "Lei e" and "Dinah" by Dick Miné. Following a graceful hula dance by Inada to "Hula Blues," the "jazz show" closed with the Moana Glee Club harmonizing on "Aloha Oe." A Japanese "Hawaiian orchestra" composed of ukulele, steel and standard guitars and bass viol accompanied the singers.

Betty also appeared in movies while under contract with Columbia Records. *The New World Daily News*, San Francisco, June 19, 1934, reported:

Betty Inada and Saburo Nakagawa. Film still from *Hodo no Sasayaki*. Tokyo. 1935. Photo courtesy of Masahisa Segawa.

> *BETTY INADA, GINZA STAR, IS BACK TO VISIT*
> *Sacramento girl who made good in Japan returns for three-month study visit of Paramount Studios in Hollywood and its motion picture technique in preparation for her coming movie work. The pretty and petite Sacramento girl, who already is the toast of the Ginza 'Broadway' arrived here on the NYK Chichibu Maru Wednesday afternoon. When asked about her future plans, she replied, 'When I return to Japan in September, I expect to remain there permanently.' After about two more years of stage life, she planned to open her own beauty salon. Inada had become, through her charm and patient application to stage work, one of the most popular entertainers in Japan. She was receiving a monthly salary of more than one thousand yen, compared to the girls in the chorus lines who received only about forty to fifty yen a month. In regard to chances of success for Nisei in Japan, Inada emphatically discouraged such thought, pointing to the fact that there are thousands of Nisei in Tokyo alone doing next to nothing and every one of them waiting for a chance to return to good old U.S.A.*

Musical Review. Tokyo. ca. 1934. Betty Inada collection.

The October 21, 1934, San Francisco *Hokubei Asahi* reported:

BESSIE INADA TO SAIL FOR JAPAN ON THE TATSUTA
Bessie Inada, Nisei blues singer from Sacramento, will sail back to Nippon on November 15 aboard the Tatsuta Maru to resume her stage career there. She expects to make two talkies for a Japanese film company when she returns.

This bulletin was followed by another in the *Hokubei,* November 11, 1934:

BESSIE INADA IN FAREWELL PARTY
Sacramento, November 7—A semiformal dance will be given by Bessie Inada at the Oak Park Clubhouse this Saturday night as a farewell party before she leaves for Japan on November 15 on the Tatsuta Maru. Roy Nikaido will serve as MC. Tom Curray and his Syncopators will furnish the music.

Upon her return to Japan, Betty Inada sang and danced the hula in *"Odoriko Nikki"* ("A Dancer's Journal"), a PCL Productions film, and starred in *"Hodo no Sasayaki"* ("Whispers on the Sidewalk"), produced by Shiro Kaga in 1935.

In a Rose McKee interview, Betty Inada described working conditions in Japan: "'Here you have to tell the orchestra exactly what to do and what you want. At home, the orchestra knows and you didn't have to worry about it. If you made a mistake, the orchestra covered it, but here, if you make a mistake, it all must be done over.'

"Miss Inada is making English and Japanese records. She says she must make the translated words fit the music—they have a habit of being too long. Although she knew something of Japanese before she came, she says it is hard to put feeling into a song when she is singing it in Japanese. So before

Betty Inada rehearsing chorus line. Tokyo. ca. 1934. Betty Inada collection.

she makes a Japanese record, she tries to find out exactly what the words mean and then she thinks very hard about the words as she sings. Sometimes, however, there is no one around to tell her what the words mean.

Betty Inada and Dick Miné. Manchuria, China. ca. 1940. Betty Inada collection.

"[She] says it is the students and the young people who like American entertainment—that the 'true Japanese in the old sense' do not understand nor approve of it. She misses the radio and the night clubs, finds that it is hard to fill in leisure time, which she has much more than she did in America."

Around 1940 Betty teamed with Kazuo Dick Miné, a topflight vocal star and the foremost proponent of Japanese popular music. Miné and Inada received much public acclaim as they toured theaters in Japan and performed for Japanese troops and civilians in Japanese-occupied Sakhalin, Russia, and Manchuria. After the cessation of World War II, they continued to sing with the Stardusters, the highly acclaimed Tokyo big band. In August 1950, Inada switched recording companies from Columbia to Teichiku

Records, where she continued for several years to produce many smash hits accompanied by **Buckie Shirakata** and his Aloha Hawaiians—"Texas Love Song," "Sophisticated Hula," "Tsuki No Yo Wa" and "Chu, Chu, Chu," a Japanese version of "Sioux City Sue."

Young George Miyakawa, a member of a prominent Sacramento family, returned from a prewar visit to Japan and reported to the community his reaction to a visit to the Florida Dance Hall: "Couldn't believe a Nisei [Inada] behaving like that. I was shocked at her dancing and prancing on stage...so brashly and boldly. What a way to make a living!"

Lily Oyama Sasaki, who had known Betty when she was a teenage flapper, found Inada in 1950, at age thirty-seven, "a changed person who had matured unbelievably into a refined woman. She spoke with a soft Japanese voice. She had toned down and had become a very nice Japanese lady."

Abandoning her musical career, Inada returned in 1958 to Sacramento, where she was engaged for a while with a partner in operating an unsuccessful Japanese restaurant. She subsequently moved to Los Angeles, where she met and married Cecil Silva; the two of them operated a modest hamburger stand. Thereafter, Inada worked several years in the photo studio of Toyo Miyatake. Virtually unknown to the local Japanese American community, Inada's star status had taken a major downturn. She no longer sang except for two special occasions: in 1979, at age sixty-seven, she was invited to Tokyo to appear in a tribute to Dick Miné. Accompanied by her former associate Buckie Shirakata on steel guitar, Inada sang "Sentimental Journey" and "Chu, Chu, Chu." On June 10, 1991, Inada again appeared onstage in Tokyo in a concert commemorating Miné's death— *"Nakama no konsato"* ("Friends of Dick Miné"). At age eighty in 1993, Betty Inada said, "I have no regrets. I did what I wanted to do in my own small way." Just four feet, ten inches in stature, but bighearted and possessed of dogged determination, Betty Inada, the Sacramento flapper, became, according to Japanese jazz historian Koichi Uchida, "Japan's most popular pre-World War II female jazz singer."

Teichiku record label. ca. 1950. Betty Inada collection.

TAFT BEPPU, A.K.A. JOHNNY BEPPU
Sojourner from Seattle, Washington

In the early '30s, Japanese college basketball teams came annually to the States to play Nisei teams on the West Coast and others in the Midwest. **Taft Beppu**, who was born in 1909 in Seattle, Washington, served as the interpreter for the Meiji University basketball team during its March 1933 stay in Seattle. After the tournament, Taft traveled with the Meiji team to San Francisco and then to Honolulu on the Chichibu Maru, arriving on March 18, 1933. Apparently a close friendship developed between Beppu and the Japanese team coach who urged Taft to enroll in Meiji University, Tokyo. Because of poor prospects for any kind of substantial employment in the States, and despite limited fluency in the Japanese language, Beppu, in good faith, made the decision to pursue studies overseas at Meiji.

Academic work made demands on Beppu, but it was not long before he organized a school jazz band and became its vocalist. Prior to his overseas venture, Beppu had gained limited experience as a solo pop singer with the Nisei Melodians in Seattle. Beppu managed to earn a degree at Meiji University, but his creative energies were directed toward being a successful singer. Jazz was making inroads into the consciousness of urban Japanese, and Beppu had an edge over native vocalists—he had grown up immersed in the sounds of popular American music. He signed a contract as an exclusive artist for Columbia Record Company of Japan and made his recording début in August 1934, singing "St. Louis Blues"—the first verse in Japanese and the second in English.

The *Jiji Shinpo*, a Japanese newspaper, reviewed the "St. Louis Blues" (translated): "Taft Beppu sings the 'St. Louis Blues' in a key that is too high; it should have been sung in a lower key. The special quality of his voice could not be heard in this recording. His voice is broad and fully-textured—well-suited to the microphone. With more care to details in his singing, he has the potential to become a top jazz singer without rivals." Beppu (now Johnny Beppu) was quoted later in an interview: "I am frustrated that there are no blues songs in popular Japanese music. I love sweet blues songs, not hot jazz. My favorite American singer, the one I truly admire, is Lanny Ross." Another newspaper article reported: "Beppu is young and ambitious; he does not exhibit the stereotypical Japanese American wildness. His speaking voice is a high baritone; on the other hand, his singing voice is a rich, low baritone—it is a charming voice. He still has no stage experience, but there is no one in Japan today whose voice compares with that of Johnny—a status he will probably continue to enjoy."

Beppu soon became an extremely popular entertainer in Japan. Accompanied by the Columbia Records Orchestra, he performed in theaters and at the Florida, the celebrated Tokyo dance hall. In an advertisement for a gala show featuring Columbia Recording artists, Taft Beppu was billed as "the new personality from America who will absolutely fulfill all of your expectations!" He was also a member of one of several troupes which traveled to entertain troops and Japanese civilians in occupied Korea and Manchuria. His appeal with audiences was very likely due to a relaxed American style of singing complemented by an authentic English diction. Local publicity ads labeled Beppu, "the Bing Crosby of Japan."

Taft Beppu, Miss Columbia (Records), Takio Niki. Tokyo. ca. 1934. Photo courtesy of Amy Matsuoka.

Despite his stellar achievements in Japan, Beppu came back to the United States around 1938 after a relatively short, but fulfilling, career in show business. His decision to return was due to several desires—to avoid being conscripted into the Japanese army, to retain his American citizenship, to resume living with his Nisei friends and to enjoy the relatively free lifestyle of America. Back in Seattle, Beppu, with brothers Grant and Lincoln, entered into a partnership in a fishing tackle business. Taft "Johnny" Beppu, jazz singer, did not resume singing; professional opportunities in music for Nisei in the U.S. were nonexistent. Japan was an abbreviated sojourn—pleasant and glamorous.

SHINICHIRO MIYAGAWA, A.K.A. RICKEY MIYAGAWA
Expatriate from Seattle

Shinichiro "Shiro" Miyagawa, also known as Rickey, was born in Seattle in 1907, the son of a well-to-do Issei businessman who had amassed a string of thirteen hotels in Seattle. According to an article in the Japanese *Jiji Shinpo,* July 2, 1934, Rickey Miyagawa had performed in the Midwest vaudeville circuit in the States in 1931. He also was very active in Seattle Japanese community stage productions. Miyagawa, called "Flo Ziegfield, the second," produced and directed the highly popular "Club Lotus" and "Nippon Garden Ideas" (variety shows) in 1930 at Nippon Kan. "With his directorial ability in such presentations unquestioned, he also sings and appears in comedies," reported the *Courier* in 1931. Virginia Kashino Tomita remembers going with her parents to a stage show in which Miyagawa performed: "I was still in grammar school then…musta been in the early 1930s. High-school girls, eating cheese chips, would scream and swoon as Shiro sang! I was really impressed with the wild behavior of the older girls…secretly wished I could join them. Rickey was so handsome…he had a great voice!"

Rickey Miyagawa. Tokyo. ca. 1937. Photo courtesy of Masahisa Segawa.

Kelly Yamada recalls: "Back in the '20s, I was the waterboy/equipment manager of the Nippon Athletic Club football team, a semipro Nisei club in the white Community League in Seattle. We traveled a lot…even went up to Vancouver to play. I remember Shinni [Shiro]. He was a good football player; he had a heavy build. I don't remember much about his singing except that he learned to sing in church, as most of us did, singing hymns. Incidentally, Shinni was the first Seattle Nisei, probably the only Nisei, to own a roadster which he drove up and down the coast, making enticing promises to pretty young ladies. Shinni was a smooth one!"

Leading an allegedly dissolute life as a spoiled only son, Miyagawa was banished to Japan by his father in 1933. It is no surprise that there he moved quickly into show business.

He débuted about the same time as Taft Beppu, also from Seattle, as an exclusive artist of Columbia Records of Japan.

Miyagawa had great appeal to Japanese jazz fans. A critic wrote the following in response to Miyagawa's March 10, 1934, début recording of "When You're Smiling":

This handsome, charismatic Nisei is a graduate of Bates College, Lewiston, Maine. His sweet crooning style is bata-kusai—evidence of extensive training and experience in America. On the other hand, his conversational interludes during his singing is an affectation that brings smiles to listeners' faces.

His "Maa-chan," recorded on June 18, 1935, is actually the 1920 hit, "Margie," made popular in the U.S. by Jimmie Lunceford. Miyagawa's rendition is delightful. He scored a big hit with the Japanese by his use of "Maa-chan" (a term of endearment derived from "Margie"). I like the energy of the small jazz ensemble. The arrangement by Takio Niki swings nicely. There are outstanding alto sax and clarinet solos by Mitsuru Ashida. The final trumpet solo was played by newcomer Hisashi Moriyama [from San Francisco], whose "Aah, Maa-chan," a soft cry at the very end, makes this record a big hit.

"Dinah," written in 1925, became well-known in Japan after its recordings by Ted Lewis and Bing Crosby were introduced into Japan. Around 1934 its popularity grew to the extent that many top Japanese vocalists competed to make recordings of the song. Rickey sings in Bing Crosby's crooning style and includes a bit of scat singing in this recording. He demonstrates an unusual, un-Japanese sense of musical perception. The arrangement as jazz is outstanding. With the baritone [saxophone] intro, followed by trumpet, guitar and clarinet solos, a very pleasing jazz combo sound is the result. Recorded on June 18, 1935.

Miyagawa ceased recording for Columbia and changed to Japan Victor following the above recordings. The *Rafu Shimpo* of Los Angeles reported in its August 23, 1935, edition that he appeared in an all-star show at the Hibiya Open Air Theater featuring Victor vocal stars. Miyagawa sang "Margie," "Gypsy Dream Rose," "St. Louis Blues" and "Dinah."

Kiyoshi Tomita of Seattle says, "I went to Japan to receive treatment for my eyes…guess it was about 1935. I used to hear Shiro on the radio many times in Tokyo. He would be the program announcer or he would sing or his recordings would be broadcast. I still remember a couple of his songs…'Dinah' and 'Caldonia, Caldonia.' Shiro also performed in skits and plays—

all the above in Japanese which he spoke very well…much better than most of us Nisei." Miyagawa appeared in elaborate stage shows featuring top entertainers and wrote Japanese lyrics to popular American hits which were in great vogue in Japan at the time. His singing was described by a newspaper scribe as an "American talking-jazz" style, i.e., interlacing conversational phrases and sentences into his songs. Miyagawa's hero was Jack Oakie, a popular Hollywood comedian with a wide smile and an easygoing singing style.

Shiro Miyagawa relinquished his U.S. citizenship during World War II. He served as a translator for the Japanese army, was married and spent the balance of his life in Japan, never returning to the States.

Rickey Miyagawa and Kyosuke Kami PCL Orchestra. Tokyo. ca. 1937. Photo courtesy of Masahisa Segawa.

CHIZUKO MIYAGAWA, A.K.A. HARUMI MIYAGAWA
Sojourner from Seattle

Chizuko Miyagawa, younger sister of Rickey Miyagawa, was born in Seattle, Washington, on June 18, 1916. She graduated from Franklin High School in 1933. "The Miyagawas lived on Beacon Hill," remembers Virginia Tomita. "I knew Chizuko because we were members of the Girls Service Guild of the Japanese Methodist Episcopal Church. All of us girls would go on Sundays to watch Nisei boys play baseball or football in the Courier League.[15] During one of the games, Chizuko's purse fell off the spectators' bench...spilling its contents onto the ground. We, being young and innocent, were shocked to see a package of cigarettes among the stuff that fell out. Chizuko was an outgoing, somewhat aggressive girl...like a tomboy. She would come up at times and kinda punch you on the arm. I don't remember her as being especially interested in music at that time—never heard her sing...though she did have a deep voice. I'm surprised to learn that she became a jazz singer in Japan."

Chizuko Miyagawa. Shochiku-Gakugekidan Show, Tokyo. 1938.

Henry Itoi, an old-time Seattleite does recall seeing Chizuko performing in a variety show at Nippon Kan. Evidently, she had some experience singing for audiences before her début in Japan. Tamiko Tai, now in her early eighties, was also a member of the Girls Service Guild with Chizuko; they played on the same GSG basketball team. Tai recalls: "Chizu was very athletic...played good basketball. I remember she and I were the first Nisei girls to get driver's licenses in Seattle; we were only sixteen years old at that time!"

The San Francisco *Hokubei Asahi*, October 16, 1934, reported:

NISEI SINGER AND DANCER TO LEAVE FOR NIPPON STAGE
Miss Dorothy Chizuko Miyagawa, second generation blues singer of Seattle, will make her final bow to the radio audience over [station] KXA on the Courier Program it was

announced today. She is to join her brother, Shinichiro Miyagawa, who is at present the Toast of Nippon in the jazz world, making Japanese and English popular recordings. She is expected to make records for Columbia Records Company during her stay in Japan. She is to be accompanied by her mother and expects to depart October 27.

Chizuko Miyagawa with Shochiku Dancers. Tokyo. 1937. Left to right: Saburo Nakagawa, Midori Amakusa, Chizuko Miyagawa, Mineko Ogura, Yo Kikumoto. Photo courtesy of Masahisa Segawa.

Chizuko Miyagawa's parents' wishes were that the eighteen-year-old would learn the Japanese language and absorb the rich culture there. However, with brother Ricky paving the way, Chizuko, as Harumi (her stage name), "caught the ninth wave" and embarked on her professional career in Japan at age nineteen soon after her arrival in November 1934, when Columbia Records of Japan offered Chizuko a contract. "Blue Prelude," composed by Gordon Jenkins and enjoying a hit 1933 recording by the Isham Jones Orchestra, was her début recording on December 31, 1935. Records at that time featured a different vocalist on each side of the platter. Harumi sang "Blue Prelude" in Japanese and English on the B side; Noriko Awaya, the Queen of the Blues, sang on side A, which was presumably the stronger side as far as potential sales were concerned—Awaya was already an established recording star. To the surprise of Columbia Records executives, "Blue Prelude" turned out to be the hit side!

In a review of the record, a Japanese critic wrote: "Literally, [this tune] is a blue ballad and [Harumi's] forte. Her sentimental, pathos-filled song style is terrific. The muted trumpet solo is played by [San Francisco expatriate] **Hisashi Moriyama** and the powerful, heart-rending tenor sax solo by Shin Matsumoto." Harumi's interpretation, strongly flavored with true English pronunciation and jazz-oriented phrasing and sung with a voice that was unique in texture, caught the fancy of sophisticated jazz lovers.

Another critic reported that "Miyagawa was a beauty with very fair complexion. Her friends and fans called her by her pet name, 'Haa yan.' Her voice was husky and her style was relaxed, effortless; she had an outstanding sense of rhythm. In a short time, she became a well-known and highly respected vocalist among the top jazzmen in Tokyo." In 1937 she was chosen to sing periodically with the house dance band of the Shinbashi Dance Hall. In the following year Harumi was the featured soloist with the Million Dollar Swing Band in a Christmas show. In 1938 she sang her favorites, "Blue Prelude" and "It's A Sin To Tell A Lie," at the Teigekijo (Imperial Theater) in the début performance of the Shochiku Band. In a 1939 concert, she was picked as the singer for the All-Japan All-Star Swing Band.

George Atsumo, in a 1993 interview, remembered accompanying his father in prewar Tokyo to the Teikoku Gekijo (a theater featuring foreign films and live stage shows) to hear Harumi Miyagawa perform on stage. She sang, among other songs, "Lover, Come Back to Me" in Japanese, but her singing sounded strange to young Atsumo because her rendition in Japanese was that of a Nisei, not a native-born Japanese. Coincidentally, Atsumo years later became the leader of a swing combo during the occupation of Japan and Miyagawa sang a few engagements with his group.

Despite the success of "Blue Prelude," what Harumi truly desired was to sing rhythmic jazz. Yet Columbia would not let her sing anything but sweet melodies. After much pleading, she finally convinced producer Goro Uchiyama to allow her to record "Sing, Sing, Sing."[16] A frenetic arrangement of this tune was performed by Benny Goodman and his orchestra in *Hollywood Hotel,* a movie released in 1938. This exciting swing version was also familiar to jazz fans in Japan. Although the score of "Sing, Sing, Sing" was available in Japan, Harumi wanted Ryoichi Hattori expressly to arrange the number for her recording. In order to ensure that this happened, she went to the Teigekijo, where Hattori was conducting, to ask him to compose the score. Her enthusiasm impressed Hattori and he agreed to write. The result was a marvelous vocal by Harumi and a fine Columbia Jazz Band accompaniment. Recorded on July 16, 1939, the first chorus was sung in Japanese and the second in English, with marvelous swingin' segments of scat singing. "The trombone solo is played by Tsuruta, the bold tone and phrasing à la [Coleman] Hawkins is by tenor saxman Shin Matsumoto, a rare vibes solo is by Kazuo Tanaka, the walking bass by Ryo Watanabe. The whole band is hotly lilting; Harumi, also on the wave, swings nicely," wrote a record reviewer.

As evidenced by accounts of prewar friends in Seattle, Chizuko's persona—assertive, athletic, individualistic, outgoing—and her naturally deep voice were basic ingredients which contributed toward her successful career in Japan. She terminated her singing career when, according to a Japanese writer, "she fell in love with Fumitaka Iino, a 'Keio boy,' married him and retired. Now she lives on the West Coast (United States) happily reminiscing about her old jazz band companions. She left only about ten recordings, but they are all superior jazz vocals."

Before her return with her husband and child to the States, she spent some time in Shanghai. George Atsumo learned from Fumiye Miyagawa, a professional pianist (no relation to Chizuko) that she, Fumiye, worked with Chizuko on dance hall dates in Shanghai. "Before World War II, Shanghai was considered the 'mecca of jazz' in Asia and served as an important training ground for Japanese jazz musicians," reports Japanese jazz historian **Larry Richards**. "There they could listen to and take lessons from real pros. Chicago pianist Teddy Weatherford gave lessons to pioneer jazz trumpeter Fumio Nanri while in Shanghai. Japanese musicians returning from Shanghai were automatically given preferential treatment and referred to as 'so-and-so, returnee from Shanghai.'" Harumi Miyagawa may well have been one thus honored.

The Iino family left Japan in the '50s to settle initially in Seattle and then in Los Angeles. After the loss of her husband, Chizuko lived for six years with Kathy Iino Neville, her daughter, in Sausalito, California. Chizuko Miyagawa, jazz singer, died in 1992 at age seventy-seven.

Helen Sumida. Tokyo. ca. 1935. Photo courtesy of Masahisa Segawa.

HELEN SUMIDA
Sojourner from Fresno, California

Following in the footsteps of Fumiko Kawabata in the early '30s, at a time when jazz attracted new fans and dance halls began to proliferate in Japan, seventeen-year-old **Helen Sumida** arrived in April 1934 to add to a number of Nisei who brought fresh breath to the Japanese jazz world and created a sensation in the recording industry. She was signed to a recording contract with Victor of Japan and débuted that July in a Victor Records All-Star Stage Review at the Hibiya Civic Auditorium in Tokyo.

Sumida was born in 1917 in Fresno, California. At an early age she began piano and ballet lessons; in time she became the pianist in her high school orchestra. In 1932 she entered a talent show at the Golden Gate Theater in San Francisco. Her outstanding tap and ballet performance placed her as one of seventeen winners among two-thousand-plus entrants. Graduating with top honors from high school, she enrolled in a drama school and soon appeared in RKO Orpheum Theater stage revues in Los Angeles and in motion picture musicals.

Sumida's voice suited her wide repertoire of vocals, from the blues to ballads; her jazz songs had a pleasant, rhythmic feel. Her dance style and technique ranged favorably from fast tap to "snaky Harlem" to soft-shoe. Sumida's song and dance talent represented a valuable asset of star quality to the stable of Victor Records artists. In order to compete with Columbia's Fumiko Kawabata, Victor began producing a series of recordings in July 1934, featuring Sumida singing jazzy vocal solos, accompanying herself on piano, and in comic vocal duets with Ichiro Fujiyama. By the end of 1936, Victor had produced and distributed sixteen Sumida records.

Nisei Goro Murata, in a special report to the *Rafu Shimpo* in March 1935, wrote:

Chubby-faced and wide-eyed Helen Sumida, who is under contract with the Victor Talking Machine Company, was once a pupil of Michio Ito, noted terpsichorean in Hollywood. In her apartment overlooking the Sumida River, Miss Sumida was playing the accordion when I went to get a little story for her friends in America, perhaps some in Fresno, her birthplace.

She danced, sang and played the accordion in "Hyakumannin no Gassho" ["A Chorus of a Million Voices"], with Katsutaro, Ichiro Fujiyama and other popular musicians of Japan. Recently she made a trip to Dairen [Manchuria] and sang there during the New Year celebration. Hers has been a rosy path, but she thinks it was just luck. Perhaps she has learned that culture [trait] called Japanese modesty.

Another interviewer, Rose McKee, wrote in 1935:

To Helen Sumida, seventeen, Japan has all been one grand experience and she has found herself chased by contracts. She came with her family with a round trip ticket expecting to return in three months. That was a year ago. She had a contract with a small company immediately upon landing and then the Victor Company asked her to sign with them for three years. She said, "One year," and they compromised on one and a half years.

She is a graduate of the Paul Gerson School of Dramatics in Hollywood and appeared in a Spanish version of "The Cardboard City," which featured Catalina Barcena. While going to her lessons with Michio Ito, she would pass the Fox Movie Studio gate every morning. Directors began to ask about the girl in brown slacks that always passed the gate, but never knocked. Finally, one day, her friend told her she better go over to Fox for they had a contract waiting for the girl in brown slacks. She did and found the contract, and she worked for this company before coming to Japan.[17]

Nisei journalist Welly Shibata reported from Tokyo to the *Japanese American News* in August 1935: "Helen Sumida is singing, but her records (as yet) are not making a great ado. She has a cute voice, they say, but the phonograph dealers state her records do not sell so well. She has been getting good publicity, however; one magazine writing her up as a great Hollywood star. She is young yet, so give her time. Her work in motion pictures will probably give her a boost."

Several years later, a music critic in Japan reported: "In the spring of 1937, Helen Sumida returned to the United States, never to return again to Japan. Because of her abbreviated stay, familiarity with her music has worn thin—very few people remember her today. Fortunately, eight excellent jazz vocal selections of this young lady can be heard on Record #4-Side A of the Victor album, 'History of Japanese Jazz and Pop: A Prewar Collection.' They are all numbers popular in the United States at the time and Sumida's interpretations of these songs contain a charming flavor. We can listen to these vocals with great pleasure."

In a letter dated July 28, 1993, **Kiyonao Okami**, a Japanese native musician who often worked on the same bill with Nisei vocalists, wrote from his present home in Great Britain: "To supply some newsy info on the Nisei jazz groups who came to Japan in the 1930s, I can add one girl singer without trying to think back—that is, Helen Sumida, whom I last saw in Los Angeles about thirty some years ago. Helen, like our Hawaiian band, Hilo Hawaiians (later Hilo Collegians), was an exclusive artist with the Victor Record Company of Japan. Helen sang with our band many times. Her main field was singing, of course, but she also played the piano and the accordion. She was a damned good jazz pianist. When we held our annual concerts, she played solo piano for us. I might add that many years later when we met with Helen Sumida in Los Angeles, she was married and holding a very important position in some industry which had nothing to do with the entertainment field she was in previously. We really were taken aback."

RAYMOND TSUTOMU "BUCKIE" SHIRAKATA

Expatriate from Hawaii

Hawaiian music and dance were introduced to Japanese audiences by native Hawaiian troupes appearing in expositions in the '20s. Subsequently, Nisei singers and musicians from Hawaii and the U.S. mainland were influential in popularizing this exotic music and the "erotic" hula in the context of the Japanese jazz age. **Buckie Shirakata** of Hawaii is given credit by ethnomusicologist **Shuhei Hosokawa** for introducing the electric steel guitar to Japan in 1935. Hosokawa also credits Shirakata with introducing the technique of tuning a guitar in A-minor instead of the usual C-major. Japanese steel guitar players were quick to adopt A-minor tuning because it facilitated playing popular Japanese songs, which were often written in the minor key. Shirakata's Aloha Hawaiians, originally a trio, played tunes which were highly syncopated and the ensemble sound, especially with the electric steel guitar, had great appeal to Japanese audiences. Not long after his arrival in Japan, he teamed with Dick Miné and later with Betty Inada to produce best-selling records with Hawaiian flavor.

Shirakata, after an initial six-month visit in 1933, emigrated to Japan in 1935. He assembled his own band, the Aloha Hawaiians, and made appearances—usually accompanying singers and dancers—with great success in dance halls and theaters throughout the country. With the closing of ballrooms by governmental decree on October 31, 1940, he joined an all-star jazz band established as an *ongaku imon dan* (musical consolation corps) to entertain Japanese troops in Burma, Java, Malaya, Taiwan and the Philippines. Upon his return to Japan after a lengthy tour, he was advised by military authorities that Hawaiian music and the steel guitar were prohibited. Unable to work on the Japanese mainland, Shirakata made additional trips to overseas territories as a sideman in Dick Miné's troupe.

Kiyonao Okami, now in his eighties, reminisces: "Shirakata was a very good friend of my brother, as well as mine. Prior to the outbreak of the war (late '30s), the Japanese government prohibited all record companies from importing Western music. Therefore, no new records were available from America. Such being the case, Buckie and my brother were asked by a company to play Hawaiian music in its studio with a view to producing records under a fictitious name such as 'Ray Kenney and his Hawaiians' or something. Of course, the singing parts were all sung in English. My brother sent me one of these records while I was studying at Stanford [in 1938]. How about that? My brother, also a guitar player, considers Buckie to be the world's best steel guitar player. As far as I know, he is still playing. He is a few years older than I am."

When the war finally ended, a sudden boom in Japan of Hawaiian music put Shirakata in the spotlight. Best known for appearances with his Aloha Hawaiians and his LP recordings of Hawaiian, American and Japanese tunes, he was consistently voted "Most popular steel guitarist" in the [Japanese] *Swing Journal* readers' poll throughout the 1950s.

HELEN YUKIKO HONDA
Sojourner from Hawaii

Rose McKee reported from Japan in 1935:

> *Helen Honda also has brought the hula from Honolulu and she is recording for the Polydor Company, making Japanese, English and Hawaiian records. She appeared recently in a motion picture entitled, "Karisomé no Kuchibeni" ("A Touch of Red Lipstick") with Miss* **Takako Irié**. *Although born in Hawaii, Honda was educated in California and has done radio and stage work in Los Angeles. She, too, is pretty and charming in a young-lady manner.*
>
> *Here are some problems of the second generation group. "Being Japanese, we are supposed to know how to behave in a Japanese manner while all our lives we have been Americans. We don't know what to do and when we make mistakes, we are pardoned because we are Americans," she explains.*
>
> *She says she misses honest criticism in Japan. "I am never scolded nor ever praised. It is hard to find what pleases Japanese audiences. At home, if I performed below standard, I was told, and when I excelled, I was praised. I like that."*
>
> *But Miss Honda finds the opportunity for study a good thing and she enjoys the novelty of Japan. When she came, she appeared at the Hotel New Grand in Yokohama for several months. Her brother arrived with her, but now she is here alone.*

In another interview, datelined Tokyo, March 1, 1935, Goro Murata wrote to the *Rafu Shimpo*:

> *Helen Honda is somewhat tired of Japan and her people. Show business is not at all smooth sailing in Japan. There are bad managers and promoters who blow the wind in the wrong direction and ruin your chance to make money.*
>
> *'The Japanese don't show any signs of appreciation for my singing,' complained Miss Honda, 'And I don't know when they are crabbing about my Hawaiian music.' Japanese music fans are not expressive, according to Helen.*

Welly Shibata, in an August 1935 column for the *Japanese American News*, wrote:

Helen Sumida. Tokyo. ca. 1935. Photo courtesy of Masahisa Segawa.

DRIPPING WITH SWEETNESS, HAWAIIAN HELEN HONDA SINGS IN TOKYO
Featured in Nippon Records.
TOKYO—*"Ka lei e, Roselaui e, He lei hui hui hui e." The 'hui' business has nothing whatsoever to do with Huey Long. It is Helen Honda, second generation from Hawaii, singing 'Gekka No Oka Ni' ('On Moonlit Hills') a Nijo record which has brought the Honda voice, dripping with Honolulu sugariness, into sudden prominence in Japanese record circles.*

Helen Honda HAS a voice, so the critics are saying. In addition, when it comes to Hawaiian music, which is popular in Japan, no one can sing it (with the proper falsetto) exactly like Honda can. Her latest offering is a recording of 'By the Waters of the Minnetonka.'

It's a hard racket, this entertainment and recording business. Fumi Kawabata is a byword. The others are not so widely know as yet outside of Tokyo, but they are up and coming. The second generation isn't doing bad at all. So give them all the breaks and watch their smoke.

A short notice in the May 29, 1948, issue of the *Rafu Shimpo* reported Helen Honda back home in Honolulu, performing for U.S. military personnel.

HISASHI MORIYAMA
Expatriate from San Francisco

Hisashi "Sash" Moriyama, born in San Francisco in May 1910, lived at 1797 Sutter Street, near Buchanan Street. He was the second of three Moriyama children, with an older brother named Iwao and a sister, Kazu. His father was a commercial photographer in San Francisco's Japantown. Teenagers periodically visited the Moriyama Studio, the Moriyama Shashin Kan, to look at the display of recently photographed newlyweds—a popular way at the time for adolescent girls to be informed of the latest in the romance department.

As a youngster, Moriyama was a bugler in Boy Scout Troop 12 drum and bugle corps;

he later played the mellophone, the French horn and the trumpet in Polytechnic High School. Hisashi loved his trumpet; each day he would saturate the neighborhood skies with brilliant, sometimes not-so-brilliant, sounds of his horn.

In 1929 Lily Oyama Sasaki scribbled on her copy of Hisashi's high school graduation photo: "'Sash' had a lot of 'S.A.,' as the girls would admit, i.e., sex appeal…large for his age, bold and shy at once, aggressive, explosive and sophisticated." Lily continued: "My high school girl friend, Elizabeth Kozono [Murata], seventeen then; drove all the way to S.F. from Sac'to [Sacramento]…taking her dad's car (some weak pretext) just to get a glimpse of him or with high hopes of running into him as he, with his family, lived in a large corner sandstone house. We took nearly four hours on the old road. When she (Eliz.) asked me to accompany her, I went, but noticed nothing happened—she was too 'chicken' to knock at his door. So we bought a few things and returned home (to Sac'to). She promptly buys a saxophone, thinking this may 'make a hit' with Sash as Sash was one of the best trumpet players among the high schools in S.F. and was sent to Sac'to to perform in the High School U.S.A. Band."

Determined to pursue a career in music, Hisashi matriculated in 1929 at the College of the Pacific, Stockton, California. Unfortunately, after several semesters, Moriyama had to terminate his studies because of financial constraints created by the Depression. He then enrolled in San Francisco State Teachers College to further his musical skills. Moriyama's extracurricular activities involved organizing his own dance band for community dances, which often took place at Kinmon Gakuen Hall. He also gave trumpet lessons to aspiring youngsters at the local YMCA and directed the Epworth League choir of the San Francisco Japanese Methodist Episcopal Church. For diversion

Hisashi Moriyama, high school graduation photo. San Francisco. 1929. Photo courtesy of Lily Oyama Sasaki.

Buchanan St. YMCA, Blazing Arrows Club. San Francisco. ca. 1929. Hisashi Moriyama, top row, center. Photo courtesy of Jiro Shimakawa.

from his music he played basketball with the Blazing Arrows, the Japanese YMCA club, and, as often as he could, went fishing, his favorite pastime.

About this time Moriyama came in contact with Japanese musicians working on transpacific Japanese ocean liners. San Francisco was a major port for travelers coming from or going to Japan. Dance-band musicians were hired to entertain first-class passengers in the elegant dining rooms of these ships. Since ballroom dancing and swing music were coming into vogue in Japan, as they had in the United States, Japanese musicians seized every opportunity to listen to jazz at its source. Thus, Moriyama was in great demand to escort them to local hotels in downtown San Francisco to listen to popular dance bands. Bolstered by talk of dance music's growing popularity and the shortage of jazz musicians in Japan, Hisashi, sensing a frustrating future here in the States, decided to take his chances overseas and left San Francisco in 1934 for Tokyo.

Soon after his arrival, Moriyama signed a contract with Columbia Records of Japan and worked in the trumpet section of the Columbia Jazz Orchestra and, eventually, recorded several sides as featured vocalist. The Columbia Records Orchestra, which included many of the leading Japanese jazz musicians of the time, also played nightly gigs for hundreds of Tokyo smoothies at the Florida. Ballroom dancing was *in* for urban male sophisticates; the Florida promised an array of attractive taxi dancers.

Roy Ashizawa of San Francisco recalled: "In 1938 my father sent me to Japan for one year of cultural exposure. It was three months of shrines, temples and museums and nine months of back alleys and dance halls of Tokyo. I frequently went to the Florida to see Hisashi and dance the jitterbug and fox-trot with hostesses at ten *sen* a dance [three U.S. cents]. Hisashi played the trumpet and during the course of the night's gig, he sang several songs in English. I remember he sang 'My Blue Heaven.' Tib [Kamayatsu] from Los Angeles played guitar in the band. They

Louis Armstrong and Hisashi Moriyama. Tokyo. ca. 1953. Photo courtesy of Kazu Itabashi.

played on the main stage and alternated with a Latin band which played from the mezzanine stage directly above the cocktail bar. The bar sold alcoholic beverages and a soft drink similar to Coca Cola called Vita Cola. Occasionally, after the dance, Hisashi, his beautiful Japanese wife, Tib and I went to a nearby Chinese restaurant for tasty bowls of noodles.

Columbia Records Orchestra. Tokyo. ca. 1935. Left to right: Fukui, Saigo, Shin Matsumoto, Hisashi Moriyama, Momo-chan. (Inscription on bass drum head: "I JUST COULDN'T TAKE IT, BABY."). Photo courtesy of Yoshio Morimoto.

"The Tokyo Theater had stage shows between movies—singers, tap dancers and chorus lines. I recall one performance in 1938. The orchestra sat on a huge revolving stage. On the right side up front, Tamaki Miura stood at a microphone singing a Japanese song named 'My Trumpet.' On the left stood Hisashi, immaculately dressed in a white tuxedo, white bow tie and white shoes. And each time Tamaki Miura sang *'To-ran-pet-to',* Hisashi raised his horn toward the ceiling of the theater and blew half-a-dozen bars in accompaniment. I was impressed."[18]

Kiyonao Okami, a member of the Hilo Hawaiians in Japan in the '30s, wrote: "1930's was a period when the Japanese military began taking over the government and the whole of Japan. They tried hard to get rid of all Western influences in our daily lives. The authorities decreed, accordingly, that students will not be allowed to enter any dance hall, and Florida was no exception, of course. Consequently, the smart manager of that dance hall procured at least one dozen coats and ties and put them in his back room. When a student quietly slipped into [the dance hall] in his college uniform, a woman at the reception swiftly figured out the size of her customer and gave him a coat and a tie. Within a minute, he became a ready-made non-student—a business man. My size was thirty-eight short at that time, but unfortunately I have out-grown that size. Through this way, I used to see Hisashi and his orchestra."

When Western music was eventually banned by government decree and ballrooms were closed in 1940, Moriyama was fortunate to be able to continue playing trumpet in an all-star band which no longer played *jazu* (jazz) but was permitted to play *kei ongaku* (light music). This government-sanctioned group was given the label *ongaku imon dan* (musical consolation corps) and entertained troops overseas in southeast Asia during its occupation by Japanese troops. After touring for about four months, Moriyama returned to Japan and, fortunately, was permitted to play "light music" with another orchestra, one of four or five which toured Japan, also under the sanction of the military.

After the defeat of Japanese forces and when Japan was occupied by American and Allied troops, Japanese dance bands enjoyed a tremendous resurgence of job opportunities. **Al Kimoto** of San Francisco was billeted with other Nisei Military Intelligence Service language specialists in the NYK Building (Nippon Yusen Kaisha) in downtown Tokyo. He recalls a couple of clubs that the U.S. occupation personnel frequented—the Tokyo Club and the Marigold, a taxi dance hall. The latter was located in the war-damaged Itoya Building along the Ginza, which had been Tokyo's most fashionable street, then dotted with buildings burned during B-29 firebomb raids. Kimoto claims that there were 150 to 200 hostesses who worked at the Marigold—each hostess receiving a small percentage of the ticket for a dance with a guest. The dance hall was a critical source of income for hostesses and their families. Because of the wartime shortage of clothing and money, many ladies reconstructed their Japanese kimonos into western-style gowns—it was a time of survival and recovery. **Mas Manbo** recalls: "My wife Emiko was with me when I went to the Marigold, and she noticed that one of the taxi dancers, while managing to find an evening dress to wear, had Japanese army shoes on her feet."

On the night that Kimoto went to the Marigold, Moriyama's orchestra was on the bandstand. (Kimoto had no inkling of Moriyama's prewar San Francisco origin.) He especially enjoyed the singing of a gorgeous Japanese female vocalist; he even remembers the tune—"Love Letters In The Sand." Says Kimoto, "She sang in English with perfect diction and pronunciation. Amazed, I later asked the vocalist about her background and discovered that her name was Yoshiko Ishii, a native of Japan,[19] and her English coach was Hisashi Moriyama, a Nisei! It was a shock to learn that the man with the horn leading the dance band was a native son from San Francisco… my home town!"

In time Moriyama worked steadily with his New Pacific orchestra, ensconced in United States military clubs in Tokyo—Tachikawa Air Force Base, Pershing Heights and Washington Heights. For the delight of American jazz fans, in addition to standard dance tunes, the band's book contained swinging blues charts of Count Basie and Woody Herman's big-band bebop arrangements of "Apple Honey" and "Caldonia," with Moriyama doing the vocals on the latter.

During his years in retirement, Moriyama happily returned to his favorite pastime, fishing, which brought him to Canada several times in search of beautiful salmon. Hisashi Moriyama died in 1990 in Japan. His Nisei-infused jazz legacy abides in his daughter Ryoko. Brother Iwao, who resides in Bethesda, Maryland, has remarked with a smile that "Hisashi would have gotten a kick to learn that he was the subject of research about Nikkei musicians. He was a happy-go-lucky guy who enjoyed life to the hilt. He had a fulfilling life playing his trumpet and leading a prestigious dance band…a rich life he probably couldn't have experienced here in the States."

RYOKO MORIYAMA

Hisashi Moriyama's legacy to his daughter **Ryoko** was the gift of song. Her 1967 singing début was a recording of her original composition, *"Kono Hiroi Nohara Ni Ippai"* ("A Field Full of Love"), a stunning best-seller. Soon Ryoko was known as "Queen of Folk," a label she felt was undeserved because "my heart was truly into popular music, not folk." Her career has expanded subsequently to successful stage appearances, which total over two thousand to date. She has also released forty-nine singles and sixty-two albums, including *The Christmas Album,* scored by Gordon Jenkins and featuring the orchestral accompaniment of the New York Philharmonic Orchestra. Ryoko is a versatile vocalist with an engaging smile and a dynamic stage presence; her repertoire includes both popular Japanese and Western tunes (spirituals, pops, jazz). Nisei expatriate Tom Oshidari (see below) wrote: "Ryoko, a beautiful, gifted, tremendously popular television star, is known for her perfect English singing, an art which no other [Japanese] star could match!"

On May 26, 1996, Ryoko performed at the Sacramento (California) Jazz Jubilee accompanied by the **J-Town Jazz Ensemble**, a seventeen-piece swing band based in San Francisco's Japantown. The Sacramento gig heralded her sensational engagement at Carnegie Hall on July 12, 1996, in commemoration of her thirtieth year as a vocalist. **Michel Legrand**, French composer and pianist, conducted a luxurious forty-piece French assemblage of soothing strings and bold brasses. Virtually unknown heretofore to American audiences, Ryoko Moriyama's U.S. début earned the adulation of a thousand new fans. Ryoko Moriyama's success may be attributed directly to her Nisei father's love of jazz and his determination to pursue a career in music. Hisashi Moriyama could have remained in San Francisco and worked in his father's photography studio. If that had been the case, would there have been such an engaging star as Ryoko?

Ad for Ryoko Moriyama/Michel Legrand Concert. Carnegie Hall, New York City. July 12, 1996. Photo courtesy of George Yoshida.

TOM OSHIDARI
Expatriate from Stockton, California

Tom Oshidari was born in Stockton, where he attended grammar school and high school. He stroked a mean banjo—a very popular instrument in the '20s and '30s. As a member of a trio, The Banjo Boys, he performed on a weekly radio show on Station KLX, Oakland, and also in vaudeville shows on the stages of theaters in the San Francisco area. He also led a short-lived Nisei dance band in Oakland with Hisashi Moriyama and John Yoshino, trumpets; Dick Motoyoshi and George Takahashi, saxophones; Mary Harano, piano; and Tom Tsuji, drums and xylophone. They were purported to have played dance music at the Peking Low Restaurant in Oakland Chinatown on weekends.

After high school Oshidari matriculated at the College of the Pacific. He majored in music theory and played the bass viol in the college symphony orchestra, the tuba in the marching band. As an undergraduate, Tom composed a symphonic poem which was performed by the Stockton Symphony Orchestra and by the college symphony orchestra which he conducted.

After graduation in 1935 from the College of the Pacific, at the height of the great Depression in the United States, Oshidari, with very little facility in Japanese language, traveled immediately to Japan. In a recent letter, he wrote: "I spoke pidgin Japanese when I arrived in Japan, where its [Western] music was still in its infant stage. I somehow survived without plucking a note on my banjo. One day a traveling [Japanese] banjo player who was eking out a living on country [music] circuits appeared. Glad of a chance to put my expensive instrument to a useful purpose, I said to the musician whose name I can't recall, 'Here, take this [banjo] and stick it out. Do the best you can in your tough musician's life…and good luck!' This event put a period to my banjo-playing career, and my luck began to change dramatically.

Tom Oshidari. Oakland, Calif. ca. 1931. Photo courtesy of Aiko Yamamoto.

"Instead of performing, I began to write, produce and direct musical shows on NHK, the major radio network which was and is still a government administered organization. One of its programs employed the Columbia Recording Orchestra, which accompanied virtually every top-name popular musician in Japan—jazz instrumentalists, pop vocalists, chanson singers and classical artists.

"During the war my show depicting the culture of Japan was valued so highly by Japanese General Headquarters that my signature could exempt members of the Columbia Recording Orchestra from military conscription. [Nisei] Hisashi Moriyama, who was single at that time, received such an exemption. There could possibly have been no Ryoko (Moriyama's daughter) if he had gotten involved in a war in which millions of Japanese soldiers died."

After the war, Oshidari inaugurated a successful radio advertising company which he headed for over three decades. He spent the last six years before retirement as the Far East Director of the Tokyo affiliate of WGN, the prestigious radio/television subsidiary of the (Chicago) Tribune Company. Tom Oshidari, the "banjo king" from Stockton, California, resided in retirement with his wife in Tokyo until his death in 1993.

THE SHO TOKYANS
The Los Angeles Dance Band's Gig in Japan

The **Sho Tokyans** were delighted when Hawaiian steel guitar devotee **Naoyuki Okami**, a Japanese native, secured a six-month contract for the band to play dance halls in suburban Tokyo—the Chante Claire and the Ballet Tabarin. Despite the promise of a working contract in Japan, personnel problems surfaced for the Sho Tokyans when Kikugawa, the drummer; Amano, the pianist; Arima, a trumpeter; and Chiye Tawa, the vocalist, elected to remain in Los Angeles.

Says Mas Manbo: "The six who decided to make the Japan trip were fugitives from fruit stands, flower shops, and farming and gardening businesses. Ages about twenty-two to twenty-nine, we constituted a pretty good cross section of the working Nisei population." Leader George Igawa, Susumu Chikami and Mas Manbo, the sax section; trumpeter Hajimu Masuda and bass player Joe Sakai were among the original members of the Sho Tokyans who decided to go overseas. After an intensive search, replacements were found: Lauro Planton on piano and Pete Pilan on drums from Filipino dance halls in the city; and Sam Najar, a nineteen-year-old Mexican trumpeter.

Naoyuki Okami, who had obtained the contract for the Sho Tokyans, strongly urged: "Bring Dolly Fujioka…she'll be a big hit over here. She's a good singer…she'll look good with a baton in her hand in front of the band." Dolly agreed to go. She had been a pop vocalist for some time. The San Francisco *Hokubei Asahi* reported on September 5, 1934: "Dolly Lee To Sing For Sacramento Cabaret. Dolly Fujioka, cabaret singer, known as Dolly Lee of this city, has been engaged by Miami Cabaret in Sacramento to sing in the opening night program there. She has a one-month contract with the cafe and is leaving here for Sacramento on Wednesday."

Thus, the team of Sho Tokyans that would travel to Japan was set except for a guitar player. The search was directed to the Olivers, a Nisei men's club. One of the Olivers suggested: "Why don't you ask Tib [Kamayatsu]…he'll probably go. Go on down to the pool hall where he hangs out…he's there all the time." Leader Igawa went. "Yup, there he was…shooting pool. And when I asked if he'd be interested in playing guitar with us in Japan, he answered without hesitation, 'Sure, I'll go!'"

Mas Manbo wrote: "We embarked for Yokohama on the Tatsuta Maru from Los Angeles in July 1937, just about the time the Japanese forces initiated its invasion of the Chinese mainland which spurred the deterioration of [Japan's] entertainment business." As stipulated in the contract, they played the Chante Claire for three months and later the Ballet Tabarin, but the original group of Sho Tokyans from the United States broke up soon after their Chante Claire engagement. The discriminatory policies of the Japanese immigration department in regard to the three non-Japanese members of the Sho Tokyans did not allow for an extension of their short-term visas. Igawa remembers the disappointment of Sam Najar, the Mexican trumpeter, when he learned that his visa extension had been denied and he had to return to the States: "Sam really enjoyed playing music with us in Japan. When he received the discouraging news about his visa renewal, he cried."

Mas Manbo continued: "We then finished our run at the Ballet Tabarin with three replacements—a trumpet player named Cruz, a drummer named Doro, both Filipino old-hands in Japan, and a Japanese pianist whose name I recollect as Yamane. While our band may not have sounded so hot, we at least looked like a million dollars with an impressive array of instruments, tuxedos or mess jackets with red cummerbunds and with Dolly in front as torch singer—a curvaceous lass who knew her way around. Anyway, the customers couldn't have cared less if we

Sho Tokyans. Kawaguchi, Japan. December 1937. Left to right: Susumu Chikami, George Igawa, Hajimu Masuda, Cruz, Masao Manbo, Tadashi Kamayatsu, Doro, Joe Sakai, Yamane. Front center: Dolly Fujioka. Photo courtesy of Masao Manbo.

hit a sour note or two; they were there mainly to cuddle with the dance hall cuties."

Igawa adds: "In the latter part of 1937, we played the Ballet Tabarin in Kawaguchi—stayed there for the balance of our six-month contract. Alternating with a tango band, with each group playing twenty-minute sets, we played six nights a week from 5:00 to 11:00 pm. We were very popular with the dance crowds at the Chante Claire and the Ballet Tabarin because we understood what we were playing. You see, Japanese musicians could read music well, but they were too tight...no feeling. We couldn't read as well, but we sounded good because we were relaxed and enjoyed ourselves on the bandstand."

Tib Kamayatsu was a great hit singing novelty songs such as "The Music Goes 'Round and 'Round" and "The Love Bug Will Bite You." He had a charismatic stage presence—a handsome smile plus an engaging singing style. Kamayatsu obviously doted on the music; dancers on the floor were delighted.

Joe Sakai remembers: "Japanese musicians begged us for copies of our music arrangements because their bootlegged copies from Hong Kong contained many inaccuracies and printing errors. The lyrics to songs such as 'Honeysuckle Rose' and 'The Lady Is A Tramp' were considered too risqué by the dance-hall management, which requested that we not play them. Dance hostesses would tip members of the band so that we musicians would direct customers to them. Patrons, in turn, would tip us so that we would introduce them to the choicest ladies of the hall. Gangsters would visit the band leader for monthly 'protection' payoffs."

In a 1994 letter, Mas Manbo threw some light on Sakai's recollections: "Maybe we had 'Honeysuckle Rose,' but not 'The Lady Is A Tramp.' I don't think anybody made a fuss about lyrics. I doubt that the Japanese knew what the lyrics in English exactly meant. I was aware there were gangsters around. When Hy Masuda made a play for a taxi dancer, he was warned [that] she was a gangster's moll. I didn't know about protection payments though. In Japan, of course, the fellows who came around to the dance halls weren't too concerned about the music very much. For many, ballroom dancing was not the attraction as much as the presence of delightful hostesses who would plaster right up against them. Earning salaries which were quite good for that time of one hundred sixty yen monthly, we played for large crowds in Saitama."

George Igawa continues: "After the conclusion of the Ballet Tabarin job, we couldn't get a new contract because I didn't have the money to grease the palms of greedy dance-hall managers. The fifty yen a week they demanded represented my entire salary for the week. I sailed back to the States early in 1938."

Upon his return, Igawa resumed his gardening work. He was later incarcerated during World War II in Heart Mountain Detention Camp, Wyoming, where he organized and led a big band.[20] Several years later, when he returned home to Los Angeles from the detention center, Igawa organized the Taiheiyo Band, which played popular Japanese music arranged mostly by Igawa himself. At age sixty, he gave up playing music and the leadership of his band because of the demanding and tedious responsibility of arranging music for ten vocalists who sang with the band. "It was too much work; it took all of my time to write parts for each instrument," Igawa said. "When a *hakujin* [white] musician friend told me that he got fifty dollars for writing out the saxophone section parts just for one tune, I was shocked. I didn't get a penny for any of my work! So, I said, 'To hell with it,' and gave it up...just too much work."

Dolly Fujioka returned to the U.S. about the same time as Igawa. But before she left Japan, Fujioka recorded a few sides for Columbia of Japan after the Sho Tokyans' contract expired. In July 1938, she recorded "Where The Lazy River Goes By," a Jimmie McHugh hit tune first introduced in a 1936 movie, "Banjo On My Knee." A Japanese record reviewer wrote: "Recordings of 'Lazy River' by Ray Noble and his orchestra and also by Midge Williams in her Teddy Wilson sessions were received well in Japan. Subsequently, the song was performed many times on Japanese stages. Midge's marvelous, pure voice has not changed a bit from the time she sang here in Japan; her great vocal style has continued to be highly imitated by our singers. Dolly Fujioka, the vocalist for a Nisei dance band, utilizes English monologue in combination with Japanese lyrics and, in this way, she creates a marvelous mood of intimacy. She is accompanied by the Columbia orchestra with a tenor sax solo by Shin Matsumoto."

In a 1993 letter, Kiyonao Okami wrote: "I didn't get to know Dolly Fujioka very well while she was in Japan. I was surprised to see her in New York [in the mid-'60s], where she was singing in a restaurant on Seventh Avenue."

Joe Sakai also returned sometime in 1938 to the States; he was married and had a family here. He resumed playing his bass viol with the reorganized Sho Tokyans. During World War II he was incarcerated in Manzanar Detention Camp in central California, where he helped to organize the Jive Bombers, a sixteen-piece big band. In the postwar years he became the leader of a small combo and gigged with other Nisei musicians. In 1995, approaching his mid-eighties, Sakai gave up his bass viol, but he still enjoys listening to jazz. His granddaughter provides him with a bountiful supply of jazz CDs—Wynton Marsalis is a current favorite. Says Sakai, "I can't get around on my own, so I don't work gigs anymore. I'm really sad 'cause music is what I live for!"

Hajimu "Hy" Masuda, unlike Sakai and Igawa, elected to remain in Japan as a professional musician. Motivated by a love for music burning within, his sojourn in the Far East resulted in an adventure of many years while he toured Japan, China and Korea before returning to his native land.

When the Sho Tokyans' Ballet Tabarin contract expired in 1938, Masuda moved to Kamakura and lived as an itinerant musician, working with several bands in central Japan and the northern provinces. About this time, Masuda quit the trumpet and took up the saxophone. In fact, he borrowed Mas Manbo's clarinet and departed for Shanghai, the prevailing hot spot for jazz in the Far East. Here he found unlimited lucrative jobs in dance halls. After a stint in sophisticated, up-beat Shanghai, he toured Korea and Manchuria with another dance band and finally returned to Japan.

Things were going very well, but Masuda's good life was short-lived. Shortly thereafter, the U.S. Naval Base at Pearl Harbor was attacked and warfare erupted between Japan and the United States. Masuda, preoccupied with comfortable living, had either miscalculated or disregarded the imminence of war. He found himself stranded in Japan—transpacific passage had abruptly been cut off.

Japanese law decreed that offspring of Japanese nationals are bona fide members of the Japanese citizenry. Since his father was born in Japan, Masuda was subject to conscription into the army despite his birth in the United States. His possession of dual citizenship created a distressing set of circumstances—suspected of being an American agent, Masuda was subjected to

The Sho Tokyans. Kawaguchi, Japan. 1937. Left to right: Masao Manbo, Joe Sakai, Cruz, Doro, Hajimu Masuda. Photo courtesy of Masao Manbo.

intense questioning, harassment and even beatings by the *kenpeitai,* the Japanese military police. Despite Masuda's strong declarations of his U.S. citizenship, he was drafted in May 1943 into the Imperial Japanese Army. Not trusted to bear arms, he was first assigned as a bugler; then, for a short time, he drove a quartermaster delivery truck. Subsequently, Masuda was transferred to Canton, China, to work at a radio listening post, sitting side-by-side with German Luftwaffe personnel, monitoring English-language news broadcasts. Masuda's service in the Japanese army nullified his U.S. citizenship.

Following the surrender of Germany, Masuda was detained by American authorities as a possible witness to testify against the Germans, who were charged with continuing acts of war after the armistice was signed on May 8, 1945. It is not known whether or not he was called to appear in court, but Masuda was eventually released from custody. When the Japanese surrender took place on August 15, 1945, Masuda's unit was demilitarized and, traveling together with Japanese nationals stranded in China, this bedraggled, war-weary group, undergoing great hardship, eventually reached Shanghai, the port of embarkation for Japan. Hy Masuda chose to remain in Shanghai, where he joined the Filipino Musicians Union and resumed his career as a dance-band musician.

In 1948 the Communist threat in Shanghai compelled Masuda to leave China. Incredibly, he was permitted to reenter Japan, even though his legal status was "stateless" when he arrived in Shibuya in October 1950. With evidence provided by his mother and his wife Hattie (née Tomimatsu), the daughter of a Japanese businessman who had befriended him in wartime Shanghai, Masuda was successful in regaining his U.S. citizenship. An additional factor which weighed heavily in support of his American status was the fateful testimony of a former Japanese army sergeant who testified that a reluctant Masuda was coerced into enlisting in the Japanese army. This sergeant who was so thoroughly supportive during the hearing was Masuda's superior during his enlistment and had often mercilessly beaten Masuda because of his being a Nisei—a suspect traitor. The appearance of the sergeant at the hearing was the result of their chance meeting in busy Shibuya after the war.

At the end of the war, the occupation of Japan by American and Allied troops created abundant opportunities for musicians to work in servicemen's clubs, dance halls and night clubs. Hy Masuda, now playing a tenor sax exclusively, led his own band, the Moon Glowers, and worked as a full-time musician at the Tachikawa Civilian Club, Camp Zama NCO Mess, Haneda Airmen's Club, Tachikawa Airmen's Open Mess, etc.

"I first met Uncle Hy in Japan during the Korean war," says **Roy Obana** of Redwood City, California. "I was then stationed at Itazuké Air Force Base and would occasionally fly to Tachikawa Air Force Base, where Hy worked leading his own dance band. He was kinda short-tempered; but, he was usually a happy-go-lucky type, *if* you didn't cross him. Guess he had an 'attitude'—like 'Don't bug me!' In his later years he quit drinking, but before he gave it up, whenever I visited, he'd always say, 'Come on, let's go out for a drink.'"

The Masudas returned to the States in 1959. Hy worked days as a gardener in Los Angeles, and rejoined George Igawa to play in the Taiheiyo Band. At the same time, he occasionally gigged dance jobs in Haruo Fujisawa's combo. Sakai, Fujisawa's bass player says, "Twenty-three years later [after I left Japan], back in the States, Hy came down to First Street in L.A., where I was working at Club Ginza. We had a *lot* to talk about.

"Shortly after Hy lost his wife in 1985, he suffered a stroke," continues Obana. "Being disabled, he moved to his sister's home in Gardena. There, he spent his final years. Uncle Hy was a person who lived just for music—his radio was constantly tuned to jazz on an FM station. He would place only the saxophone mouthpiece to his mouth and blow quietly, making strange sounds, reliving his days playing in dance bands. And that's kinda like how his life ended."

Hajimu "Hy" Masuda, pioneer Nisei music maker, personable and charming, was born in Los Angeles on June 8, 1915, and died in Gardena, California, on August 5, 1990.

Masao Manbo, who also remained in Japan, wrote: "I hung on with trumpet player Hy Masuda and joined expatriate San Franciscan Charlie Kikugawa's band at the Pacific dance hall located near the Yokohama waterfront. Musicians of the P & O Line [Pacific and Orient] would visit the Pacific to sit in with the band. Here I met an Englishman for the first time—a really nice chap named Bill Hoare, who was a saxman in a ship's orchestra. I remember every time things became dull on the gig, Charlie would have our best trumpet player named Oishi bust out with 'Somebody Stole My Gal'.

"It was after the Yokohama job folded that I worked with Archie Grant, Japan's last prewar black entertainer, in

Masao Manbo. Yokohama, Japan. ca. 1937.
Photo courtesy of Masao Manbo.

the Hawaiian-Negro Band on tour of outlying spots. The band, justifying its name, had a few veteran Hawaiian performers besides Archie, the lone black who played the piano. Archie was a small man with graying hair and a little mustache who carried himself with dignity. He must have been around fifty at the time. He had been a Los Angeles mail clerk before he landed in Japan; liked what he saw when he stepped off the boat and decided to stay. Archie and I hit it off right away as we were both from L.A. and spoke the same language. Members of the troupe used to say we were like father and son.

"The Hawaiian-Negro Band was part of a motley stage show that included a couple of fading opera singers, a handsome Korean tenor who rendered popular songs and a few dancers. The band would open with a chorus of 'Song Of The Islands' and the Hawaiian fellows would play and sing other numbers. Archie was no Teddy Wilson at the keyboard, but he would put on a funny act, perfected no doubt through appearances in the Osaka area as a sort of poor man's Sammy Davis, Jr. Donning a rumpled sailor suit, he would blare out a few bars on a trombone and then tap dance furiously. Mopping his brow and gasping for breath, he would holler, *'Ahh, shindo!'* The exclamation in Kansai patois—equivalent to 'Boy, am I bushed!'—was a sure laugh-getter.

"One night Archie demonstrated how quick he was on the uptake. I was trying to explain to a maid how my not-common surname Manbo was written [in Japanese] and I began in the usual fashion, *'Ichiman no man,'* meaning *'man'* as in the Japanese character for 'ten thousand.' And then Archie quickly chimed in without missing a beat, 'And "bo" as in hobo!'

"While performing in Hiroshima, whom should I spot in the audience one day but my aged grandfather, owner of a farm close to the city, sitting with a young relative. When the fellows in the band got wind of this, they urged me to get up and play a solo. I did so, rendering an unaccompanied version on my tenor sax of 'I Can't Give You Anything But Love.' No doubt it stank out loud. I always did love jazz, but was never much of a performer. After the day's show, though, a kid—a solitary schoolboy in a somber, black uniform—approached me as I was leaving the theater, thrust out an autograph book and said in good English, 'May I have your signature?' I signed with a flourish for my only fan, adding 'Hollywood, Calif.' after my name. I had lived in the movie capital before coming to Japan and was proud of it. But I didn't want to return there to my old occupation, which meant pushing a lawn mower.

"Following the Hiroshima engagement, the troupe performed in Hofu, a town in Yamaguchi Prefecture, and in Moji, a Kyushu port, where it disbanded as the end of 1938 neared. I never saw Archie and the Hawaiian fellows again; this was also the time when I gave up the saxophone—to nobody's regret. It was soon after that I met Pete Takahashi, the chief proofreader of the American-run *Japan Advertiser* in Tokyo, who offered me a job as an assistant proofreader. Takahashi, a Nisei, was the older brother of the Takahashi sisters, Helen and Dorothy, who were pro jazz singers back in the States. I saw them perform at the Paramount Theater in Los Angeles. I still remember one of their songs—'I Only Have Eyes For You.' Dorothy later married the Chinese fellow who appeared with them. Dorothy and Tony Wing subsequently worked as 'Toy and Wing,' a [ballroom dance] duo.

"I worked for the *Japan Times* after it took over the *Advertiser* in 1940. When the latter folded, I was ready to go back to the States as it looked like there would be a war, but then I decided to stick it out. During the war I changed my citizenship to Japanese as the police were making things tough for the Nisei. I then followed Pete into the Domei News Agency, where I remained throughout the war. I tried to do some playing, but soon did not have any instruments. Hy Masuda, who began singing Japanese popular songs in Asakusa, borrowed my tenor sax which fell into the hands of a Japanese guy who was the manager of an all-girl orchestra. Later Masuda borrowed my clarinet and then went off with it to Shanghai. Actually though, if I had the instruments all along, they would have been destroyed when the Akasaka section of Tokyo was engulfed in flames during a B-29 air raid in May, 1945. I barely escaped being burned to death in the raid."

In the postwar years, Manbo married a native Japanese woman and served at various times as a journalist for the *Jiji Press,* the International News Service of the United States, the Kyodo News Service and the *Japan Times*. Much of his writing covered jazz, music and sports events including baseball, boxing, pro wrestling, bowling and swimming. Other assignments included magazine articles and occasional columns overseas to the *Pacific Citizen,* the Japanese American Citizens League organ. Says Manbo of the written material turned out during the occupation: "The story that gave me the most satisfaction was the one about Nisei GI musician **Jim Araki**, whose musical genius truly blossomed in Japan." Expatriate Manbo's interest in jazz, rooted early while growing up in Hollywood, had not diminished as he pursued his new career as a journalist in Japan. In his mid-'80s, Masao Manbo lives today [in 1996] in retirement with his wife in Tokyo, enjoying a warm relationship with his grandchildren.

Tadashi "Tib" Kamayatsu was the third member of the Sho Tokyans to remain in Japan with the hope of making it in music. The States certainly could not provide him with opportunities for a career in the entertainment world—hanging out in pool halls in the Los Angeles wholesale produce district was an easily dismissed lifestyle. In an interview by David Jampel in the May 29, 1956, issue of the *English Mainichi*, Kamayatsu recalls the time when the Sho Tokyans arrived in Japan:

> *It was the most [exciting experience]. We wanted to see the country of our ancestors. We settled down at a dance hall just outside Tokyo for the six-month contract. It was quite different then. Swing was just getting a toehold in Japan, whereas, we played what has been described as hotel music. The people liked us. [Coming to Japan was an exciting] idea—so many places to see. Up to the time we came here, we had been financially dependent upon our parents. Here, we found a little independence. We were just at the age of growing into manhood and it felt good to be on our own. As a matter of fact, I got married here.*

Tadashi "Tib" Kamayatsu. Los Angeles. 1937. Photo courtesy of Vincent Uyeda.

After the termination of the Sho Tokyans' contract, Kamayatsu became the guitarist and vocalist for Shin Matsumoto's orchestra at the prestigious Florida Dance Hall in Tokyo. Blessed with an exceptional sense of rhythm and an easy American style of singing, Kamayatsu with his ready smile soon became a popular attraction for the dancing crowd.

Wartime in Japan, after the dance halls were darkened by government decree in 1940, seriously affected the livelihood of musicians. Kamayatsu had no choice but to go on tour with a band that played only traditional Japanese music. "It was bad," he recalls in the 1956 interview. "I was questioned at every small town and had to register with the police on my arrival. My house was being constantly searched by the *kenpei* [the military police]. [The psychological pressure was so great] I became a Japanese citizen, and a year before the war ended, I was inducted into the army. Since I could drive, I was put into the Transportation Corps and was sent to the Hankow district of China. Later [upon the surrender of Japanese troops], as a POW [prisoner of war], I was ordered to teach English to Chinese youngsters."

Upon repatriation to Tokyo in 1946 Kamayatsu rejoined his former colleagues, Shin Matsumoto and Hisashi Moriyama, who were co-leading the New Pacific Band. The terrible war was over; dance halls were again going full blast! Back on familiar ground, Kamayatsu worked for two years with the New Pacific Band, then joined the Stardusters for a seven-year stay.

In 1951, Kamayatsu headed the jazz department of the Tokyo Seisen Ongaku Gakko (Seisen School of Music), where he taught guitar and singing. "There weren't too many people around who could teach," Kamayatsu said in an interview in 1956. "This was especially true for vocalists. They would learn the [American] melody, but the enunciation [of English]...well, I figured I could help them." Staffed with outstanding Japanese musicians and popular vocalists, the school attracted a new generation of Japanese youth eager to acquire the intricate skills to play and sing jazz. Moreover, the success of the school, presumably, was secure in the light of the new musical phenomenon making its appearance in the States—rock 'n' roll.

The Jampel interview revealed further: "Tib, whose vocals are mostly rhythm songs, adds, 'Naturally, I like Bing Crosby. That man's got rhythm in his voice.' About [Louis] Armstrong, he says, 'He's not a singer, but he has the phrasing and feeling.' Frank Sinatra is also singled out by Tib for his phrasing. In addition, he observes, 'Frank sings like an ordinary guy. He makes everyone think they can do it.'"

Mas Manbo reported in the April 4, 1980, *Pacific Citizen* that Kamayatsu became ill in mid-1979 and died on March 10, 1980, of cancer of the esophagus, at age sixty-eight. His funeral service was conducted in a church in Setagaya-ku, Tokyo. Peggy Hayama, popular vocalist and a prime product of Kamayatsu's lessons, rendered farewell solos; and Buckie Shirakata played "Aloha Oe" in tribute to Kamayatsu. Before the funeral, the boxed urn containing his ashes had been placed on a covered table in a room of his apartment. Next to the urn were some of his favorite things—a bottle of imported whisky, his pipe and a deck of cards. His white guitar lay in what appeared to be his favorite chair. An old album on a shelf contained photographs of Tib in his younger days with members of the **Oliver Juniors,** the downtown L.A. club to which he belonged years ago.

Tib Kamayatsu, a charismatic entertainer and a fugitive from the wholesale produce markets of Los Angeles, played a significant part in the Japanese jazz boom in the postwar years. He was a Nisei expatriate who pursued a nebulous future in a very foreign land and succeeded in a uniquely American profession which was denied to pioneer Nisei musicians in their native land.

Kamayatsu's son, Hiroshi, growing up in the shadow of his guitar-playing father, gravitated, unsurprisingly, toward popular music and the guitar. Hiroshi's inspiration was not jazz, but rock 'n' roll which in the early '60s exploded in a tremendous proliferation in Japan of *gurupu saunzu* (the Japanese corruption of "group sounds"—the general term for small instrumental/vocal rock combos). Elvis was "king" and made-in-Japan copies sprouted like weeds after fresh spring rains. Paul Anka and Neil Sedaka tunes were played and sung to hordes of teenage fans, mostly female. Young Kamayatsu, captured by the excitement of this new music, joined in its worldwide adulation. He traveled to Los Angeles to study and to indulge in the ferment of rock 'n' roll at its source and played with local rock groups for a short while. Upon his return to Japan, Kamayatsu achieved prominence as a member of the very popular Spiders, a '60s soft-rock band, and continues his involvement in the entertainment world as a singer and a composer of popular songs.

JAMES ARAKI

In the March 4, 1948, issue of the *Japan Times,* Masao Manbo, Hollywood expatriate, reported:

> *HE BLOWS HIGH…HE BLOWS LOW!*
> *Lieutenant Araki, Nisei Musician, Is Talk of Local Swing World. The proficiency of a young Nisei soldier-swingcat who plays a number of instruments with remarkable skill is the talk of the Japanese jazz world today. Musicians declare that Araki on saxophone is far superior to any Japanese player, which includes jazzmen who were blowing horns while he was still in rompers. If Araki should turn to playing jazz professionally in this country after his army life is over, he wouldn't exactly starve. While Japanese office workers are clamoring for a 3,000 yen basic wage, average musicians receive about 20,000 yen monthly from dance halls with one sideman reportedly getting as much as 50,000 yen. Araki plans to leave for California this summer to continue his education and has his eye on the big time—a seat in a name band in the United States.*

Manbo went on to describe the musical activities and aspirations of **James Araki**, twenty-two years old, who was creating waves sitting in with local Japanese jazz musicians. Nisei Yoné Fukui, stationed in Tokyo at the same time as Araki, recalls: "Japanese jazzmen admired Araki so much, they called him *kamisama* [god]!"

Araki was one among many Nisei servicemen who served in the Allied Translator and Interpreter Section of General Headquarters in postwar Tokyo. Because of his Japanese language skills and his deep understanding of jazz, Araki, in his spare time, managed to convey the most

James Araki, U.S. Army. Tokyo. 1948. Photo courtesy of Janet Araki.

current jazz concepts and technique to native Japanese musicians. Professor Shoichi Yui, cofounder of the Hot Club of Japan, described Araki as "the great alto sax player who first introduced bebop to Japan." The January 31, 1948, *Rafu Shimpo* of Los Angeles reported that Army Lieutenant James Araki was making guest appearances with the Gay Quintet, Tokyo's most popular jazz band, at the Tokyo Correspondents Club. It also added that "APO 500" and "Night in Pakistan," both composed by Araki, were leading the jukebox parade in Tokyo.

In April, 1949, Mas Manbo again wrote:

TOKYO—A hep little guy named Jim Araki is the No. 1 Japanese American Swingcat. Araki lately has been playing hot guitar in Sgt. Johnny Baker's jive combo, heard over WVTR Armed Forces Radio. Aided by Japanese players, he has cut records with the tenor saxophone, and when he sits in with a local band, he may play the piano. However, the talented young jazzman regards the alto sax as his best instrument. To cap his amazing musical versatility, Araki has been creating swing numbers for Japanese bands. These include "Melancholy Mood" ("A rush number I dashed off in about ten minutes.") and "Swing in Orange," both of which were recorded recently by Hiroshima and his Stardusters, a top Japanese band.

In the fall of 1959, Japan Victor Co. issued an Araki album, *JAZZ BEAT—Midnight Jazz Session, JV-5006*, a multi-dubbed recording with Jim on alto [and tenor] sax and piano, George Kawaguchi on drums and Mitsuru Ono on bass. Etsuzo Yoshida, a veteran recording engineer, described this experience (excerpted): "The instant the two late-night recording sessions were over, I felt totally drained. I have never conducted a session like this that exhausted me both physically and mentally. But the energetic drive of the three musicians caught up with me as I sat at the mixing equipment, and I forced myself to keep up with them. I believe that a mutuality between the performers and the mixer is necessary to produce a good recording, but I didn't realize how much labor and energy would be required to record a session with Jimmy tripling and quadrupling as a musician. On several numbers, Jim alone dubbed four saxophone parts as well as the piano part.

"Only because tape-recording has become technically advanced were we able to produce a multiple-dubbed record album. On some of the numbers, only after making five recordings of the same tune could we know if it had turned out all right.

"I am apprehensive of the forthcoming reviews of this album. Multiple-dubbed recordings like this one will become more frequent in Japan. I am very happy that I was able to be a part of the team that created the very first."

Thirteen numbers are included in this album. Several are standards, e.g., "Take The A Train," "Harlem Nocturne," "I'm Beginning To See The Light." Others are Araki originals. All were arranged by Araki; solos on the alto and the piano also by Araki. This recording in 1958 took place during Araki's third visit to Japan as a student of Japanese literature. He had completed his two-year research and returned to the States soon after, "leaving this recording as a parting gift."

---

7 The Japanese term *"bata-kusai"* means, literally, "reeking with butter," but in usage connotes "very Western or un-Japanese." It is not pejorative.

8 Japanese boogie-woogie compositions, unlike true American boogie-woogie based on the twelve-bar blues scheme, were patterned after the thirty-two bar A-A-B-A pattern of most popular American music. A pseudo boogie-woogie sound was derived from a light eight-beats-to-the-measure pattern created by the rhythm and implied by the melody. It did not have the powerful, driving essence of boogie-woogie music performed by black American artists.

9 In Japan, Americans of Japanese ancestry were labeled *gaijin* (foreigners) by Japanese natives.

10 The Columbia Records Orchestra accompanying Williams included Hisashi Moriyama, the San Francisco-born expatriate Nisei, in the trumpet section.

11 At this time ten Japanese sen was equal to about three cents in U.S. currency.

12 Barton Crane was an American reporter for the *Japanese Advertiser*, an English language paper devoted to Japanese commerce. He was an amateur singer who sang American hit songs using his own Japanese lyrics at social gatherings.

13 Some American jazz historians consider the Casa Loma Orchestra with its precise syncopated arrangements as being the prototype white swing band.

14 "Betty" spelled "Bette" was the influence of Hollywood and the Americanization of Nisei—wanting to be sophisticated Americans.

15 The athletic league was sponsored by James Sakamoto, the editor and publisher of the *Japanese American Courier*, the first all-English Japanese American weekly paper. Sakamoto was an illustrious journalist who had become totally blind as a result of retinal detachments sustained earlier during his professional boxing days.

16 Louis Prima's "Sing, Sing, Sing" became a jazz classic when the Jimmy Mundy arrangement which included Fletcher Henderson's "Christopher Columbus" was played by Benny Goodman and his orchestra at their illustrious and extraordinary Carnegie Hall Concert on January 16, 1938. This rendition of "Sing, Sing, Sing" featured, among others, Harry James's exciting, crisp trumpet solo and an intense, extended duet by Goodman on clarinet and Krupa on tom-toms, followed in

ethereal contrast by pianist Jess Stacy, who, according to Kolodin of Columbia Records, "drops into a new groove to play one of the most original solos of his life."

17 One of her earliest works for Fox consisted of a minor film role in the fall of 1939 as a Malayan girl.

18 "My Trumpet" was a hit "jazz ballad" composed by Ryoichi Hattori and first recorded in October 1937 by the Columbia Jazz Orchestra. This recording featured Noriko Awaya, the Queen of the Blues, with a solo by Fumio Nanri, pioneer Japanese jazz trumpeter. The lyrics suggest a deep love for the sweet sounds of a trumpet which at times torments and yet consoles one's heart with its lovely swing.

19 Yoshiko Ishii is still performing and is presently a well-known chanson singer.

20 During World War II about 120,000 persons of Japanese ancestry living in the Pacific West Coast were unjustly incarcerated in ten detention camps established by the U.S. government .

CHAPTER TWO 117

The Jivesters. Topaz Detention Camp, Utah. 1943. Left to right: Sadie Towata Tajima, Tak Enomoto, Yutaka Yoshida, Ich Sasaki, Ike Nakamura, Kazu Maruoka, I. Matsuhara. Photo courtesy of Kazu Maruoka.

CHAPTER 3

Of Jive Bombers and Stardusters

DANCE BANDS IN "ASSEMBLY" CENTERS AND DETENTION CAMPS

BUDDHAHEAD BLUES

Going to sprout my wings and fly right over that fence,
Going to sprout my wings and fly right over that fence,
'Cause staying in here don't make no sense.

Buddhahead boy, what makes you so yellow?
Buddhahead boy, what makes you so yellow?
You seem like an ordinary fellow.

Dream every night of a big roast and candied yam,
Dream every night of a big roast and candied yam,
The food they give me here is a no-good sham.

Beat down, sun; blow, wind, through my hair,
Beat down, sun; blow, wind, through my hair,
Who said life's any kind of fair?

Searchlights shining in my face always give me a start,
Searchlights shining in my face always give me a start,
Makes me feel like Cagney or a Humphrey Bogart.

Call me a taxi, call me a limousine,
Call me a taxi, call me a limousine,
I want to go riding—out where the grass is green.

Oh, big, red sun, you going away tonight,
Oh, big, red sun, you going away tonight,
When you come back tomorrow, I'll be clean out of sight!

Want to ask Jimmy Rushing to sing these blues,
Ask the Count and Jimmy to wail these blues,
Dream on, baby; ain't nothing left to lose.

Oh, I don't know why
I want to cry,
I want to die.
I'd sure get tight
If there were gin in sight
For me.

—ERNEST MICHIO MASUNAGA
SANTA ANITA "ASSEMBLY" CENTER, 1942

"*The sign on* the telephone pole ordered us to assemble nearby on Saturday with just our bedding and clothes…just stuff we could carry. I could NOT leave my records…put about fifty of my favorites—Tommy Dorsey, Artie Shaw, Duke Ellington—into a case. Clutching my lifeblood…sighed a heavy-hearted 'good-bye' to East L.A."

—George Yoshida, April 1942

"*With such hot* 'jives' as 'Back Beat Boogie,' '9:20 Special' and 'Basie Boogie' being featured, the Down Beats will open the local Dance Week tonight at Barrack #1020 from 7:30 pm with a Swing Concert. The Down Beats band leader, Riki Matsufuji, claims he will have the audience 'cuttin' the rug' before the evening is over."

—*Tulean Dispatch*, June 14, 1943
Tule Lake Detention Camp

The entry of the United States into World War II initiated a series of unprecedented events which changed forever the lives of Japanese Americans living on the Pacific Coast. Anti-Japanese bias and extreme hysteria fed by unfounded rumors of enemy attacks and espionage led to a hasty response by the U.S. government. In violation of their constitutional rights, all Americans of Japanese ancestry were excluded from the Pacific coastal areas. "Once a Jap, always a Jap. You can't trust 'em. Put 'em all away!" was the sentiment of the time.

On February 19, 1942, President Roosevelt signed Executive Order 9066 which led to the forced removal and detention of 120,000 Japanese Americans. Since permanent quarters were not ready for their occupancy, the first groups of evictees were corralled into nearby, temporary "assembly" centers—horse stables and utility buildings of local fairgrounds and racetracks. In Northern California Japanese Americans were taken to the Tanforan racetrack in South San Francisco; the Los Angeles internees were temporarily billeted at the Santa Anita racetrack. The persistent stench of horse smells, the windowless stalls, and barbed wire fences completely encircling each center created a jail house ambience that aggravated the anxiety and suffering of people whose only "crime" was to have a Japanese face.

By 1943, 120,000 persons of Japanese descent, two-thirds of whom were American citizens, had been forcibly uprooted from their homes and interned in ten permanent U.S. camps dispersed in desolate, barren, arid tracts of land generally away from the West Coast. My desert home, Poston, in southwestern Arizona (110 degrees in the shade!), was a tar-paper-covered wooden barrack. Living space for the five of us—my father, mother and two younger sisters—was a rectangular room, approximately 20' by 24', with exposed wood framing, a hanging light fixture (a 60-watt bulb), an oil-burning stove for heat and no furniture except for five metal cots with straw-filled canvas mattresses. Generally, four of these rooms comprised a barrack; twelve to fourteen barracks made a block. Each block contained a communal mess hall, a laundry room, a recreation hall and segregated showers and latrines. All detention centers were self-contained cities with populations of 10,000 to 20,000 per center. Detainees provided the bulk of necessary services—medical, police, fire fighting, education, mail, recreation, and so on.

The psychological impact of being incarcerated because of racial origin was devastating on youthful citizens—"Didn't we pledge allegiance to the American flag all of our lives? Hey, we're Americans, you know—apple pie, baseball and Chevrolets! Aren't we?"

Needless to say, the daily "busy-ness" of survival in detention camps could not erase the hate message that was deeply etched and submerged in our psyche: "Japanese Americans are enemy aliens and not to be trusted!" Yet, despite the bad taste in our mouths, with hope in our "red, white and blue" hearts, we continued to buy U.S. War Bonds, to sing "God Bless America," and to send sons and brothers off to the hills and fields of Italy and France and to the jungles of New Guinea to defend the American Way of Life—to bleed and even to die a "glorious" death. "Yes, yes, yes, we are Americans!" we shouted in concentration camps surrounded by barbed wire.

It is no wonder that in this physically and psychologically depressed ambience, dance bands spontaneously and swiftly came into being. The vacuum created by the need for sustenance of hope, for distraction and for the uplifting of wounded spirits was satisfied for many by music and dance. Artists are healers—youthful Nisei provided the balm to disheartened souls. Youngsters who earlier had acquired some ability to play musical instruments joined together in an attempt to recreate the great sounds they heard over the radios in their barracks late at night: "From the beautiful Palladium Ballroom located in the heart of Hollywood, California, we bring to you the music of the Sentimental Gentleman of Swing, Tommy Dorsey and his orchestra!" The sweet sounds of Dorsey's trombone would float over the air; but that music was being played on the *outside*—forbidden territory to us "enemy aliens."

On the *inside* in the sweltering mess hall of Block 36, we heard the not-too-bad-not-too-good music of the **Music Makers,** the camp band. Twelve collective voices of saxes, trumpets and 'bones accompanied by a barely adequate rhythm section, playing their theme song, their version of Glenn Miller's "Moonlight Serenade." Girls in their neatly ironed dresses and white saddle shoes and young men in clean Levis and polished boots would glide, not too gracefully, on rough linoleum-covered floors in the dim mess hall decorated with niggardly strips of bright red crepe paper.

In one especially dark corner of the room would congregate a cluster of strongly judgmental, pimply-faced, shy stags eyeing the non-dancing girls who were sitting demurely across the room, waiting to be invited to dance. The only cure for this commonly occurring impasse was the pronouncement: "The next dance will be the last dance." This forced a desperate action on the part of anxious youths who, emboldened with sudden courage, walked forward to seek a special partner: "May I have this dance?" Proceeding to shuffle in a soft embrace, rocking very slowly from side to side, disregarding the rhythm flowing from the band, they, before long, experienced terrible disappointment. The band, after playing for some time, had come to the end of the last chorus. The evening ended much too soon!

On a given Saturday night in the summer of 1943, there may have been as many as ten such dances taking place. Dance bands, all playing identical arrangements of ballads and swing tunes, performed for crowds of young couples in isolated barbed-wire-enclosed cities. The response to the quality of music of individual orchestras ranged from a non-committal "It's OK" to a fervent "The jive is jumpin'!" The number of advanced students in music, especially in jazz, was limited and band leaders had to be content with whoever showed up for rehearsals. Nevertheless, frivolous as it may seem, dance bands proliferated for a while during the wartime incarceration of Japanese Americans. It was a matter of survival and a subconscious affirmation of self—a way to express through music: "I am an American!"

George Akimoto. *The Stag*. Rohwer Detention Camp, Ark. 1943.

Pete Ohtaki, obviously a devotee of swing bands, regularly reviewed the status of their music and its practitioners in the *Manzanar Free Press*. November 28, 1942:

> *PLATTER CHATTER*
> *Ups and downs in the band biz has been experienced by practically every musical organization in the country, including top favorites who you would think needn't have been down in the dumps before they began clicking. Harry James, who left Benny Goodman several years ago with the latter's best wishes, was no exception. It was only seven months ago that James put out "You Made Me Love You," and now, he is the top band of the country and every platter of his is a sure seller. Columbia Records won't lose money with James' "Strictly Instrumental," which is sure to go over—a pleasant arrangement with [Corky] Corcoran's sax solo plus solid brass filled by the maestro's versatile trumpet. "Manhattan Serenade" features Helen Forrest on the femme vocal, being in the slow tempo category.*
>
> *Harry James is now seen in a pic called, "Springtime in the Rockies," Claude Thornhill will be seen in the movie "Calgary Stampede," and Sammy Kaye's ork already is all over the country in "Iceland." Harry James is at the Hotel Lincoln…Gene Krupa at the*

Hollywood Palladium…Bonnie Baker announced her engagement to Orrin Tucker, now in the service, early last month…Claude Thornhill has been called into the Armed Forces, holding a 1-A rating for some time…Clyde McCoy also, will be wearing unies [uniforms] soon…Judy Starr, petite femme chirper, is now singing for Bob Allen's band, both being former vocalists for the late Hal Kemp…When pianist Eddie Duchin, now a lieutenant, left his band, he asked Frankie Carle to take over, but the ivory tickler for Horace Heidt refused, since he has a financial interest in the Musical Knights.

"Praise the Lord and Pass the Ammunition" is going around like wildfire, and Kay Kyser didn't overlook his chance to put it over. His Glee Club takes the spotlight, giving it a harlem background. "I Came Here to Talk for Joe" may be a sure fire with Harry Babbit coming across with the romantic vocal for Kyser's revised dance style. Shep Fields has also recorded the same song—in medium tempo with a male vocal, novel guitars and nine saxophones is his idea of "talking for Joe."

Apparently, Pete was a most knowledgeable observer of the contemporary music scene. His coverage in the *Platter Chatter* enjoyed an extensive readership. Popular American music was an essential, pervasive influence in the Americanization of Nisei.

Bill Nikaido's story illustrates what happened to Nisei musicians who returned from a sojourn in Japan. Suddenly, their desire to work abroad was considered suspicious; they found themselves caught between two worlds of warring nations.

"In 1932 I accompanied my mother to Japan; she was seriously ill and wanted after her death to be buried in the family plot in Japan. I enrolled in Meiji University, Tokyo, and commuted to school for three years. I majored in political science, but my heart was not in studying. Every chance I had, I would go to the Florida Dance Hall or to the Shinbashi Dance Hall or to the Ginza Dance Hall. You see, I got to know the band leaders and they would let me sing since I knew a lot of American songs and I had the experience back in Sacramento. I didn't get any pay, but, instead, got free dance tickets…didn't mind that a bit. As a matter of fact, one of the girls, a hostess, was stuck on me, but I wasn't ready for any kind of [commitment] then. I just wanted to sing. I remember seeing Betty Inada singing and dancing the hula at the *Nippon Gekijo;* Betty was from Sacramento. Helen Sumida was another very popular vocalist; she was from Fresno. I remember Sash Moriyama [from San Francisco] playing trumpet in a band at the Shinbashi Dance Hall. These Nisei musicians were doing OK in those days.

Dance band arrangements. ca. 1940. Courtesy of George Takamoto.

"With two friends, we auditioned for Columbia Records; we were rejected, and that was that. Another problem I had was that, although I wanted to become a professional singer in Japan, my sister gave me absolutely no support. She objected because she had it in her head that anyone in the entertainment business was low class.

"In Tokyo, while in school, I joined the Nisei Club, made up of about thirty Nisei, many from Hawaii. One Christmas I organized a choir of club members, about fifteen of us, and on Christmas eve we jumped into three cabs to sing carols at St. Luke's Hospital and the U.S. Embassy. Ambassador Joseph Grew, who headed the embassy, rewarded us with twenty yen for our singing. We bought candy with the money, then went to Sumida-gawa [Sumida River], where destitute boat-people lived; we sang carols and gave candy to the kids.

"When I left Meiji, I had to make a decision about my future—Should I stay? Should I return to California? I did locate a good-paying job in a watch manufacturing company, but I would have had to give up my American citizenship and serve in the Japanese army for two years with no assurance of getting my job back after discharge. That was a helluva lousy deal, so I knew I was gonna go back to the States. On top of that, since I was a Nisei, the military police began to harass me more and more. They suspected me of being a spy or something. They would routinely come to question me about my background, my whereabouts, and so forth. Things were getting so uncomfortable in Japan, I decided to return in 1934.

"It took twelve long days crossing the Pacific on the Taiyo Maru. Upon arrival in San Francisco, I was isolated and detained for five hours on Angel Island. I wasn't allowed to see any of my relatives who had come to greet me upon my return home. Again, I was suspect as to my loyalty and status—this time by the FBI. Even though they had in their hands my U.S. passport, they asked me where I was born, what schools I attended in California, why I went to Japan, what I did in Japan, what I studied, where I stayed…just a bunch of irritating questions. I was really upset being treated so bad…they were so suspicious. I remember saying something crazy like, 'Why are you asking all those silly questions? I was born here! I'm an American citizen! I wanna talk to the President!' Boy, was I mad!

"I finally ended up in Sacramento. In 1941 when war with Japan was declared, I was offered a job teaching Japanese at the University of Chicago. The pay was not enough to support my family…had a wife and a child, so I didn't take the job. We were then, unfortunately, confined in Jerome Detention Camp, Denson, Arkansas, with about ten thousand other Japanese Americans. There in camp I was again questioned by the FBI—'Do you want America to win the war or Japan to win? Do you say *banzai* to Hirohito?' All kinds of outrageous questions—made me so mad! I kept on protesting, 'I'm an American! I'm an American!' The only good thing about Jerome Camp was the dance band led by Frank Tashima. The band was called the Densoneers and, once more, I had a chance to return to the music I loved."

THE STARLIGHT SERENADERS
Santa Anita "Assembly" Center, Arcadia, California

By June 2, 1942, the Santa Anita "Assembly" Center, hastily constructed at the Santa Anita racetrack in Los Angeles, was the thirty-second largest city in California, accommodating 18,527 internees from Los Angeles, Hollywood, Beverly Hills, San Diego, Santa Clara and San Jose. The *Pacemaker*, the center newspaper, announced the anticipated début of a 12-piece band, the **Starlight Serenaders**, at the community dance, which took place on Saturday evening, June 12, 1942, in front of the racetrack grandstand. Members of the band were: leader Yukio Miyamoto, Francis Ikezoye, Glenn Jiobu and Susumu Chikami, saxophones; Ernie Arima, Roy Nishimura and Jim Nakanishi, trumpets; Nob Okuno and Harry Kitano, trombones; Akira Ohno, guitar; Eddie Inouye, drums; and Dorothy Takii, piano. (Chikami, Arima and Ohno were former members of the pioneer Sho Tokyans.) Vocalists were Yoshiko Iwashika and Bob Kinoshita. The center's administrative officers were guests of honor. Only couples and their parents were permitted to attend the affair. Everyone was asked to be careful of the camouflage nets hanging near the dance area; the nets posed a hazard to dancers.[21]

On the same day, the *Pacemaker* reported an incident illustrating that even camp conditions couldn't curtail the resourcefulness of a frustrated musician:

> *JOE'S TRAPS ADD EXTRA OOMPH*
> *A boogie-woogie recording with a little extra 'oomph' emanated from the electric shop and stopped several music lovers on their way to the regular Sunday evening concert. The more curious who investigated the source of the extra oomph discovered a drummer banging away on a homemade set of drums. The set consisted of a salvaged wash tub, a large grease can, a group of small cans and two tin plates.*
>
> *Joe Shimada, unable to send for his set at home, and missing his daily habit of taking it out on the skins, has assembled the pieces, including a clever foot pedal for the bass tub. Joe gave the classical concert a little competition.*[22]

The Starlight Serenaders provided dance music on June 27, 1942, for the Graduation Ball feting three hundred graduates of grammar schools, junior and senior high schools, junior colleges and universities. The ball took place on the tiled area in front of the grandstand. Diplomas had been presented to many graduates at commencement exercises on the previous night. Again, couples only were admitted to the dance, and parents were cordially invited. (One wonders how many Issei parents attended. Did they dance? Or were they there solely for crowd control?)

While internees were making painful adjustments to incarceration in "assembly" centers, permanent detention camps to house them were nearing completion in ten diverse sites in the United States. For most "assembly" center residents, relocation to their permanent "homes" took place within six months after their arrival. In August 1942, large contingents left the center for transfer to far-off camps. Dances to commemorate their departure were organized. At one Saturday night community dance an overflow crowd of two thousand was present to honor the former residents of San Diego who were leaving Santa Anita for an undisclosed destination. A "Sayonara Ball" for the transferees of San Jose, Santa Clara Valley, Hollywood and part of Los Angeles was held the following Saturday night. Other farewell gatherings were held until Santa Anita "Assembly" Center was emptied of its last detainee.

For the remaining War Relocation Authority staff and clean-up crews, the rapid death of what was once a bustling city-within-a-city must have been an eerie experience. Although detainee occupation time spanned just a few months, the Santa Anita "Assembly" Center had been a hectic locale where babies were born, where the elderly and ill died, where teenagers jitterbugged, where young families anxiously pondered their uncertain future, where faithful Buddhists recited their sutras, and Christians prayed and sang their hymns of hope.

Band members of the Starlight Serenaders, anticipating musicians of similar predilection for big-band music and jazz, packed their instruments and were dispersed with their families to new detention centers. Yukio Miyamoto discovered a spot in Poston, Arizona, where his tenor sax became an asset to the Music Makers; Harry Kitano found himself in Topaz, Utah, where he blew his 'bone with the Topaz Tooters; and Yoshiko Iwashika continued her singing with a group called the Music Makers in Gila Butte Camp, Arizona. For several Nisei musicians, these early camp experiences served as springboards for careers in American pop music.

THE MUSIC MAKERS
Poston Camp #1, Arizona

Eventually ten permanent detention camps were built—most in desolate wastelands far from the Pacific Coast. Nine out of the ten centers had dance bands. Actually there were more than nine bands. Poston consisted of three separate sites and each had a band. Gila River Center consisted of two sites with a band in each.

In Poston Camp #1, population 9,483, young dancers enjoyed the rhythms of the **Music Makers**, an eleven-piece ensemble directed by seventeen-year-old **Hideo Kawano**. Kawano had

The Music Makers. Poston Camp #1, Ariz. 1943. Left to right, front row: Jack Wada, Frank Oshima, Tug Tamaru, George Yoshida, Paul Matsuda, Yuki Miyamoto. Back row: Haruo Fujisawa, Shig Aramaki, Hideo Kawano, Tom Murakami, Raymond Sunada. Photo courtesy of George Yoshida.

arrived in Poston with relatively extensive experience in jazz and swing music. He was an unusually talented jazz drummer as a youngster and had been featured prominently in talent shows in Los Angeles's Li'l Tokyo. With the Music Makers he played the trumpet and served as its musical director—a responsibility he assumed with skill and confidence.

Rounding out the brass section were Tom Murakami and Raymond Sunada on trumpets and Shig Aramaki on trombone. The three had transferred from Camp #2 when its band called it quits. Yuki Miyamoto and Tug Tamaru played tenor saxes; Paul "Pancho" Matsuda and I played alto saxes. Yuki was generally the soloist for the Music Makers—his improvisations were more imaginative and his instrumental technique more advanced than those of other musicians. On guitar was Frank Oshima, a "cowboy" singer from San Bernardino. Jack Wada, a quiet young man from Redlands and the captain of the Poston Fire Department, played the piano. Haruo Fujisawa from Imperial Valley was our drummer.

The Poston Music Department supported the band by purchasing portable music stands and music arrangements. The Music Makers' theme song was Glenn Miller's "Moonlight Serenade" and its repertoire contained a good mixture of up-tempo tunes such as Woody Herman's "Blues on Parade" for jitterbugs and slow, romantic numbers such as "Dream" for the love-struck. Band members wore sport coats and ties. No one received any pay. Our reward was the joy and satisfaction in playing music we loved and the affirmation received from appreciative couples who danced the night away in the dreary mess halls. Outside in the dark night, the brilliant desert moon and the brightest of stars would illuminate row upon row of identical black, tar-paper-covered barracks in the quiet city in the desert. Concerned mothers anxiously awaited their teenage daughters' return home.

Pianist **Jack Wada** of Redlands, California, was the oldest of five boys in the Wada family; there were four sisters. His brother Bob says, "Jack loved music. Before Poston, Jack was a gardener by trade. He was a loner. Whenever he wasn't out working on his route, he'd sit in his room, all by himself, and play his guitar. I suppose he was a self-taught musician; I remember seeing stacks of music books in his room. Jack showed me how to finger a few chords, and I tried studying his books, but I never did get the knack of playing a guitar. Frank Oshima would come over from San Bernardino every Sunday and the two of them would spend hours playing and singing 'cowboy' songs—just having a ball! Frank wore Western clothes and cowboy boots; he was tall, handsome, and looked the part of a romantic 'cowboy' singer. I heard he was on friendly terms with Roy Rogers.

Poston Music Makers. Poston Detention Camp, Ariz. 1943. Left to right: Frank Oshima, Tug Tamaru, George Yoshida, Paul Matsuda, Yuki Miyamoto. Photo courtesy of George Yoshida.

"Jack had an unusual hobby outside of music. He built a boxing ring and put up punching bags in our garage in the back of the house…called it the Redlands Athletic Club. Jack was the owner and trainer. Most of the guys who came over were Mexicans. Some of them were good enough to box at the semipro level at nearby civic auditoriums. Our next-door neighbor, Milton Kanatani, a teenager at the time, used to come over to train seriously. He was a tough bantamweight who boxed professionally for a short while before being sent to Poston."

Bob continues: "Since my brother was the captain of the Poston Fire Department, a few of us were allowed to hang out at the fire station. A major benefit of being familiar with the fire station was having access to the schedule of dances regularly listed on the station bulletin board. It was the responsibility of the firemen to inspect dance sites for potential fire hazards. We hangers-on, knowing where dances were taking place, would go to check out the action; not necessarily to dance, but to see who was there, to check out the girls, and, if we were lucky, to watch a sporadic fight, minor fisticuffs, among young camp *yogores* [rough necks]. That was a kick!

"The fire station is where I also became acquainted with [Paul] Pancho Matsuda, a fireman who played the alto in the Music Makers. Paul, who was older than I, would always be practicing his alto sax and clarinet at the station. He was a short guy; in fact, it seemed as if his saxophone was bigger than he was. Since I enjoyed music and always admired people who could play instruments, I would sit and listen to Paul practice—even enjoyed hearing him just going up and down the scales. One day without his permission, I picked up his clarinet, put it to my mouth to try blowing a few notes. Paul caught me and angrily scolded me—he didn't want anyone to ruin his favorite reeds which were hard to get in camp. But he was nice enough to give me an old one he didn't want. He taught me how to finger a few simple notes and would let me blow his clarinet for a short while.

"What I really liked to do was to go to Foozie's place to hear him work out on his drums. Foozie was the drummer of the camp dance band; I thought playing drums in a band was great! I loved to watch and listen to the Music Makers. I come from a small town where there were only two other Japanese families, so it was such a shock, however pleasant, to see a dance band made up entirely of Japanese faces! I was inspired by Foozie's drum playing so much that I joined Poston Boy Scout Troop 100 (so named in honor of the all-Nisei 100th Battalion) drum and bugle corps and later enrolled in the Poston High School music program to play in the orchestra and band. I didn't continue my music after I left camp. Guess my brother, Jack, was the only one in our family who took up music seriously."

Haruo "Foozie" Fujisawa from El Centro, Calif., reminisced: "I first started out in junior high school with the alto sax, but changed over to the drums and continued on through high school playing in the orchestra and band. I also played in the school dance band where I picked up a lot of experience in big-band music. In 1942 I ended up in Poston with the rest of the Japanese families from Imperial Valley. After my arrival there, I had my entire drum kit sent to camp where I got a job as a teacher and drummer in the Music Department. I remember Sachi Amano and Ritsuko Kawakami were also on the staff. They both played the piano for many events, gave piano lessons to youngsters and also directed vocal groups. We were paid the top scale of $19.00 a month; I was the only person in the Music Makers to receive pay. My favorite drummers were Buddy Rich, who played for TD [Tommy Dorsey], and Gene Krupa, who played for BG [Benny Goodman]. I really enjoyed Glenn Miller's music…guess his orchestra was my favorite."

Post-camp days found Fujisawa first in Chicago in 1945 playing drums in Koichi Hayashi's band. Later, upon returning to the West Coast, he continued to play with a variety of groups in Los Angeles: Tak Shindo's band, Tets Bessho's Nisei Serenaders, his own combo with Joe Sakai on bass and Jim Araki or George Atsumo on piano and saxophone. "As a trio we played shows at the New Ginza on First and San Pedro Streets in Li'l Tokyo. Later, in the '80s for seven straight years, four or five nights a week, I led a five-piece combo—tenor sax, trumpet, bass, piano and drums—at the Mama Lion Club, located at Beverly and Western Avenues. Basically, we played music for lively dance crowds—popular American, Japanese, Latin and Hawaiian tunes. The place used to jump on weeknights as well as weekends. The beauty of that job was I didn't have to take home my drum set every night after the gig. (The curse of all drummers—packing it up

"Jammin.'" Poston, Ariz. 1943. Left to right: Tug Tamaru, Haruo Fujisawa, Frank Oshima. Photo courtesy of Haruo Fujisawa.

and moving!) My final music gig was a trip to Hawaii around 1986 with a thirteen-piece orchestra made up mostly of Hawaiians and a few mainland Nisei to play American and Japanese pop tunes accompanying several Hawaiian Japanese vocalists.

"I had several day jobs during all those years I played drums, so I wasn't dependent on music for paying rent and putting food on the table for my family. But I sure spent a lot of time on gigs. Some of them were a drag, but I also got my kicks, too. Don't regret it at all. I still listen to my collection of big-band music and jazz…have about a thousand of 'em. Funny thing, lately I'm beginning to listen more and more to classical music, like Bach and Beethoven. As a matter of fact, I just came back from Branson, Missouri, where there are about thirty-five clubs featuring great live musical shows—country/western, rock 'n' roll, dixieland, Glenn Miller's music, Andy Williams's pop vocals…and I enjoyed them all. Guess I'm getting old…getting to like all kinds of music. You know, music means everything to me!"

Poston Music Makers. Poston Detention Camp, Ariz. 1943. Left to right: Haruo Fujisawa, Shig Aramaki, Hideo Kawano, Tom Murakami, Raymond Sunada. Photo courtesy of George Yoshida.

Watsonville Y.B.A. Orchestra. Watsonville, Calif. Jan. 1, 1942. Left to right: Arthur Izumizaki, Ben Tada, Walter Moriya, Tom Murakami, Kenji Torigoe, John Kado, Helen Iwanaga, Harumi Nagase. Photo courtesy of Helen Iwanaga.

THE CAMP #2 BAND
Poston Camp #2, Arizona

Poston #2's Instructor of Music, **Helen Okamoto Iwanaga,** was born on August 30, 1914, in Stockton, California. Her father, Naoichi Okamoto, studied and taught *utai* (classical songs of the Japanese noh theater); her mother, Yoshikiku Iwahashi, learned to play the organ and the piano in a women's finishing school in Japan in 1912. Helen remembers: "As soon as I could sit on a piano stool, I was given piano lessons. My teacher was a strict, elderly Englishman who came once a week." Motivated by her genetic and environmental influences, Helen's interest and progress in music blossomed. After attending elementary and secondary schools, she matriculated at the College of the Pacific (COP), Stockton, where her goal was a degree in music with a major in piano performance. In 1935 she married Reverend Yoshio Iwanaga, who was then the religious leader of the Stockton Buddhist Church. Helen graduated from COP in 1936, gave private piano lessons and led choral groups in the church until 1940 when Rev. Iwanaga was transferred to Watsonville.

Poston Camp #2 Band. Jack Matsuoka, artist. Poston, Ariz. 1942. Courtesy of Jack Matsuoka.

Classical Western music was Helen Iwanaga's great love. Yet, in order to capitalize on the interests of young Buddhists, mostly high school students, she organized the Watsonville YBA Orchestra (Young Buddhists Association). She purchased stock dance-band arrangements of the '40s—Miller, Dorsey, Shaw. After many rehearsals, their ensemble work attracted the attention of YBA friends who invited them to play for dances. Their meager earnings from dance jobs provided more band arrangements, music stands and uniforms.

Wartime removal placed Iwanaga first in the Salinas Fair Grounds "Assembly" Center, where families from Salinas, Monterey and Watsonville were gathered. Months later they were boarded on a train and transported to Poston Detention Camp #2 in southwestern Arizona, where, as Instructor of Music, she organized a dance band consisting of many former Watsonville YBA Orchestra members. They performed in talent shows and dances in mess halls; band members did not receive remuneration for their efforts. Iwanaga says of the band, "We didn't play too well, but the music sounded good, especially some of those Glenn Miller charts. And, we did have fun!"

In postwar years, Iwanaga utilized her creative energies in promoting religious music in Buddhist churches. She wrote and arranged choral music; conducted choirs for special occasions. In all she devoted fifty years of music education to the Buddhist Churches of America. She enjoys a personal sense of accomplishment today from that experience.

"I love to sing, I go to the opera, I love symphonic music!" exclaims an energetic, youthful Helen Iwanaga as she approaches her mid-'80s.

Tom Murakami is today a semiretired strawberry grower in Watsonville, California. Murakami and I were both members of the Poston Camp #1 Music Makers; he says I wouldn't recognize him today, even if we stood face to face. He's bald—he's lost his bountiful head of jet-black hair! He doesn't touch his trumpet anymore. The last time he played was in 1949 or 1950 when the Watsonville YBA Orchestra played a dance in Mountain View.

Says Murakami, "I've played trumpet since my grammar-school days when I was twelve years old. In time my technique improved and I was able to join the Watsonville High School marching band. I didn't play in the dance band, but a bunch of us at the Buddhist Church got together for the fun of it and with the help of Mrs. Iwanaga, we formed the Watsonville YBA Orchestra: three saxes, two trumpets, a drummer and a pianist. We rehearsed on Friday nights at the church and played tunes like 'Deep Purple' and 'Alice Blue Gown,' a pretty waltz. Our theme song was 'Moonlight Serenade'—the Glenn Miller sound with the clarinet lead on the melody, a favorite of us all. The orchestra played most of the time for Buddhist Church dances in Watsonville, Salinas and Monterey. I remember going up to San Francisco in 1940 to play for the Young Buddhists Festival on Treasure Island, for the Golden Gate International Exposition...we all had a great time there!

"When World War II broke out in 1941, Watsonville Japanese Americans were assembled first in the Salinas Fair Grounds, then transferred by train to Poston Camp #2, where a dance band was organized with the YBA Orchestra as the nucleus and augmented by musicians from Salinas and Monterey. We played a few dances, then disbanded because several members left camp to work or to go to school. Raymond Sunada and I, trumpets, and "Sugar" Aramaki, trombone, played for a while in the Music Makers of Camp #1. After a few dances I left Poston for the Midwest where I was soon drafted into the army.

"Upon being discharged from the service, I returned to a farmer's life in Watsonville. Marriage and family responsibilities restricted my participating in the YBA Orchestra, which had reorganized after the war. Young members replaced older members as the latter dropped out. I suppose I played a bit after I came back here. As I said earlier, none of us were super-musicians. We just got together and enjoyed playing dance music and swing. It was the popular music of our time."

THE RHYTHMAIRES
Poston Camp #3, Arizona

I had a long, fascinating conversation with **Noboru "Nobi" Nakamura**, who played tenor saxophone in the Camp #3 band in 1942. Nakamura is a successful architect in active practice for many years in Oakland, California, but hasn't blown his sax in fifty! Yet he still has his horn. On his sax case, lettered in white paint, is "**Rhythmaires**."

Rhythmaires was the name of the nine-piece dance band at Poston Camp #3. The band was a component of the recreation department. Each member received $16.00 a month, rehearsed weekdays and worked gigs on weekends—very much like professionals. They played what other camp dance bands were playing—stock band arrangements of Miller's "String of Pearls," Dorsey's "Song of India," Shaw's "Begin the Beguine."

Nakamura's story is a bit unusual. He was born in Japan and immigrated with his family when he was seven years old to Reedley, California, a rural community in the San Joaquin Valley. Before long, he was speaking English fluently; he even learned to play the violin in grammar school. In high school, he gave up the violin to play the bassoon. Music was a great source of pleasure for Nobi.

In the spring of 1942, Nakamura was removed with his family to Poston Camp #2. Says Nakamura, "There I learned that a dance band was being formed; however, since two alto sax players were already identified, a call was issued for a tenor sax man. I was disappointed. I wanted to play the alto, because I already knew how to finger the clarinet, and it would be a relatively simple transition to play the alto. I wanted badly to join the band, so I reluctantly consented to switch to the tenor saxophone—bought one by mail order from a music store in New York City.

"I discovered, as I became more familiar with the horn, that the tenor was not a bad instrument. In fact, the heavier, throaty sound of the larger saxophone began to be more and more appealing as time went by. I listened carefully to tenor players on all of the records I could get my hands on. Corky Corcoran of the Harry James band became my role model. The unique tone of Corky's horn and his improvisations sounded awfully good to me. I spent many hours studying and imitating Corky.

"My technique improved rapidly. We played stock arrangements of Herman, Dorsey and Miller. I don't remember any tunes that had special appeal to me since I played fourth tenor, which *never* had the melody line; the second tenor takes all the solos and the fourth just sucks on the reed. Life in camp, nevertheless, was satisfying, carefree—practicing my horn and playing dances for happy dancers."

But that life was not destined to continue as it was. With the loyalty of Japanese Americans no longer a question, the War Department, reversing its original position, encouraged internees to relocate to distant cities in the Midwest or the East for work and for education. The war in the European and the Pacific theaters was raging furiously. The military draft of Nisei was reactivated and young men and women enlisted into the ranks of the 442nd Regimental Combat Team, the Military Intelligence Service and the Women's Army Corps.

Nakamura opted to enlist in the U.S. Army even though he had earlier been classified as an enemy alien. His motivations were twofold: first, to contribute to the national war effort and, second, to obtain U.S. citizenship. Nakamura volunteered for the Army in Denver, Colorado, and was assigned to the Military Intelligence Service Language School at Camp Savage, Minnesota. Young recruits were trained to act as interrogators of Japanese prisoners of war and translators of strategic military documents. The Japanese language course was extremely intense—great demands were made on the students' intellect and stamina. Upon completing the language training,

Nakamura was soon engaged in the crucial work of providing military intelligence services in the Philippines. U.S. forces had begun their offensive to reverse the tide of the war against the Japanese in the Pacific theater. Early in 1944, Nakamura's secondary goal of enlisting in the U.S. Army was achieved. Noboru Nakamura, taking his oath of allegiance in Minneapolis, Minnesota, became a bona fide citizen of the U.S.A.

Nakamura still has his mail-order tenor saxophone. When asked why he prizes the ancient instrument which hasn't been played in fifty-plus years, he responded, "Several reasons. First, the horn is a part of my history—it represents many memories of Poston, where we made something out of a bad situation. Secondly, I've always loved music—the horn is my connection to that love. Thirdly, the horn is a reminder of many happy and carefree days of my youth."

THE HARMONAIRES
Minidoka Detention Camp, Idaho

At the close of summer 1941, the Mikados of Swing returned to Seattle in triumph from their successful musical journey to California, but the euphoria they experienced was short-lived. A few months later, Japanese bombs fell on Pearl Harbor. By early 1942, all Seattle citizens of Japanese descent were forcibly sent to the Washington State Fair Grounds in Puyallup. As soon as their families settled into their temporary housing—horse stalls and other barely adequate accommodations—-the Miks reorganized. The band's name, Mikados of Swing, was changed to **Harmonaires**, a more politically acceptable one ("Mikados" smacked too much of Japan, our enemy). The section of the center where they were housed was called Camp Harmony—thus, Harmonaires. A Nisei scribe wrote: "Taking advantage of the situation, the Harmonaires hepped out with the solid stuff almost nightly for the evacuated cats in Puyallup 'Assembly' Center."

The wholesale transfer of Puyallup internees to Minidoka Detention Camp, Idaho, took place several months later. The Harmonaires resumed their band work with relish—rehearsing and playing for weekend dances. A bizarre situation was created when the Harmonaires, "enemy aliens" by U.S. government definition, were invited to play for high-school proms in neighboring towns of Twin Falls and Filer. These youthful musicians with Japanese faces had to file through a guarded sentry gate, past barbed-wire enclosures, then driven on buses to entertain white high-school seniors celebrating their graduation. Yoshio Tomita, a member of the Harmonaires, remembers: "We were a great hit!" But the excitement of their brief "parole from prison" ended much too soon.

The wartime shortage of farm labor was critical. Internees were recruited from relocation camps to harvest the crops of farms located outside the centers. For the young men who volunteered, it was a welcome opportunity to escape the constrictions of life in camps, and an opportunity to savor, just for a brief spell, the sweet taste of freedom they so cherished. This movement in and out of Minidoka complicated the rehearsals and performance schedules of the Harmonaires. Eventually, it caused the dissolution of the group which once had been acclaimed "the best Nisei band in the land."

THE STARLIGHT SERENADERS
Gila River Canal Detention Camp, Arizona

Canal Camp of the Gila River Project, for a brief spell, enjoyed the dance music of the **Starlight Serenaders**. Leader **Tom Ishii** first announced the formation of a band by posting bulletins throughout the camp. The response was adequate enough to organize a group to provide music for a few dances. The *Gila News-Courier* announced that "the Starlight Serenaders will present 'Sketches in Rhythm' for dance fans on September 26, 1942, at Mess Hall 16 from 8:30 pm. Five cents will be charged at the door."

Ishii says that it was just an eight-piece combo; it lacked a piano, bass viol and guitar. Nevertheless, fans liked them because their music was live; it was better than records. "Tuxedo Junction" and "Jumping at the Woodside" were a couple of favorite tunes; the last dance was always Glenn Miller's "Moonlight Serenade" repeated two or three times. Ishii remembers Danny Kuwahara on trumpet; Frank Onishi, Sak Yamashita and Ted Iseri, saxophones; and Roy Teranishi, violin. There were others. Mary Oino Shibata did the vocals. Many Gila internees remember even today Mary's "terrific" rendition of "Sleepy Lagoon," accompanied by her sister Yumiko on piano. In postwar years Mary resumed her intense interest in singing by taking voice lessons and participating in classical choral music.

Tom Ishii had played drums in his high-school orchestra. He was the only member of the Starlight Serenaders on the Recreation Department payroll. His drumming in camp was hampered drastically because his set consisted sadly of just a snare drum and a lonely cymbal. Ishii's career as a dance-band drummer coincided with the short life of the Starlight Serenaders. He did not play drums after the breakup of the camp band.

Canal Camp's Presidents Ball on February 29, 1944, was unique in regard to dance music in detention camps. Since the Starlight Serenaders had disbanded, Bert La Mar and his five-piece orchestra from Phoenix, Arizona, were invited to provide music for the Presidents Ball. La Mar was described by the camp newspaper as "a polished trumpeter who was formerly featured soloist for Raymond Scott, Leo Reisman and Jack Denny." La Mar returned to Canal Camp for several subsequent dances.

THE MUSIC MAKERS
Gila River Butte Detention Camp, Arizona

One evening in August 1993, three former members of the Gila River Music Makers and I met at China Station, a restaurant in Berkeley, California. **Tad Yamamoto** was in town from Des Plaines, Illinois, to visit his sister. He and Jack Kusaba, trumpet players, and George Hara, a trombone player, were reunited. Tad had not seen them since "camp" fifty years ago. Time had exacted its unconditional toll—wrinkles, memory recall difficulties, graying-to-white hair and, of course, except for Yamamoto, who continues to play gigs with his alto, no chops. Yet much youthful energy was in evidence. The conversation centered on the **Music Makers,** the band that played dances in Butte Camp at Gila. It was time to indulge in nostalgia.

Tad Yamamoto led the band and also played most of the solos on trumpet or alto. The band consisted of standard dance-band instrumentation of saxophones, trumpets and trombones. Unfortunately, the rhythm section suffered serious shortcomings—no string bass, no guitar, no drums, and most of the time, no piano. It was a rare occasion when Yumiko Hojo, the Buddhist minister's wife, could assist on the piano.

With no drumset or drummer, Yamamoto in frustration persuaded his friend Yosh "Boku" Tsukahara to keep time with a beater on just the bass drum. Boku loved his new role, limited as it was, as a dance-band drummer. Tsukahara is today a retired dentist whose days are very much consumed by his responsibilities as mayor pro tem and councilman of Gardena, California. He is extremely concerned about the disintegration of the community spirit in Gardena, and is struggling to stabilize a transitional, ethnically diverse population. Listening to the big-band music of his youth helps him to revive sagging spirits. "What a tonic! It was a kick playing bass drum in Gila…I enjoyed being a member of the band with my friends!"

Dances were lively affairs despite the shortage of bottled drinks, as suggested by this announcement in the *Gila News-Courier* on December 23, 1943:

The Music Makers. Gila River Butte Detention Camp, Ariz. 1943. Left to right, front row: Tak Ogino, Haruo Hayashi, Ben Tamaki, James Araki. Back row: Paul Suzuki, Ichiro Ino, George Kikuchi, Yoshimura Araki, Yoshio Migaki, Mitsugi Kawamoto. Photo courtesy of Mitsugi Kawamoto.

BUTTE DANCE—"AS TIME GOES BY"
New Year's Eve Dance at Club 41. Limited number of bids at 65 cents per couple. Boys are requested to wear sport coats or suits. One bottle of RC Cola, 7-Up, or Pepsi Cola will be given to each person in addition to other refreshments. Caucasians as well as detainees are invited to greet the new year as time goes by.
(Note the invitation extended to non-Japanese Gila River Center staff.)

As in other centers, the young replaced the old as internees left camp, forcing changes in band personnel. George Kikuchi, a trumpet player, joined the Music Makers when he was thirteen years old. High-schoolers "Ich" Ino and Paul Suzuki completed the trumpet section. Yosh Araki and Yoshio Migaki formed the trombone section. Ben Tamaki, Haruo Hayashi and Jim Araki joined Tak Ogino, the only old-timer remaining from the original Music Makers, making up the sax section. A healthy roster of three trumpets, two trombones and a four-man sax section comprised a well-balanced horn and reed section. But alas, as before, the rhythm section suffered serious deficiencies—no drummer, no piano player, no guitar, no bass viol. Eventually, the youthful Music Makers located a drum set, primitive as it was—no cymbals, just a bass drum and a field snare. Mitsugi Kawamoto, who replaced the first drummer, confessed that he, too, had no training or experience playing drums. Says Mits, "I just kept time." Shades of Boku, the one-armed drummer.

As for piano, someone in the band later discovered John Fuyumi. When John relocated to the East Coast, he was replaced by **Suzi Tamura Ochi**. During her many years as pianist and music educator, Ochi spent only two playing popular music. Those two years were in Gila River, where, as a teenager already well-versed in classical piano, she was persuaded to join the Music Makers.

Suzi began her long career in music at age three as a student of the *koto,* a Japanese stringed instrument (her mother was an expert *shamisen* and *koto* player), and then at six commenced piano lessons. Today Ochi is an accomplished concert pianist, but her relatively short involvement in popular music directly influenced her future. Classical piano is somewhat of an individualized activity in that one practices in isolation hour upon hour. Then the "finished product" is presented to a subdued audience which proffers polite accolades. The pianist usually has very little, if any, emotional contact with his or her listeners and often no feedback from them—their only response might be courteous applause.

From these sober experiences, Ochi was thrust upon a stimulating and intoxicating musical adventure in Gila River. She played for public dances in a dance band, accompanied vocalists in talent shows, played for Buddhist Church worship services and pounded out joyful boogie-woogie which excited her highly excitable teenage peers! "Gila provided opportunities that were new and exciting," she recalls. "I played with a dance band for the first time in my life and did a lot of solo work. I learned to play popular tunes, including a lot of boogie-woogie, without having to read orthodox music sheets. I learned how to improvise, utilizing modern chord progressions. I used a lot of 7th, 9th and 11th chords. All of the above in the context of satisfying public performances. The self-confidence that resulted from these performances was powerful. I came to a realization that music might be for me the ideal career choice!"

The guys in the band called her "Pine Top." You see, Pine Top Smith, one of the best of all boogie-woogie pianists, had composed "Pine Top's Boogie-Woogie" in the mid-'20s, a number which gave the boogie-woogie style its name.[23] At Gila River, Suzi initially learned "Pine Top's Boogie-Woogie" from a written arrangement and loved to play it because of the energy it provoked. It was great fun; it was exhilarating!

"Guess I'll have to give Pine Top some credit for leading me to my long, satisfying career in music," she adds. "Playing all that heavy boogie-woogie bass-line in camp gave me such a strong left hand, it caused an imbalance in relation to my right hand…a major handicap that I overcame in time. But Pine Top put the fun in music for me and gave me the confidence to play to audiences…that made all the difference!"

Ochi recalls her earliest experiences with the Music Makers: "The band didn't sound too good—poor intonation, disregard of dynamics, out-of-tune instruments and lackluster interpretations. When Tad Yamamoto, leader of the original Music Makers, returned to Gila for a short visit, he took over rehearsals of the band. He was a taskmaster…forced us to rehearse for hours after school and weekends! Wouldn't let us go to movies or anything! But he did it…he cast a magic spell! The results were astonishing. The band truly sounded like a dance band should."

Suzi Ochi retired in 1991 as a music consultant to the Santa Barbara City School District. She now devotes her time to traveling, performing intermittently in concerts and enjoying life in general.

Haruo Hayashi, who played the saxophone and clarinet, led the sophomoric Music Makers when Yamamoto left Gila. He remembers the unique response of dancers in their début: "The kids enjoyed our music so much, they threw chocolate candy at us! Don't remember whether we rushed to pick up the goodies, or whether we were too embarrassed to do so…anyway, it was great fun!" Hayashi, fifty years later, a semiretired farmer in Arroyo Grande, California, still enjoys big-band music and jazz. He bought a new tenor saxophone not too long ago and, when it is convenient for all, he gathers his four adult sons who play piano and other instruments for an informal jam session. "We try to play arrangements. We start off together quite well, but during the course of playing the rest of the music, we somehow manage to go in different directions… hopelessly lost. But it's a great source of enjoyment for me…wish we could do it more often."

James Araki first played the clarinet in Gila River. He possessed an extraordinary talent for music and progressed to a level where he was invited to play both clarinet and alto saxophone in the camp dance band. This early introduction to swing was the beginning of an exceptional, lifelong career in jazz. When conscripted into the U.S. Army, Araki became a student in the Military Intelligence Service Language School at Ft. Snelling, Minnesota. There, in 1945, an unplanned reunion of several former members of the Gila Music Makers took place—James Araki, George Hara, Hiro Goto and Yoshio Migaki were reunited as members of the Ft. Snelling dance band, the Eager Beavers. The subsequent blossoming of Araki's jazz development, both conceptually and technically, was phenomenal. His dynamic presence in Japan during the Occupation as a major influence in the development of postwar jazz in Japan has been highly acclaimed by Japanese musicians and jazz historians.

DEEJAYS AND HEPCATS
Rohwer Detention Camp, Arkansas

Rohwer did not have a dance band, according to artist **George Akimoto,** originator of "Lil Daniel," a clever cartoon series of a Nisei lad's experiences in camp. Phonograph records of popular big bands provided music for dancers. One of the more popular deejays in camp was Charley Wakai of Lodi, who owned a respectable stack of 78 rpm records which he played on a phonograph unit capable of relatively heavy bass response—"high fidelity" components were an uncommon concept for the masses in prewar days.

Akimoto made an interesting observation regarding the dance styles of Nisei in Rohwer. He noticed that Los Angeles couples at first danced with slow-moving, short shuffles, holding on to each other rather closely; whereas couples from the Stockton/Lodi area took longer steps and moved actively on the dance floor. Akimoto discovered that after several weeks of social interaction at dances, a change in dance styles of these two groups, urban vs. rural, occurred. The L.A.

The D-Elevens. Jerome Detention Camp, Ark. 1943. Left to right, front row: Haru Yoshikawa Goya, George Nakatani, Tom Nakamichi, Frank Tashima, Mackay Yoshimura. Back row: Sam Seno, Hank Yoshikawa, Buddy Hirasuna, Jimmy Hirasuna. Photo courtesy of Mackay Yoshimura.

crowd began to navigate faster around the floor with drawn-out steps and the Stockton/Lodi dancers gradually slowed down, eventually, to a shuffling drag!

Moreover, many Los Angeles hepcats arrived in Rohwer, affecting the "pachuco" (young urban Mexican American) zoot-suit style in vogue at that time, i.e., a long coat with wide-shoulders plus a pair of pants with a waistline high on the chest, wide knees and tight cuffs. The latter were called "drapes." Los Angeles mail-order specialty shops were busy filling orders from young men in camp eager to be among the in-crowd.[24]

THE DENSONEERS, A.K.A. THE D-ELEVENS
Jerome Detention Camp, Arkansas

Led by Frank Tashima, the Densoneers was an eleven-piece dance band consisting of three saxes, a violin, two trumpets, one trombone, a guitar, piano and drums. The vocalist, Bill Nikaido, made it eleven. In a 1995 interview **Mackay Yoshimura,** who played the clarinet and tenor sax, could not recall details of the band's performances except that they played for camp dances and talent shows: "We played all stock arrangements of popular bands—enjoyed playing the Miller stuff. We were not members of the recreation department. I guess the band received a few dollars for playing dances, but individually we didn't get any money for playing."

Yoshimura continues: "I loved music quite early; first learned how to play the clarinet in Washington Intermediate School in Honolulu and went on to McKinley High School, where I played clarinet in the orchestra and symphonic band. During high school days I played some dance music in Nisei and mixed bands…you know, Japanese, Portuguese, Chinese kids. With the advent of Pearl Harbor, my family, with several hundred other Japanese families, were rounded up and sent to a detention camp on the Mainland. You see, our fathers were active in community affairs—mine was the president of the local Buddhist Church and also head of the Japanese language school. We were herded onto the 'Kota Agoeng' (I still remember that name after all these years), a troop ship of Dutch registry, disembarked at the Port of Oakland [Calif.] after a tedious ocean voyage in cramped quarters. Then, from Oakland by train to Arkansas…took a whole week to get there. Other trains had priority; we had to pull our window shades down when they passed by or when we traveled past train stations.

"I remained in Jerome, played in the Densoneers for about a year, from February 1943 to June 1944, then left for Chicago to enroll in the Chicago Musical College. My major was music education; my intention was to teach music in a high school. For four years I studied harmony, music history, instrumental music, basic academic courses and discovered upon graduation many opportunities to teach. About that time, I met June Ezaki, originally from San Francisco, who was studying piano at the college. She and I were married later.

"While a student at the Musical College, I played tenor and clarinet in Koichi Hayashi's dance band…a mixed band, mostly Nisei, with a few black and white musicians. **Elsie Itashiki** sang a couple of gigs with us; 'Shoo Fly Pie & Apple Pan Dowdy' was one of her favorites. About the only thing I remember about that time was when we played a Nisei dinner dance and never got paid as promised. Boy, was I mad!

"As I mentioned earlier, I received many job offers when I graduated. I chose a job in Bridgeport, Nebraska, at their high school at a salary of $3,200 per year, organizing orchestras, marching bands, etc. That lasted just a year, from 1948 to 1949. I didn't enjoy teaching high school, so I went into the retail music business in Scottsbluff, Nebraska, until 1951—sales, teaching and instrument repair. I returned to Chicago and subsequently moved to California, where I continued teaching and instrument repair, finally owning my own music store in Sunnyvale.

"During this time I played occasionally as replacement in different dance bands and even played a Miss California Pageant in Santa Cruz. I also organized and directed a Japanese Community Youth Service band in San Jose, an all-Sansei symphonic band consisting of about thirty-five members ranging from elementary grades through college levels. We rehearsed at the San Jose United Methodist Church. Out of this group, we formed a dance band, called it the Amber Saints—four saxes, three trumpets, a trombone, piano and drums.

"I used to collect jazz records years ago…started out with people like Sidney Bechet, Bix Beiderbecke and Louis Armstrong. Of course, during the swing years I liked Benny Goodman for his jazz and classical stuff—Mozart, Debussy's Rhapsody. Bought a lot of records by Glenn Miller, Artie Shaw and Bob Crosby. But my favorite was Jimmie Lunceford…he swung so much! I remember hearing Lunceford in a great stage show at the Regal Theater in Chicago. I liked Count Basie, too.

"What does music mean to me? Well, I feel sorry for people who don't really feel the music…they're missing so much. I mean, music is more than just the melody…more than the tune itself. There's phrasing, intonation, dynamics, expression, etc. We go to the San Francisco Symphony concerts…purchased season tickets for twenty years, but we're giving it up now. I'm seventy-one years old now. I'm sorry I can't play my clarinet anymore, but I still enjoy music… all types! Music has truly given me meaning in my life."

Sam Seno, the guitar-playing member of the Densoneers, remembers: "Ty Saito, who worked in Community Activities in nearby Rohwer Camp, heard that we had a live band. He had tried to organize a band there, but they didn't have enough musicians. So, after he heard about us, he said that they would be privileged to have us come and that they'd have a dance for the whole community. We went over a couple or three times, as I recall. The distance to Rohwer from Jerome was about twenty miles or so. The guys who drove the trucks were from the Jerome Motor Pool; they were happy to get out [of camp]. Everyone was happy to get out.

"Since coming back to L.A. [after the camps were closed], we met people who say they were in Rohwer and they remember us coming with the band. I guess it was a big thing in those days. The rest of the time our band in Jerome performed at dances and things, usually in some mess hall. We played old Tommy Dorsey standards. Our theme song was 'Dream.' I used to sing it. It was a slow romantic kind [of song]."

THE POMONANS
Pomona "Assembly" Center, California

Life in disordered, makeshift and tentative "assembly" centers was lightened by distractions such as movies and talent shows, thanks to Nisei creativity and organizing skills. On May 28, 1942, more than three thousand appreciative movie fans jammed the Pomona Center athletic field to view their first center movies. Father Clement of Maryknoll Missions, donor of the films, showed several short features and *Spring Parade* starring Deanna Durbin. He was impressed with "the orderly behavior of the massive crowd."

To accommodate camp talent shows, a sturdy stage was built, backdrops designed and installed, and dressing rooms provided backstage. "The second weekly Talent Revue came off with a bang last Friday night on the athletic field before an eager crowd of about 3,000," reported the *Pomona Center News,* June 2, 1942. Highlight performers were Tets Bessho, a clarinet player from Montebello; the Aloha Serenaders led by Frank Hayami and hula dances by Margaret Nagakura. Other talent included **George Igawa,** saxophonist; "Chick" Ikezoe, harmonica player; and Mary Watanabe, vocalist.

The talent show helped to identify those with a propensity for playing dance music and singing pop songs. Just one week after the second talent show, the Pomonans, a newly formed dance band organized by George Igawa with the assistance of recreation director "Buck" Dimon, made its début at the third talent revue. The center news headlined "Band Makes Hit—Crowd Clamors For More" and added, "The warblist for this musical outfit was petite June Yoshino, who brought down the house with her two numbers." The members of the orchestra were: George Igawa, Tets Bessho and Toyo Niitake, saxophones; Yoneo Fukui and Bill Furukawa, trumpets; Frank Hayami, guitar and Eiko Watanabe, piano. This seven-piece ensemble formed the nucleus of the future dance band in Heart Mountain Detention Camp. Pomona internees were transferred there in the early months of 1943.

THE GEORGE IGAWA BAND
Heart Mountain Detention Camp, Wyoming

Upon arrival at Heart Mountain, the Pomonans continued entertaining camp crowds as the **George Igawa Band.** Igawa had been the leader of the Sho Tokyans, the Los Angeles dance band which toured the West Coast and worked dance halls in Japan in 1937 and 1938. With the original Pomonans augmented by five new members, the sound of the band greatly improved.

George Igawa Band. Heart Mountain Detention Camp, Wyo. Dec. 17, 1943. Right to left, front row: Takako Kunimatsu, Haruko Satow, Harry Takamura, James Toyama, Tetsu Bessho, Susumu Chikami, George Igawa, George Azuma, Tami Hirashiki, Yutaka Yamamoto. Back row: unknown, Jimmie Akiya, Harry Shimoto, Walt Hayami, Yone Fukui, Frank Hirahara, Max Koga, Tomo Fukui. Photo courtesy of Yone Fukui.

At its peak it boasted six saxes, five trumpets, three trombones, piano, guitar, string bass and drums—truly a *big* band. When vocalist June Yoshino relocated out of camp, she was replaced by a succession of female singers—Beverly Kawata, Joy Takéshita and, finally, Takako "Tubbie" Kunimatsu. For a short time, Lyle Nakano also sang with the band.

Yoneo Fukui, veteran trumpeter, recalls: "Band members were employees of the recreation department and were paid $12.00 a month as unskilled laborers. We had the luxury, however, to put in a lot of rehearsal time and played talent shows and dances on weekends. To improve public relations with our neighbors outside of camp, I remember being bussed to nearby towns to play for War Bond Drives, local lodge gatherings and high school dances. The townsfolk liked our music; there were no comparable groups out there."

Fukui, a retired public accountant, began his lifelong musical career in a San Francisco grammar school where he was first introduced to the harmonica. Then, as did other urban Nisei, he played the bugle in a Boy Scout drum and bugle corps. In junior high school Fukui played the trumpet and has continued to play the horn to this day except for a short respite following camp. "When I first started, my trumpet hero was Harry James; my favorite swing bands were led by Glenn Miller, Harry James and Tommy Dorsey. Today, Count Basie's band is my top favorite. I never took a [formal] lesson in my life; I'm a self-taught musician," says Fukui. He now rehearses weekly with the Musicians Union concert band, a "German" band, an Adult School concert band, the San Mateo Elks Lodge concert band and has time for twice-monthly rehearsals with the 17-piece J-Town Jazz Ensemble in San Francisco. "Have to keep my chops up and, of course, I enjoy the music," says Fukui, approaching his seventieth birthday.

"Tubbie" Kunimatsu. Heart Moutain Detention Camp, Wyo. 1944. Photo courtesy of Tommy Hirashiki.

The median age of Nisei in camp was nineteen years. Many of them had crowded social calendars. The energy to make new friends and to search for distraction and fun could not be suppressed despite the psychological impact of being brutally uprooted from their homes to be incarcerated in segregated badlands.

The *Heart Mountain Sentinel*, dated November 27, 1943, provides a sampling of these events:

ORALS SPONSOR BIG GOBBLERS' JIG
In keeping with the Thanksgiving holiday atmosphere, a "Gobblers' Jig" sponsored by the Original Orals was enjoyed by members of the Faicoms, Starlettes, Cardinals, Falcons, Shamrocks and special guests last night at mess hall 9-27. June Sugiura and Ayako Takagi were in charge.

A number of novelty dances including a spot dance, broom dance, reverse dance, and a card matching dance were featured. Skits performed by members of the Original Orals were presented during the intermission.

Chairmen of the various committees were Mari Tsuyuki and Alice Hamada, refreshments; Alice Taketa, program and Mits Shimizu, general chairman. Miyoko Fukuyama is advisor of the group.

ORIGINAL ATTIRE FEATURED AT DANCE
With "Priority Stomp" as the theme, a social held by the Girl Reserves at the high school auditorium Wednesday night attracted more than 200 girls who appeared garbed in original costumes. As an initiation for the members, girls were required to wear these comical clothes throughout the day.

A singspiration led by Hisako Takehara preceded the program dancing emceed by Pauline Shinta and Alice Taketa. Prizes were awarded to the following: Kana Magara, Reiko Ohara, jitterbug contest; Claire Sudderth, Miyo Hayami and Dorothy Honda, novelty lemon number; Kitch Yasunaka and Maye Wada, best-dressed couple; Arlene Mukai and May Osuga, most original couple, and Margaret Hiura, most unfortunately dressed girl.

Inclement weather forced the girls from Powell and Cody to decline the invitation.[25]

WINTER CARNIVAL SET TONIGHT FOR 22 YOUTH ORGANIZATIONS
With approximately 300 persons expected to attend, last-minute preparations are being made for the huge "Winter Carnival" which will open 7 pm tonight at [barrack] 12-30 with the Herculites playing host to 22 youth organizations. The guest list includes the Gingers, Junior Misses, Radelles, Starlettes, Bell Sharmiers, Faicoms, Debonnaires, Royalettes, Victories, Kaletas, Original Orals, Heart-teenans, Hi-Jinx, Royal Dukes, Aristos, Weightlifters, Shamrocks, Appollites, Royal Aces, Club Chattanooga, Broncos, and the Jackrabbits.

The affair will be informal with a "Come As You Are" motif, and guests are urged to arrive early as doors will be closed by 8 pm.

In charge of general arrangements will be Jim Yamaguchi, Lyle Nakano, and Isamu Ujiiye. Lane Nakano will be master of ceremonies.

Certainly, there was no scarcity of social opportunities—something for just about any lad or lass. Still, there were concerns about the youngsters' grasp of etiquette. *The Heart Mountain Sentinel,* January 15, 1944, printed the following editorial:

DANCE MANNERS AND HABITS ARE IN NEED OF OVERHAULING
Heart Mountain social functions can be made more enjoyable if offenders of social graces would put their manners and habits on the repair rack for a complete over-hauling.

The Heart Mountain stag line is not only an eyesore, but a definite nuisance. To begin with, it is always too long. It doesn't know how to behave. Its chief offense is converging toward the center of the floor, crowding dancers and forcing them to navigate in an ever-decreasing area.

At community stag and stagette affairs and at mess hall socials the stag line is especially obnoxious, being the ruination of many an otherwise good social. It is the opinion of many girls that this center can well afford to do without these affairs.

To add insult to injury, many of the stags are crashers, the social enemies No. 1 of the camp. Crashers will stop at nothing and stoop to everything to break into a social. To their way of thinking, every party, no matter how private, is an open affair. Crashers display their worst manners when it's refreshment time, having the crass [nerve] to ask for seconds when there's hardly enough to go around once.

Clothes do not make a dance, but proper dress would certainly raise the much-needed dignity of some socials, especially those stag and stagette functions. A boy wearing a sport coat over a dirty pair of jeans has a distorted sense of individualism. Garish, outlandish outfits simply stamp the wearer as being on the "queer" side. Some fellas take the "come as you are" parties too literally, showing up in engineer's boots and in sloppy jeans rolled almost half way up their legs. Some girls do not disapprove of jeans just so long as they are clean.

And there are other ways in which dances can be made more enjoyable. The tagging technique of some boys can certainly stand a lot of brushing up. And surely, there is always room for more courtesies at dances, especially the small courtesies which count more than the big ones. And every dance can do without the loudmouths.

Some observers decry the lack of spontaneous zest for fun. Crowds are dead in many instances, with participants seemingly trying to dare the hosts or emcee to entertain them. At some parties, the emcee has to give a pep talk every time to get the dancers out on the floor.

Yes, a little more cooperation, common sense and manners can do much to elevate the standard of center socials.

George Akimoto. "Lil Daniel." Rohwer Detention Camp, Ark. 1943.

These highly critical statements above applied to social life in camp over fifty years ago. Those uncouth stags, wherever they may be today, most likely have become respectable citizens. Yes, may even have become highly critical fathers of "uncouth" teenage sons—the cycle continues relentlessly.

Nisei jazz fans in camp were not neglected by enterprising outside business interests. The following ad appeared in the *Heart Mountain Sentinel*:

JERRY BERGER'S—EVERYTHING IN MUSIC
Rare Collectors Series Albums [78 rpm] Buy while available
All Brunswick Records of Cab Calloway—4 records, $3.70.
Jimmy Noone, Dean of Hot Clarinetists—4 records, $3.70.
Boogie-Woogie Piano—4 records, $3.70.
Red Nichols and his Band including Jimmy Dorsey, Glenn Miller, Benny Goodman,
  Gene Krupa, Jack Teagarden and others, $3.70.
Duke Ellington—4 records, $3.70.
Chicago Jazz Classics, Benny Goodman—4 records, $3.70.
Harlem Jazz—4 records, $3.70.
Pine Top Smith, Boogie-Woogie Piano—2 records, $2.10.

On July 5, 1994, I visited the Japanese American History Archives in San Francisco to research prewar Nisei social activity in the city. Just outside the office door, seated at a tiny table, was an attractive, neatly dressed woman with a tablet and a pencil in hand, age somewhere between forty and sixty (Nisei women are ageless), casually flipping the yellowed pages of the *Heart Mountain Sentinel*. "Hi," I said.

Joy Teraoka looked up and replied, "Hi." She was documenting her family's history and looking for information pertinent to her two-year search. I introduced myself, remarking that I had a photograph of the Heart Mountain dance band—"Did you by any chance hear the band in camp?"

Talk about serendipity—this lady in her reading glasses at the table bounced back, "I was the vocalist in George Igawa's band!" What followed was an animated interview over a vegetarian tempura dinner. I had sensed from her expressive face—eyes that danced—that music was very special to her.

Joy Takéshita Teraoka was born in Los Angeles. "When I was very young, I idolized Shirley Temple. For 'show-and-tell' in elementary school I would sing 'Animal Crackers In My Soup' and 'On The Good Ship Lollipop.' Later, at the Hollywood Japanese Presbyterian Church, I occasionally sang in duets and trios with my girl friends. The teenage years transported me into an exciting new world of delight—popular big-band music! I won't ever forget those times just before the war, when, although I was underage, I went with my friends to the Palladium Ballroom in Hollywood to dance and listen to the wonderful music of Tommy Dorsey, Glenn Miller and Gene Krupa. Those were unforgettable, happy times.

Joy Takéshita Teraoka. Heart Mountain Detention Camp, Wyo. 1943. Photo courtesy of Jimmie Akiya.

"In the spring of 1942 under the cloud of World War II, along with my fellow internees, my family was incarcerated in the Pomona Fair Grounds "Assembly" Center. Then, in September of the same year, we were all transported many miles eastward in vintage trains across desolate prairies to Heart Mountain, Wyoming, a permanent detention camp. There, at sixteen, I became the vocalist for the camp dance band. My girl friends had urged me to try out...I did and was chosen. Was I excited! My father who sang and taught *shigin* (stylized Japanese poetry reading) shared my joy. My mother preferred classical music; nevertheless, she gave her consent as long as I kept up my school work. It was a dream come true...to sing with a big band, just like Helen Forrest with Harry James or Peggy Lee with Benny Goodman. Some of the tunes I enjoyed singing were 'Dream', 'At Last', 'I Had The Craziest Dream', and 'Mr. Five-by-Five.' Incidentally, when I appeared with the band, I wore my older sister's clothes and heels so that I would look more grown-up.

"George Igawa, the leader, played the tenor saxophone. I also remember Tets Bessho on clarinet, he took the solos; Yoné Fukui on trumpet; and Eiko Watanabe, piano. Besides camp functions, we were invited to entertain adults and students outside of camp in places like Lovell, Powell, Worland and Thermopolis—all small towns without big bands."

The *Heart Mountain Sentinel,* March 20, 1943, reported:

IGAWA'S ORCHESTRA WILL PLAY AT LOVELL CHURCH DANCE TONIGHT
Music as styled by George Igawa and his orchestra will be heard in Lovell tonight as the musicians play for a Mormon Church reunion dance. The orchestra is fresh from a triumphant debut at Powell a week ago when some six-hundred persons jammed the American Legion Hall and contributed $210.00 to the Shoshone Chapter's Red Cross fund drive.

Joy Takéshita, vocalist, will accompany the orchestra, while other entertainment will be provided by Alfred Tanaka's Surf Riders.

Among other requests following the Powell performance are invitations from the Powell High School Junior Prom Committee, Lovell Junior Chamber of Commerce, a group from Cowley and several other districts.

Paul Douglas, commander of the Powell American Legion, expressed his compliments to the musical groups in a letter which reads in part: The assistance given by the people of Heart Mountain Center to the Shoshone Chapter has been a big boost in putting our War Fund quota over the top in such grand manner. The people of Powell really appreciate good music and we seldom have the opportunity of obtaining such a large number of artists to appear on one program. We hope this dance has paved the way to full cooperation between the people of Powell and our American Friends of Heart Mountain.

When asked about the attitude of Powell citizens toward the internees, **Jimmie Akiya,** drummer of the Igawa orchestra, replied, "Shopkeepers, especially, welcomed visitations of Heart Mountain residents who were occasionally granted permission to go shopping in Powell. After all, it was *not* business as usual. Thousands of potential customers eager to purchase all kinds of consumer goods were suddenly thrust upon the merchants—it must have been a godsend.

"The crowds in those small neighboring towns were very receptive to our music. We had the distinction of being the only big band in the state of Wyoming. We didn't go out to solicit dance jobs. They came to us after they discovered our band and would donate a few dollars to us when we played—from fifty to a hundred dollars. It was a mutually agreeable arrangement. We called ourselves the George Igawa Band; our music stands were lettered 'GI' to denote the leader's initials. Many of our white fans thought that we were a U.S. Army band because of the 'GI' on our stands. The popular usage of 'GI' then was in reference to U.S. military personnel, military supplies and equipment. Of course, we straightened them out whenever we discovered this misunderstanding. Sure was ironic, though—'enemy aliens' going outside of a concentration camp to play for the dancing pleasure of white Americans, who often mistook us for an Army dance band!

"The music played by the Pomonans and the early GI Band consisted of simple stock arrangements readily purchased from music stores. In Heart Mountain, after the band solidified into a presentable unit, the music began to take on the sounds of many well-known orchestras—Glenn Miller, Harry James, Tommy Dorsey, Count Basie, etc. [Authentic] arrangements were not available then; but, undaunted, George Igawa rearranged practically the entire band library to reflect the distinctive sounds of the various big bands, including our theme song, Glenn Miller's 'Moonlight Serenade.'

Tetsu Besso. Heart Mountain Detention Camp, Wyo. 1943. Photo courtesy of Jimmie Akiya.

"I remember **Tets Bessho,** who played the alto sax. An outstanding star soloist, he was called the Nisei Artie Shaw. His rendition of the clarinet solos in Artie Shaw's 'Frenesi' and 'Concerto for Clarinet' will be long remembered by those who heard him play. **Yoné Fukui** was the ultimate showman and a fantastic trumpet player à la Harry James—his ad lib solos did justice to any trumpet player around. George Igawa played the tenor sax and was *the man.* Without George and his many talents—leader, arranger, superb tenor sax playing—there would never have been the GI Band of Heart Mountain.

"The GI Band, playing on the average once every two weeks for the many dances in the center, added in time a new dimension to our performances. We planned a variety show of Japanese music and dance aimed toward the many Issei in camp. To our basic band was added a trio of talented players of the *shamisen, koto* and *shakuhachi.* A few ensembles today routinely incorporate occidental and oriental instruments, creating a most pleasing sound; but fifty years ago, it had never been tried. This blending of two culturally different types of instruments presented an unforeseen problem—music scores were unavailable. Again, Igawa's talent provided the solution. He painstakingly listened to Japanese phonograph records and wrote the score for each instrument of the augmented band. The success of his efforts was apparent in the response of audiences who packed the mess hall performances, many returning several times for the same show. Hearing their favorite Japanese songs and seeing familiar dances evoked in Issei an intense and enjoyable sense of nostalgia."

Jimmie Akiya subsequently relocated to Cleveland, Ohio, where he played drums for a few years with several dance bands. He recalls with affection a jazz quartet which included Tom Nakashige on tenor sax, Mabel Sugiyama Eto on piano, Mark Ota on trumpet and himself on the drums. Says Akiya, "I haven't played drums in any way since 1949, but my interest in music is still with me. My main music involvement now is working with the Santa Clara Vanguard, a nationally renowned, award-winning competition drum and bugle corps that has been described as 'a group presenting a ballet-opera-musical on a football field.'" Actually, the Vanguard is a musically superior and superbly trained group of young men and women who are extremely serious about their commitment toward their goals of top-quality musicianship and showmanship.

"Jammin'." Cleveland, Ohio. 1949. Left to right: Mabel Sugiyama Eto, Mark Ota, Tom Nakashige, Jimmie Akiya. Photo courtesy of Jimmie Akiya.

The *Heart Mountain Sentinel*, April 17, 1943:

ORCHESTRA PLAYS AT THERMOPOLIS
Spreading music and good will, George Igawa and his band traveled 130 miles to Thermopolis last night to play at the Junior-Senior Prom. The busy band members furnished music at the Lovell war bond drive dance last Monday, April 12, at which more that $10,000.00 worth of War Bonds were sold. The affair was sponsored by the Lovell Women's Club, the Junior Chamber of Commerce, and other community groups.

"Going out was special," says Joy Teraoka. "Getting out of the confines of camp was a treat in itself, but many times we would have a chance to eat 'outside' food—a welcome change from the camp fare of egg foo-yung, dried fish or baked spaghetti. Once we were even treated to a banquet of succulent venison. The goodwill we established among the townsfolk with our music was valuable beyond measure.

"In August 1943, my singing with George Igawa's band ended when I relocated with my parents, first to Salt Lake City, then to Denver, and finally to Washington, D.C., where in 1944 I graduated Calvin Coolidge High School. I sang 'Embraceable You' at the Senior Banquet—my swan song for some time to come. Several years later, after marriage in Honolulu and the births of two children, I enrolled in a voice class at the University of Hawaii. About this time, I became acquainted with Carl Jones and Paul Conrad. These two professional musicians taught me how to phrase lyrics, to sing on pitch, to be aware of time and meter, and to convey emotions suggested by popular songs—basic training that I had earlier lacked in Heart Mountain.

"My singing became much more expressive; I felt more confident. Sensing the progress I had made and the love I had for this music, my husband challenged and encouraged me to sing publicly. My first professional job entailed weekends at Leroy's on Ala Moana with Twerp Nakayama's five-piece band for about a year. At the same time I sang at weddings, parties, proms and conventions. I then worked, in turn, with Larry Fukunaga's Ebbtides at the Tripler Officers Club, the La Parisienne dinner club in the Reef Hotel, then five nights a week at the Pearl Harbor Non-Commissioned Officers Club for one hectic month into 1969, when I quit singing. Burnout? Boredom? I don't know…for many years there was no singing.

"I'm into the karaoké scene now with friends who introduced me to beautiful Japanese songs. I take weekly lessons in Japanese singing to improve my language and diction—a never-ending process. Our karaoké club, about twenty of us, meets each Tuesday at the Ala Wai Golf Clubhouse to sing and to listen to each other…it's great camaraderie. We often go to nursing homes to entertain old folks who give us a warm welcome each time and that's nice, too. But I must admit that American standards are what I really prefer. Japanese songs are usually sung rather straight…can't ad lib very much. What I *really* miss is the interplay between my singing and the live accompaniment of a creative jazz pianist or band. What a *wonderful* feeling it is when two or more people work in the same groove! Oh, well…guess I can't complain. I feel fortunate to have lived my dreams those many moons ago." Joy Teraoka was well-named. Born with a song in her heart, she brought joy to her audiences with her songs of love, and joy to herself as well.

Heart Mountain Center was closed on November 15, 1945. During the months preceding the closure, individuals and families relocated to other centers, to the Midwest or back home to the West Coast. Due to dislocations created by the impending camp closure, the personnel of George Igawa's band was gradually decimated. When Igawa relocated, Tets Bessho took over the vestiges of the band now composed only of high-school students. The latter ushered in a new year, 1945, with a dance in the high-school auditorium. According to the *Sentinel,* no stags or stagettes were to be permitted to attend this sports-formal affair. The dance would begin at 8:00 pm and continue until 1:00 am. Special instructions were directed to the celebrants: "All dancing will be done counter-clockwise to avoid confusion. Corsages will be permitted, but none will be available at the dance." As detainee relocation accelerated, the longevity of Bessho's band was clearly on the wane; it was time truly for *"the last dance."*

JIVE BOMBERS
Manzanar Detention Camp, California

Soon after Manzanar internees were settled in their permanent "homes," a Conservatory of Music was established in Music Hall 24-15. (Pretentious labels assigned to primitive tar-paper-covered barracks.) The *Manzanar Free Press,* October 31, 1942, announced: "Lessons on nearly all musical instruments will be given free to anyone interested." Dr. Shunzo Mitani was the director. His staff consisted of Shinta Kadona, sax/clarinet; Fukiko Komatsu, piano; Roy Nakama, guitar and mandolin; Joan Nagao, piano; Henry Onishi, sax/clarinet; Yoshiko Hibino, piano; Isaye Terazawa, piano; and Bill Wakatsuki, voice and trumpet.

The schedule of music classes listed a Glee Club, a class in Harmony, a Concert Band, Mandolin and Guitar lessons, an Orchestra and a Swing Band. Torao Kusaba, a trumpet-playing member of the swing band, remembers: "Because Dr. Mitani, our leader, was schooled in classical music, we played dance music that was rather conservative and staid. We played only for the white administrative staff; we did not play for Nisei dances. The **Jive Bombers** came later."

"The name 'Jive Bombers' was my idea," says Joe Sakai, former member of the Los Angeles Sho Tokyans. "At the time, Japanese *kamikaze* pilots were bombing and diving into our battleships in the Far East." The band was first led by **Bill Wakatsuki** on trumpet. *The Canteen Cowboy,* a gossip column in the October 31, 1942, *Manzanar Free Press* asked: "IS IT TRUE WHAT THEY SAY about Bill Wakatsuki? If so, he's really on the beam. Confirmed reports say that one morning a person heard someone playing "Sleepy Lagoon" on the trumpet à la Harry James, identical style except with no other musical accompaniment. Interested party was told that the ace trumpeter was Mr. Wakatsuki."

What a way to be greeted in the morning! One would surmise that being awakened by "Sleepy Lagoon" would be much more palatable than "reveille"—the standard U.S. Army wake-up bugle call. "Sleepy Lagoon" was a lyrical waltz, tops with the young dance crowd. The Jive Bombers' leader greatly admired Harry James's trumpet technique and style.

Leader Wakatsuki was assisted by Joe Sakai on bass and Henry Onishi on the saxophone—two of the older, married men in the band. Onishi, thirty-seven years old then, was an experienced dance-band musician who had been a member of the 1929 Sacramento Night Hawks; Sakai, a former Sho Tokyan. The others were high-school students. Yoshiteru Murakami, alto sax player, led the Bombers when Wakatsuki left. Murakami eventually relocated to pursue studies in music at St. Olaf College, Minnesota.

The Jive Bombers was truly a *big* band—it consisted of four saxophones, two trombones, four trumpets, a guitar, a piano, drums and a bass viol. Being a member of the Los Angeles Musicians Union, bass-playing Joe Sakai was able to obtain dance-band arrangements gratis from the union. He remembers with a smile: "A favorite pastime of the Bombers was to amplify *real loud* our playing the Cole Porter hit, "Don't Fence Me In"…directing the speaker toward nearby Army barracks where camp sentries bunked. Don't know if any of the guards caught on to what we were doing, but we sure got a big kick out of it!"

Because the mood created by "Dream," their theme song, was incongruous with the implied vigor of "Jive Bombers," it was replaced by Woody Herman's up-tempo arrangement of "Blues on Parade." Vocals were provided by a trio of young ladies—Kazuko Nagai, Lillian Uyemura and Machiko Sasaki—who sang their songs in the fashion of the Andrews Sisters, a top swing era vocal group with nineteen gold records and record sales numbering several millions. Junko Yoshimoto later replaced Machiko, who relocated with her family to Tule Lake Detention Camp.

The Jive Bombers. Manzanar Detention Camp, Calif. 1943. Left to right, front row: Yoshiteru Murakami, Yoshindo Shibuya, Gordon Sato, Katayama, Joe Shikami. Second row: Kiyo Nishi Tanaka, Roy Nakagawa, George Maeda, Bill Wakatsuki, Bruce Kaji, Torao Kusaba. Back row: "Zush" Matoba, Joe Sakai. Inset: Bill Wakatsuki, leader. Photo courtesy of Mary Nomura.

Bruce Kaji was given the demanding task of playing solos for the Bombers—"Star Dust" and "Blue Moon" were a couple of his favorites. Kaji recalls his start in instrumental music: "I played the bugle with Boy Scout Troop 197 around 1938 at Chuo Gakuen, a Japanese language school in East Los Angeles. Mr. Arnold directed our drum and bugle corps; Iwao 'Wahoo' Oyama acted as drum major. George Yoshida and I were in the same corps; I remember how much he loved playing the field snare drum. About that time, when I was a student in Hollenbeck Junior High School, I quietly approached my parents and hinted that, maybe, it would be nice to own a trumpet (didn't want to be too forward about wanting one; times were tough then). To my surprise, they agreed without question. I became the proud owner of a beautiful, golden Conn. I was really happy with my new horn. I kept it brightly polished all the time and carefully oiled the valves so that they would work smoothly. I enjoyed playing trumpet in the junior high school orchestra.

"When the wartime removal of Japanese Americans thrust my family into Manzanar Detention Camp, I played in the high-school orchestra and the Jive Bombers. I have pleasant memories of playing dances with the Bombers. My trumpet heroes then were Charlie Spivak, Harry James and Bunny Berigan. I gigged about two years with the camp band—from 1942 through 1944, when I left Manzanar for Iowa to attend college. No sooner had I arrived in my new home when Uncle Sam, in February 1945, pointed his finger at me: 'I want you.' After basic training, I was transferred to attend the Japanese Language School of the Military Intelligence Service at Ft. Snelling, Minnesota. Upon graduation, Army travel orders sent me first to Japan and then to the Philippines to serve as translator/linguist during the War Crimes Trials of former Japanese officers. I was discharged from the Army in 1947 and enrolled soon after at University of Southern California (Los Angeles) to study accounting. At this time I resumed playing my trumpet in Tets Bessho's Nisei Serenaders. We rehearsed weekly at the All People's Church and played many Nisei dances at the Palms Hotel in downtown L.A. I think we were paid only about $10 each for a four-hour dance job...not much, but it was worth it 'cuz the collective sound of a big band was such a joy!

Jive Bombers. Manzanar Detention Camp, Manzanar, Calif. 1943. Left to right, front row: Yoshiteru Murakami, Yoshindo Shibuya, Gordon Sato. Second row: Torao Kusaba, Bill Wakatsuki, Bruce Kaji. Back row: Joe Sakai, "Zush" Matoba. Photo courtesy of Torao Kusaba.

"I don't play the horn anymore…no instrument…no desire. [During my basic training in the Army] the loud rifle fire on the firing range blew out my ears. The inner nerves are shot in both ears…I have constant ringing that interferes with my hearing. That's probably one reason why I quit playing my trumpet. Still, I enjoy listening to all kinds of music."

In addition to playing bass for the Jive Bombers, **Joe Sakai,** with George Kitahara on banjo and George Stanicci[26] on guitar and vocals, organized the Hot Shots, a trio which delighted the Manzanar audiences with pop and country tunes. Of interest to jazz fans might be Sakai's association in prewar years with members of the Sims family who lived nearby in Hawthorne, California. The four Sims brothers were accomplished musicians: Ray on trombone,[27] George on guitar, Bobby on trumpet and **John ("Zoot") Sims** on tenor sax. Their father was a former circus drummer and mother Sims played the piano. Sakai, who lived in Redondo Beach, went with his bass and a bottle of red wine to their house for informal jam sessions, which often continued into the early morning hours.

Joe Sakai. Manzanar Detention Camp, Calif. 1943. Photo courtesy of Torao Kusaba.

Says Sakai, "Jackie [Sakai called John 'Jackie' then; 'Zoot' came later] started playing the tenor sax when he was a teenager. With a horn borrowed from Max Hartwell, he taught himself how to play. Later, I took Jackie down to a pawn shop on Main Street in Los Angeles and bought him an old Conn horn for ten bucks. He loved the tenor, worked hard, became pretty good at jammin'—he was about fourteen then. Once in a while, I'd take Jackie to a seedy club in downtown San Pedro for an all-night session of hard jazz. He couldn't read, but he could really blow!" Zoot Sims eventually developed into a world-renowned solo artist on the tenor saxophone—a vigorous, imaginative improviser who played with incredible swing!

THE STARDUSTERS
Merced "Assembly" Center, California

In June 1942, among the thousands of internees temporarily incarcerated in the Merced County Fair grounds was **Paul Higaki,** a seventeen-year-old San Francisco high-school lad. As a youngster, Paul blew the bugle in Boy Scout Troop 12 drum and bugle corps and had advanced to the trombone in junior high school. Obsessed with the sound of the horn and with swing music of big bands and jazz, he efficiently and quickly organized a dance band in the "assembly" center. He called it the **Stardusters**. The personnel he was able to muster consisted of five saxophone players, two trumpeters, Paul on the trombone, two female violin players, a female pianist, and a female drummer who played a huge bass drum and a field snare drum—sorry remnants of a drum and bugle corps. Sumi Kawamura, pleasingly plump with a big smile and nicknamed affectionately "Kate Smith" for her beautiful voice, was a joy to those who heard her sing with the Stardusters.

Jack Teagarden's jazz improvisations on trombone were a great inspiration for Paul. He also idolized trombone-playing Tommy Dorsey for his beautiful tone and phrasing on ballads. Paul borrowed Dorsey's theme song, "I'm Getting Sentimental Over You," for the Stardusters. He obtained stock arrangements of dance-band music, skillfully rehearsed the band and in time played for young dancers in Merced "Assembly" Center. Nob Kuwatani, a sax-playing member of the orchestra, remembers young Higaki as being a perfectionist who demanded faultless performances from all of his band members. "He was a task master!" says Kuwatani. Higaki scribbled in his scrapbook below the photograph of his Stardusters—"[This is] my first band. Organized at Merced "Assembly" Center in June, 1942. Leo Kikuchi (second sax man from the right) was killed in action with the 442nd Regimental Combat Team. The band stunk, but we got our kicks anyhow."

The August 7, 1942, *Mercedian,* the center newsletter, announced:

> "GIRL DATES BOY" HOP SET
> *Public opinion requested another dance, initiating the "Girl Dates Boy" theme, so here you are. The Mercedian Staff will again sponsor an affair where the girl takes the initiative. This dance is to be held Saturday, August 8, from 8-11 pm at the Administration Building. Professor Paul "Waldo" Higaki and his high-stepping "Stardusters" will furnish the music which will be sweet and soft. Tsugimé Akaki will act as Mistress of Ceremonies.*
> *Only couples will be admitted, so girls show that fine spirit of cooperation again and*

enjoy an evening all for yourself. To accommodate those undecided persons, a blind date bureau has been set up in F-2-2.

Girls, especially you hesitant ones, sign up and arrangements will be made. So far the boys are right in the spirit of it and the date list is growing longer on their side, but where are the girls? Girls, make this affair another success to assure continuance for future dances. Come one, come all…sign up and drag them.

Several months later the Merced "Assembly" Center was closed and its inhabitants were transferred to the Amache Detention Camp in Colorado, a permanent residence for approximately eight thousand internees.

The Stardusters, Merced "Assembly" Center, Merced, Calif. 1942. Left to right, front row: Miyo Mizutani, unknown, David Higaki, Paul Sakuma, Henry Wada, Leo Kikuchi, Nob Kuwatani, unknown, unknown. Back row: Sumi Kawamura, Paul Higaki, Satoshi Hirano, Ben Kuraya. Paul Higaki collection.

MUSIC MAKERS
Amache Detention Camp, Granada, Colorado

Joe Shiro, currently a resident of Mill Valley, California, grew up in Grimes, an isolated rural town near Marysville in northern California; his father grew rice. There was only one other Japanese family in this expansive farming community. As did many other Nisei, young Shiro played the harmonica, a Hohner Marine Band. He was self-taught and played simply for his own pleasure. Shiro did not have the opportunity to play in an organized drum and bugle corps, but he did become the bugler for his Boy Scout troop—played simple calls such as "Taps" and "Assembly." "No big deal," he says, but it was a move up the musical ladder and an introduction to a brass instrument.

In Pierce Joint Union High School, Shiro, a freshman, was assigned to play a baritone horn. The baritone was not the instrument of his choice, but soon he discovered the pleasures of ensemble music. Little did he know then that in a few years he would play in a dance band—a concept that was beyond his imagination at the time. Despite the limited extent of his initial experiences in music, Shiro's musical development replicated that of other Nisei described above, following a progression from harmonica to bugle to high-school music to camp dance band.

Shiro and his family were incarcerated in Amache Detention Camp, adjacent to Granada, Colorado—just a whistle-stop with a tiny railroad station, a minimal post office, a warehouse. Shiro remembers an enterprising Nisei Coloradoan opening a modest grocery store in Granada soon after Amache began housing West Coast detainees. Internees were given permission to shop at the Granada Fish Market, which stocked precious Japanese staples among other grocery items. The market was located about three-quarters of a mile from Amache—walking distance, but most shoppers managed to hitch rides from one of many trucks that commuted from camp to Granada.

Shiro was awarded a Pierce Joint Union High School graduation diploma despite his being forced into the detention center a few weeks short of his scheduled graduation day. He joined the **Music Makers** as a trumpeter and played in the camp band from 1943 to 1944. There were two others playing trumpet, two trombone players, and Nob Kuwatani, the leader, and his younger brothers, Tad and Yutaka, making up the saxophone section. The rhythm section consisted of a drummer, a guitarist, a bass viol player and a pianist. There was also a violinist in the band at one time. As did other camp dance bands, the Music Makers played stock arrangements—"As Time Goes By," "Moonlight Serenade," "I'll Be Seeing You," "Pennsylvania 6-5000."

The Music Makers played for block dances and were even invited to play at the local U.S. Army Post social hall for GIs stationed as sentries at the Amache Detention Camp. Shiro observed that many of the men assigned to guard duty appeared to be "castoffs"; not the standard able-bodied GIs eligible for regular Army duty. Nevertheless, they and their guests enjoyed the up-beat swing music of the Music Makers. In contrast, Nisei couples in camp preferred the slow-tempo, romantic ballads. Says Shiro, "Everybody liked our music. They would stand in front of the band and delight in just listening to us. It was my first experience playing for dancers...I enjoyed the happy, appreciative response of the crowd!"

Shiro was called to active U.S. Army duty in September 1944; he reported for basic training at Camp Hood, Texas. Replacements were critically needed for the 442nd Regimental Combat Team, which had suffered tremendous casualties during their assignment to rescue the lost Texas Battalion in France. Shiro did not resume playing his trumpet after leaving Amache; the Music Makers was an experience that he remembers fondly.

Nob Kuwatani, leader of the Music Makers, recalls: "Besides musicians in the band, I want to give credit to two guys who did a remarkable job making music stands with the [scarce] material available. Johnny Arishita cleverly designed and constructed stands which came apart easily and were easy to transport. Tak Kameoka made functional music-stand lights from Gerber's baby food cans, allowing the lights in the gym to be turned down low, creating a crowd-pleasing atmosphere.

"By the time we became organized, started rehearsals and played a few dances, the movement of people leaving the center for seasonal work, for school and general relocation grew heated. This sadly forced the band to call it quits."

Several years later Kuwatani returned home to Tiburon, California. In 1946 he organized the Music Makers, an eleven-piece, racially diverse group in San Francisco. It rehearsed at the San Francisco Buddhist Church and played for Nisei dances in San Francisco, Marysville, Gilroy and Sebastopol. Each member received about $10.00 for a four-hour dance job. The band was short-lived—it existed for about two years and then disbanded.

Kuwatani started playing the tenor sax in his junior year at Tamalpais Union High School, Mill Valley, California: "I was forced to choose a class in the music, art or drama departments. I had no interest in art or drama; that left music...I was not ecstatic. The music teacher needed a tenor sax for his band. I had no choice but to learn, reluctantly, to play the tenor. Yet it was a chance happening which opened exciting new horizons for me. Playing in swing bands became one of the great joys in my life!"

AMACHE CENTER SCHOOL MUSIC PROGRAM

Tad Hascall was the Director of Instrumental Music of the Granada Project Schools in 1943. He wrote about his experiences there as a teacher. The following account is an excerpted version of a comprehensive article which was published in the *School Musician,* a professional music education magazine, dated March 1943:

I TEACH MUSIC TO THESE JAPANESE
12 year old 7th grader, Jimmy Hirano (pseudonym) blinking away tears asked, "Please, Mr. Hascall, I like the clarinet. May I just keep it another week and try a little harder?"

He was not bitter because his family no longer had any source of income whereas they could buy him a horn. He was not angry, not disheartened. He just wanted to "try a little harder."

There are several explanations of this wholesome feeling. One is that they (the Japanese American internees) all seem to have the characteristic of doing a thing well or not at all. Then, too, this is the first time that most of these youngsters have been encouraged to participate in instrumental music since they have all come from schools on the west coast where their race has been decidedly in the minority. But the attitude is more permanent than that of a child with a newly found toy. Their music is gradually becoming a part of their regular life. Instead of "coking" [drinking colas], dancing, and the scores of other things many children engage in after school, these kids go home to their barracks and play their horns. This is one of their forms of recreation. They are obviously living and enjoying music.

Six months ago there was no Amache, Colorado. There was nothing here but cactus and western Colorado prairie. Today it is a town of approximately 7,600 inhabitants; Japanese and Japanese Americans who have been evacuated from the west coast. A quick glance at this town reminds one of any Army camp. Amache is made up of one-story barracks laid off in blocks with one larger building in the center which houses the laundries, mess halls and lavatories. A recreation hall is at the end of each block. It is in one of these blocks that the three Amache schools are located. The elementary, the junior high and the senior high schools, with a total enrollment of about 1,700 children, are squeezed into twelve barracks (six rooms in each), a mess hall building and three recreation halls. The instrumental music department serves about two hundred of these students and forty-five night school adults in one of the "large" rooms of the barracks. It measures 20 x 24 feet!

We sometimes wonder what our students' ideas are concerning this new environment; students who were born in this country and are citizens of the United States just as you and I. It is hard to get them to express their feelings in words but their attitude is not a bitter one that you might expect. In our department is George Kubota, a Japanese American teacher who majored in clarinet and received his degree at San Jose State College. Paul Higaki, a trombone major, and Tom Hattori, who has repaired instruments for fifteen years, also helps. All of these men receive the maximum wage for detainees, $19.00 a month!

In addition to making the teacher's desk, the bookcases, the instrument cabinets and the music stands, Hattori's job is to keep all of the instruments that are owned by the school in playing condition. This is quite a task when you consider that these 70-odd instruments are all second, third and fourth-hand student-type instruments and that each instrument is shared by two and, in some cases by as many as five people.

The largest part of our music library is made up of music that schools throughout the state have donated to us; music that has been cluttering up some director's library for years. Some had parts missing that needed to be copied; some was obsolete; some was nearly worn out. But we are repairing and copying until nearly all of it is again being used.

We gave our first concert on February 26. It was a Victory Concert. The "auditorium" (a large mess hall) was packed by about 500 detainees who had all purchased Defense Stamps in order to be admitted (About $1,800 in U.S. War Savings Bonds and Stamps were sold). Following the concert we sponsored a dance which netted us enough to buy a few new tunes and a used street drum for our marching band.

Although handicapped by limited facilities, the instrumental music department in the Amache schools is conducting a broad program. We three teachers, jointly direct fifty-five classes a week—a beginning and an advanced band, and a beginning and an advanced string orchestra in the senior high and four similar classes in the elementary and junior high schools. Two nights a week we meet a beginning and an advanced band made up of interested adults. In addition to his daytime duties, Mr. Higaki directs a ten-piece dance band. It was Higaki and his swingsters who furnished the music, gratis, for our benefit dance.

In spite of the difficulties and the problems to be solved, I am enjoying my work here more than I ever have before. Why? Certainly it isn't because the work is easier. I think it is because this is a situation where the fog of a speeding, 20th century world has been lifted and one can see clearly the wholesome results of music.

TULE LAKE DETENTION CAMP, CALIFORNIA

The Tule Lake Center enjoyed the music of two dance bands—the **Starlighters**, led by **Mickey Tanaka**, and the **Down Beats**, led by **Woodrow "Woody" Ichihashi**. Why two bands? Was there an excess of qualified musicians or were there differences in musical concept? Probably the latter. Nevertheless, two bands existed side by side competing for the patronage of Tule Lake dancers and swing band aficionados.

THE STARLIGHTERS

The *Tulean Dispatch*, the center newspaper, announced on April 14, 1943:

> *TULE LAKE STARDUSTING by Jobo Nakamura*
> *Heaven came down to earth and in the spraying mist of stardusts, a dance orchestra was born last Saturday at [Barrack] #2308. Before an eager and appreciative crowd of 240, Mickey's sensational new band made its début, thrilling the crowd with scores of new musical arrangements. Suma Tsuboi received the first prize of $2.50 scrip book and the distinction of naming the band: Star Lighters. Master of Ceremonies Harry Mayeda revealed that half of the band members still are high school students. Saxophone player, Tadashi Funakoshi, who is only 14, is the youngest member of the band. Others in the orchestra are: Bryan Mayeda, drummer; George Yamamoto, guitar; Haruko Sato, pianist; Americk Ishikawa, Hayao Motoyama, Richard Hamada, Tom Sasaki, saxophones; Norman Ishimoto, Roy Hatamiya, George Sumida, trumpets; Yutaka Hamamoto, Tets Ito, trombones and Art Kozono, vocalist.*

Band leader Mickey Tanaka said in a recent interview, "When I was eight or nine years old, I enjoyed listening to Richard Okumoto's Syncopaters [in Sacramento]. My brother, Harry, was the drummer in that band. Later, at fifteen, I took alto sax lessons from Richard and played in the high-school symphonic band. Swing music came later. I liked the sound of Jimmy Dorsey's alto sax. My favorite bands were Glenn Miller and Freddy Martin, who had a nice tone on his tenor. My band, initially named the Starlighters and later, the Stardusters, played good dance music. We had a great following in camp!"

THE DOWN BEATS

The Down Beats, a name derived from *Downbeat* magazine (read avidly by jazz and dance band fans in the '40s), was a swing-oriented dance band à la Count Basie or Tommy Dorsey. Its first leader, Woody Ichihashi, loved the syncopated sounds of Jimmie Lunceford—ideal for the frenzied gyrations of excitable jitterbugs. As far as Ichihashi was concerned, "Glenn Miller's arrangements were an abomination—saccharine, sentimental slush! Tommy Dorsey had a better band, but they didn't get the publicity." Ichihashi's music choices confirmed with a passion Duke Ellington's thesis: "It don't mean a thing if it ain't got that swing!"

The Down Beats. Tule Lake Detention Camp, Calif. 1943. Left to right, front row: Mabel Sugiyama Eto, Richard Muraoka, Al Nitta, George Nakao, Tosh Makishima. Back row: Sam Mayeda, Riki Matsufuji, Don Johnson, Norman Ishimoto, Frank Suzuki, Sam Himoto. Photo courtesy of Sam Mayeda

Ichihashi, a university student in architecture at the time of his incarceration in Tule Lake, had played the trumpet in junior high school and high school in Palo Alto, California. Louis Armstrong was a trumpet hero. One day, during a high-school stage band competition, he found time to catch Cab Calloway and his band on stage in San Francisco—admission eighty-nine cents. The great Chu Berry was on tenor saxophone; the music was exciting and seductive. It was the first live performance of a swing band Woody had experienced and he was hooked! He became a frequent visitor to Sweet's Ballroom in Oakland, where top-name bands of the country—Charlie Barnet, Basie, Tommy Dorsey, et al.—delighted jazz fans and happy dancers.

In Tule Lake Ichihashi posted camp notices announcing the formation of a dance band and eventually assembled a well-balanced ensemble of three trumpets, three saxes, a trombone and a full rhythm section. Says Ichihashi, "We obtained standard stock arrangements that other camp bands probably included in their book. Ours were somewhat heavy on upbeat swing numbers. As I think back to those days, I know we rehearsed and worked hard...all us enjoyed playing. In a conversation with George Nakao [alto sax player] two years ago, he mentioned how we improved as a group through hard work and determination. I'm certain that the fellows you talked to [regarding the history of the Down Beats] were too modest to mention their accomplishments in the [U.S. military] service. George Nakao, Al Nitta and his younger brother, Sam Mayeda and Frank Suzuki all did very well serving Uncle Sam."

Ichihashi assumed leadership of the Down Beats for nine months, from its inception in the summer of 1942 into 1943 when he left Tule Lake for work in Detroit. His departure also signaled the end of his active participation in dance-band work. He tried the tenor sax for a while in college, but "not much happened." Riki Matsufuji, who played the bass viol and did the vocals, replaced Ichihashi as band leader.

In retrospect, Ichihashi says, "I would have loved to make it as a professional jazz musician, but I didn't have the talent. That didn't stop me from enjoying Basie, Lunceford and Calloway. Of course, there were many good white bands—Shaw, Goodman, Barnet, Kenton, Herman and countless others. As for my preference for black over white bands, I had more exposure in person to black bands. While working in Detroit in 1943, I lived within earshot of the old Greystone Ballroom on Woodward Avenue and had a chance to see and hear Count Basie's band for over a month. The Paradise Theater, also on Woodward, a predominantly black movie theater, featured [on stage] many black bands and combos. I'm seventy-six years old now...retired. I still love to hear big-band arrangements with the Basie sound. I always enjoy a good rhythm section.

Remember Jo Jones [on drums], Walter Page [on bass], Freddie Green [on guitar] and Count on the piano? Still get my kicks listening to that stuff—they swing so-o much!"

The *Tulean Dispatch,* the center newspaper, announced on June 14, 1943:

SWING CONCERT STARTS CITY DANCE WEEK
With such hot "jives" as "Back Beat Boogie," "9:20 Special" and "Basie Boogie" being featured, the Down Beats will open the local Dance Week tonight at #1020 from 7:30 pm with a Swing Concert. The Down Beats band leader, Riki Matsufuji, claims he will have the audience "cuttin' the rug" before the evening is over. Members of the Down Beats are: Mabel Sugiyama, piano; Al Nitta, George Nakao, Tosh Makishima, Hayao Motoyama, saxophones; Frank Suzuki, Norman Ishimoto, trumpets; Sam Himoto, trombone; Richard Muraoka, guitar; Don Johnson, bull fiddle; Sam Mayeda, drums. Dance Week, sponsored by the Recreation Dance Department, will feature Japanese classical dancing, a variety show, June Jive Dance, and Sadie Hawkin's Hop during this week.

Sam "Blackie" Mayeda, Down Beats' drummer, reminisces: "We were employees of the camp recreation department, paid $14.00 a month. It was a good setup 'cuz we rehearsed on Tuesday, Wednesday and Thursday, then played dances and shows on Friday, Saturday and Sunday. The band received $5.00 for an evening's work; dance sponsors charged ten cents admission. We bought uniforms and music arrangements from the money we earned. Mabel Sugiyama was our pianist. She was really good; she played like Count Basie—called her 'The Countess.'"

Mabel Sugiyama Eto says, "When I was twelve years old, I started my classical piano training…I worked hard. Three years later in junior high school, popular music began to have great appeal. I picked up on the basic 1-4-5-1 (tonic, sub-dominant, dominant, tonic) chord progression—played all the popular Hit Parade tunes by ear. I did solo work, loved boogie-woogie and accompanied singers. My piano heroes were Count Basie and Mel Powell. Three years later in Tule Lake, I was playing piano just for fun in an empty recreation hall. Some fellows who happened to be walking by heard me playing, came in and liked what I was doing. They invited me to join their band, the Down Beats. I was thrilled. It was my first band experience!"

Riki Matsufuji, who replaced Ichihashi as the leader of the Down Beats, announced in deference to the preference of the majority dance crowd, "We're gonna play *dance* music!" According to drummer Mayeda, "He toned the band down—more Glenn Miller, less Woody

Herman." Matsufuji, after leaving Tule Lake, became a professional vocalist. He worked the Midwest dance-band circuit in the '40s as "Dick Wong."

Tule Lake High School music teacher Don Johnson organized several vocal ensembles which were featured with the Down Beats in highly entertaining concerts. These programs included a great variety of vocal and instrumental numbers of popular '30s and '40s music—both sweet and hot—most of which live on as great American standards:

Tule Lake High School Choir led by Don Johnson with the Down Beats. Tule Lake Detetion Camp, Calif. Nov. 11, 1944. Photo courtesy of Sam Mayeda.

MUSICAL REVUE

November 11-12, 1944

High School Auditorium

Co-sponsored by Community Activities Athletic Dept. & Youth Social Activities

PROGRAM

1. WOODCHOPPER'S BALL . . . . DOWN BEATS
2. STARDUST . . . . SEPTET
3. DANCING IN THE DARK . . . . HOWARD TAKAO
4. I'LL NEVER SMILE AGAIN . . . . JOE SAKAMURA & SEPTET
5. DON'T BE THAT WAY . . . . DOWN BEATS
6. AZURE . . . . DOWN BEATS
7. MOONGLOW . . . . QUARTET
8. SOLITUDE . . . . TOSHI KISHI
9. NIGHT AND DAY . . . . CHOIR

INTERMISSION

10. SWINGING ON A STAR . . . . TRIO
11. I'LL GET BY . . . . DOWNBEATS
12. GOLDEN WEDDING . . . . DOWN BEATS
13. I'LL SEE YOU IN MY DREAMS . . . . HOWARD TAKAO
14. HOME . . . . QUARTET
15. I'LL WALK ALONE . . . . JOE SAKAMURA
16. I DREAMT I DWELT IN HARLEM . . . . DOWN BEATS
17. 920 IN THE BOOKS . . . . DOWN BEATS
18. SMOKE GETS IN YOUR EYES . . . . SEPTET
19. MY MELANCHOLY BABY . . . . TOSHI KISHI
20. DEEP PURPLE . . . . CHOIR

THE TANFORAN TOOTERS
Tanforan "Assembly" Center, California

Among the internees of Tanforan "Assembly" Center in South San Francisco were many capable people who were highly motivated by their interest in music, both popular and classical. Although the Tanforan racetrack was just a temporary site, an effort was made as early as the first month of detention to organize musical activities. The following articles were culled from the *Tanforan Totalizer*, the center newspaper:

May 23, 1942 Recreational Items...Musicians, attention! All persons who would like to play in our city's newly formed band or in the 'sextet' are asked to contact Tom Tsuji, Barrack #19-2.

May 30, 1942. Classes in Music get under way...the Education Dept. has opened a music studio at the former Tanforan tavern near Mess Hall #7 for those interested in continuing their musical education, particularly in violin, piano, voice and theory. Over 100 pupils have already registered and are availing themselves of the opportunity to use the piano and the private rooms for practice and instruction, according to Frank Iwanaga, studio director.

June 6, 1942. Saturday, 7:30 to 10 pm program dancing at the Social Hall, couples only. Betwixt the numbers, Fochy Takasuka will pound out some torrid boogie-woogie. No boots.

June 20, 1942. Dance Band...To our scene is now being added a dance band of eleven members: Hoagy Ogawa, Yoneo Kawakita, alto sax; Tom Nakashige, tenor sax: Frank Ono, Tad Ishida, Kiyoshi Kawahata, trumpets; Sawai Ichisaka, trombone; Hisashi Tani, baritone; Itaya Kurita, piano; Mark Bando, drums; Katsuso Arima, guitar. Directed by Tom Tsuji, the band is featuring Ellington arrangements and tenor Nakashige is blowing the [Ben] Webster solos.

July 4, 1942. SWINGPOSIUM—Connoisseurs and students of American jazz will sit down to a Swingposium Friday night, July 10, from 7 to 10 pm at the Tanforan High School. The evening's program will touch upon several phases of jazz such as New Orleans jazz, the blues, boogie-woogie and modern day swing. There will be discussions and recordings and the public is invited. Arranging the program are Tom Tsuji, Midori Shimanouchi, H. Tsuchida, Jiro Suenaga, Kaz Kariya, Bill Hata, Mike Morizono, and Tyler Nakayama.

Music in all of its diverse facets lured a huge cadre of enthusiastic volunteers who offered information, instruction and organizational capabilities. **Tom Tsuji** established a dance band. He learned to play drums in junior high school and later studied the xylophone. Yoshio Kasai remembers waiting for what seemed like hours for Tom to finish his xylophone practice, which was strictly monitored by a determined mother. Tsuji developed into an outstanding artist on that instrument and performed in many recitals in the San Francisco Bay Area. He moved on to study timpani in New York City after his detention in Topaz. Eventually, he became the chief timpanist for the New Orleans Symphony Orchestra, retired and moved north to Worcester, Massachusetts, where he now resides.

In 1991 he wrote in a letter: "We were known as the Tanforan Tooters. I think we were the Topaz Tooters when we moved to Utah. Tom Nakashige, the assistant band leader, picked and ordered the band arrangements. He is a little younger than I and thus was closer to his fellow musicians. Our music library had a lot of old standards which were very easy to dance to. Our theme song was 'Rose Room' and I still remember the enthusiastic reception we received at the first big dance in Tanforan."

The *Tanforan Totalizer* announced:

August 15, 1942. It has been decided that the "Summer Formal" on August 22 will require bow ties and coats for the men, party dresses for the girls. Gardenias will be given to the first 300 couples. The Tanforan orchestra under the direction of Tom Tsuji will play for about half the evening, at the beginning and the end, and recordings will fill the rest of the program. For couples only.

"Couples only" created problems for some—

August 18, 1942. Letters to the Editor…How about some publicity on a campus-wide problem? We are a bunch of sad guys who have no dates each Saturday night. What would be the feasibility of a date bureau in each recreation hall? Let us have some ideas from the readers. There should be some way for girls and fellows to meet so they would not be frustrated in their mutual desire to attend the couples only Saturday night dances. How about it?

(Signed) Lonesome Wolves

The Jivesters. Topaz Detention Camp, Utah. 1943. Left to right: Sadie Towata Tomita, Kazu Maruoka, Takeshi Enomoto, Ike Nakamura, Ich Sasaki, I. Matsuhara, Yutaka Yoshida. Photo courtesy of Kazu Maruoka.

George Akimoto. "Lil Daniel." Rohwer Detention Camp, Ariz. 1943.

August 20, 1942. To the lonesome wolves…Don't be discouraged if 1 or 2 or 3 girls refuse you dates. But when you do get one, be sure to greet her parents when you call for her. Too many Nisei forget this little courtesy. Make a good impression the first time and you are sure to get another date.

August 30, 1942. After the Ball…We've heard of strict parental control, but the little incident we've learned of recently really takes the cake. The story runs that a boy and a girl went to a dance in the social hall. When the dance was over, just outside the hall door were standing their mothers to see them home safely.

THE TOPAZ TOOTERS
Topaz Detention Camp, Utah

Tom Tsuji continued in his '91 letter: "We started awkwardly in Tanforan—God, the band was raw and inexperienced when we first got together. They couldn't even tune themselves. However, by the time we were settled in Topaz, we were off and running. I remember the Tooters played for the Topaz High School Senior Prom. A couple asked for a waltz; we didn't have one in our book, so we played a fox trot, only slowly to see if the kids would go for it. You should have seen the puzzled expressions on their faces while dancing. We also played twice in nearby Delta for a U.S. War Bond rally and a Delta High School senior prom. We also took a trip to Salt Lake City for a Japanese community dance." Tad Ishida, a member of the band at the Delta High School dance, recalls today: "We did not play many up-tempo tunes, because Delta was a farm community and its students did not jitterbug—we had to play schmaltzy music."

The ebb and flow of detention center population made it impossible for dance-band personnel to remain constant for long. Even in the transition period from Tanforan to Topaz, there were changes. Young musicians replaced older ones who left centers for work or schooling.

THE JIVESTERS

Tom Tsuji's Tooters was replaced late in 1943 by the **Jivesters,** an entirely new band. Made up of high-schoolers, this seven-piece ensemble was led by tenor sax player **Takeshi Enomoto.** Other Jivesters were: Ike Nakamura, Kazu Maruoka and Yutaka Yoshida, trumpets; I. Matsuhara, alto sax; Sadie Towata Tajima, piano; and drummer Ichiro Sasaki, whose set consisted of heavy field drums and cymbals. Its snare drum and cymbal stands were handmade from scrap lumber by Sasaki. Sasaki's love of jazz endures. As recently as 1996, he was still playing rhythm guitar in the seventeen-piece J-Town Jazz Ensemble of San Francisco.

Kazu Maruoka played trumpet with the Jivesters and continued with Sasaki's Rhythm Kings. His initial band experience in Topaz was the beginning of an outstanding musical career which extended well into the '90s. **Sadie Towata Tajima** also has been active in music performance throughout her adult life. Her talent is still treasured today. Tajima plays popular music "by ear" and volunteers her services to the delight of old folks in senior residences and serves as pianist for several Christian churches in the San Francisco Bay Area.

On January 8 and 9, 1944, the staff of the Topaz High School year book, *1944 Ramblings*, sponsored "Musical Fun-tasia," a variety show featuring vocalists, dancers, comedy skits and the Jivesters jazz combo. Admission: ten cents for children under ten years and student body card holders; fifteen cents for other residents. The follow-up news coverage described the event:

> *It was perfect! The faculty and student participants gave the audience two jam-packed hours of worthwhile entertainment. The football varsity and the Joker Hada-Clem Nakai skits were slightly on the embarrassing side to the feminine spectators, but the majority of the audience was "rollin' in the aisles." Giving a big thrill to local gals was the breathless crooning of the Japanese Frankie [Sinatra], Stan Shusho. On the other hand, singers Elsie Itashiki, Florence Nagano, and Yo Ikeda gave the boys a rare treat. Red hot music was supplied by the Jivesters, a terrific five-man swing band. Mabel Sugiyama entranced the audience with her solid sendings a la boogie-woogie.*

Another news reporter, a self-styled music critic, composed a special column devoted to the performances of pianist **Mabel Sugiyama** and the Jivesters:

> *Although the microphone distorted the tone of the piano greatly, Mabel Sugiyama held the audience in ecstasy. Her first number, a medley sounding very much like "the Earl" was played in a style typical of Pete Johnson, combined with some influence from Jess Stacy and Teddy Wilson. Her second number, "Star Dust," was played well, but she should have played it first as her medley would have brought the audience to a feverish pitch, which is the ideal time to exit.*

Yo Ikeda Sumimoto. Berkeley, Calif. 1946. Photo courtesy of Kazu Maruoka.

The climax of the show was the presentation of the Jivesters. The five-piece outfit includes a reed, two trumpets, a guitar, and a drum. Their theme opened with the reed man playing the clary in Artie Shaw style. They jumped right into their first number, "Blues on Parade." It was the same arrangement as used by Woody Herman. The tenor man, Enomoto, took the first solo. He has a good tone, but should not have [followed] the orchestration so closely. This was followed by Kaz Maruoka's trumpet solo. Then the tempo was changed with "Moonlight Serenade." Again the tenor sounded off first, followed by a change to the "licorice stick" by the same man. This instrument seemed to bring out his defects in breathing and in cutting the notes too sharply.

The guitar pounded out a good solid beat. Next came "Let's Dance," the B.G. [Benny Goodman] orchestration. Enomoto took off on the clary with an attempted imitation. He should have tied his notes instead of cutting them so sharply. The tempo was unsteady. The tenor has a good tone, but there isn't much originality to his ideas. The trumpet man should try to take a hot solo without a vibrato.

The finale was a medley which included "Music Makers," "Little Brown Jug," and "One O'Clock Jump." The tenor took off again. His tone seemed much better than on the other numbers for he had a slightly rough [Ben] Websterish tone. The trumpet was also improved as he did not have a vibrato. In the climax there was a riff between the trumpet and tenor men. The drummer took a very disgusting solo, which didn't sound like anything worth talking about.

This outfit has very good potentialities in the tenor and trumpet men. If they get a good pianist and also a drummer with imagination, a good beat and technique, and fill in with a few more sidemen, the band should turn out well.

Kazu Maruoka kept this news article in his scrap book. Fifty years later, when asked about this review, he replied, "Enomoto was really mad and upset! He and I went to look for the writer. I forgot whether we located him or not, but Tak was angry! Using musical standards established by professional jazz bands, such as Woody Herman's big band, to judge an amateur group of young high-school kids just starting out was too much! In retrospect, I suppose, the guy who wrote this article, a small frog in a big pond, was croaking loudly for attention—attention to his misguided hipness."

The creative energy and the cooperative attitude of performers and producers of Fun-tasia deserve to be acknowledged. As many have experienced, producing programs requires painstaking attention to details anticipated and unanticipated—just plain hard work. Kudos to young Nisei in detention camps for their intelligence and commitment to live a creative life in collective harmony despite the gnawing irritant of being incarcerated unjustly as enemy aliens.

On February 4, 1944, the following appeared in the *Topaz Times*:

Dear Editor: The Jivesters have been challenged by another group of musicians to engage in a battle of bands. Little is known about the other band, except that it is composed of former members of Tom Tsuji's orchestra with some valuable additions from Tule Lake. If the Jivesters wish to accept the challenge for a friendly "musical battle," they can name the time and place. A notice through the Ram-Bler will suffice.

The Jivesters ignored the challenge flung at them by the mystery band. No musical battles were fought, but the news item heralded the formation of an all-new combo in Topaz—the **Savoy Four.**

THE SAVOY FOUR

The Savoy Four lineup: **Tom Nakashige,** tenor saxophone, and Jimmy Kikugawa, drums, both from Tsuji's early Topaz Tooters band; and Mabel Sugiyama, piano, and Frank Suzuki, trumpet, transfers from the Tule Lake Down Beats.

The Savoy Four was different from other Topaz groups in that their repertoire was jazz-oriented as opposed to the dance music of their predecessors. Mabel Sugiyama came with "Count Basie piano credentials" and Nakashige idolized Ben Webster. Some of their favorites were: "Basie Blues," "Tuxedo Junction," "Jive At Five," "Tea For Two" and "The Man I Love"—tunes that provided the context for improvisation, for jammin'.

Amy Morizono Eto remembers, as a young girl in Oakland, listening to Nakashige woodsheddin' in the back room of his father's grocery store: "Tommy would sit on sacks of rice, playing his tenor along with Coleman Hawkins's classic recording of 'Body And Soul.' He loved jazz; he was obsessed with the sound of the tenor!" Nakashige also affected the porkpie hat and dark glasses—de rigueur for those "hep to the jive." He was cool!

THE RHYTHM KINGS

More changes—Ich Sasaki, drummer for the Jivesters, formed his own band, the **Rhythm Kings**. The Topaz newspaper announced:

SPRING INFORMAL SLATED, APRIL 27
TO FEATURE SASAKI'S RHYTHM KINGS
The "Spring Informal" couples only dance, sponsored by the CAS, will be held Friday evening, April 27, 1945. The dance, the last to be held in the civic auditorium, will start at 8:30 pm and admission will be 50 cents a couple. The music will be supplied by Ich Sasaki and his Rhythm Kings. The six-piece band includes Mrs. Maas on the piano; Kaz Maruoka on the trumpet, tenor sax and clarinet; Al Noda on the trombone; Hid Sakashita on the bass; Tak Nakayama on the drums and Ich Sasaki on rhythm and Spanish solo electric guitar.

The Rhythm Kings. Topaz Detention Camp, Calif. 1945. Left to right, front row: Mrs. Maas, Ich Sasaki, Kazu Maruoka, Al Noda. Back row: Hid Sakashita, Tak Nakayama. Photo courtesy of Kazu Maruoka.

The significance of this event is implied in the phrase, "The dance, the last to be held in the civic auditorium…" The U.S. government was putting pressure on all internees to leave their camps, which were to be closed as soon as possible. For some time, just prior to the German and Japanese surrender, the U.S. War Relocation Authority had adopted a policy of permitting internees to leave centers at will for areas other than the Pacific Coast. There was no dispute as to the loyalty of Japanese Americans. U.S. military forces were successfully subduing the remnants of German and Japanese armies. The Japanese American 100th Infantry Battalion and the 442nd Regimental Combat Team encountered the enemy with exceptional valor while suffering extraordinarily high casualties. Nisei servicemen as interpreters and translators in the Military Intelligence Service facilitated victory in the Far East. Nisei women provided precious assistance in the war effort as WACS and as nurses. What more could Japanese Americans do to prove where their allegiance lay?

Wartime incarceration in camps was the cause of wrenching physical-psychological trauma for 120,000 persons of Japanese ancestry. The music of resourceful, enthusiastic Nisei musicians provided a reassuring cushion for many young internees against complete spiritual annihilation—a thin ray of hope in the darkness of a frightening, unpredictable future. Camp dance bands exemplified a fitting truism—"Music washes away from the soul the dust of everyday life."

---

21 About 1,242 internees were engaged in the camouflage net fabricating project as a contribution to the national war effort.

22 Joe Shimada was the drummer of the Japanese Sandmen, the L.A. dance band of the early '30s.

23 Boogie-woogie consists of a propulsive, percussive, repetitive, rolling left hand joined by the often delicate, contrapuntal, upper register notes of the right hand—a twelve-bar blues basically in the tonic and dominant mode.

24 The pachuco style was a phenomenon throughout the camps. Men's high fashion note from the *Gila News-Courier:* "Every chain and plug has been taken from each laundry tray in the washrooms. It is reported that these are being worn as watch chains. We are not proud to associate a people once noted for honesty with the moral level that is characteristic of zoot suits."

25 Powell and Cody were "civilian" towns outside of Heart Mountain.

26 Stanicci was a bona fide internee. His father was of Italian/Japanese origin and his mother of English/Japanese origin. Executive Order 9066 ordering all persons of Japanese ancestry into detention camps included regulations requiring detention of persons who were ethnically as little as one-sixteenth Japanese.

27 Ray Sims became a professional trombonist and played with Les Brown's band for many years.

CHAPTER THREE 189

"Paul Higaki Day." San Francisco, Calif. July 10, 1950. Left to right: Paul Higaki, Haruhisa Kawada, Hibari Misora, Lionel Hampton. Courtesy of Mrs. David Higaki.

CHAPTER 4

Going to Chicago Blues
FROM WAR TO PEACETIME

"Leaving Poston was release from prison. Chains were exchanged for wings...time to fly. My destination was Chicago—friends and, hopefully, jobs awaited me. Still, I could not dismiss the thought of Uncle Sam pointing his forefinger at me saying, 'I want you!'"

—GEORGE YOSHIDA,
POSTON DETENTION CAMP, APRIL 1943

My first breakfast on the *outside* was so beautiful, I will never forget it. It was April 1943. It took place in the American Friends Service Committee hostel in northside Chicago—temporary housing provided by the Quakers for Japanese Americans relocating out of detention camps. The bright spring sun warmed the breakfast nook just off the main dining room. Sitting at the table, alone, without being called to breakfast by nerve-racking clangs of an iron triangle, was joy in itself. I don't remember what I ate that morning. I do remember putting a slice of white bread into an electric toaster, patiently waiting for it to complete its chore, picking up the toast when it popped up, and carefully knifing onto it a dab of *real* butter…it was a memorable ritual, so long in coming. The first crunchy bite of the delectable morsel was a *heavenly* experience.

After a year in Poston Detention Camp, along with many other detainees, I had received official clearance to leave. I packed a few pieces of clothing and a toothbrush in a raggedy suitcase, said my goodbyes to family and friends. A group of us were loaded onto a truck and were taken to a lonely railroad station in Parker, Arizona. Following an interminable wait, we boarded a slow train to *freedom*. I was on my way to Chicago! Free, unwhite and twenty-one…eager to taste for the first time what it meant to be a man with mom and dad well out of my life! It was a *wonderful* feeling coupled with grave misgivings.

Just as the exclusion of Japanese Americans and alien Japanese from the West Coast was born out of political pressure, politics prolonged the return to their homes. Executive Order 9066, the exclusion act, was based on theories and recommendations from General DeWitt and the Western Defense Command along the order of: 1) The loyalty of the Japanese was solely determined by ethnicity—"Once a Jap, always a Jap." 2) The Japanese were so alien that it was impossible to distinguish the loyal from the disloyal. Therefore, exclude them, Issei and Nisei, from the West Coast for the duration of the war.

The War Department in Washington had a third theory—it was impossible to conduct individual loyalty reviews in 1942. However, prior to the Pearl Harbor debacle, special State Department investigator Curtis B. Munson's report to President Roosevelt and to the Secretary of State stated that Japanese Americans possessed an extraordinary degree of loyalty to the United States. Years of secret surveillance by the F.B.I. and Naval Intelligence corroborated the report.

Internees were permitted to relocate out of camps to destinations in the Midwest and the East as early as the spring of 1943. Yet the debate as to the total closure of the concentration camps continued until after the 1944 election of Franklin D. Roosevelt. Finally, on December 17, 1944, Public Proclamation Number 21 was issued. In essence, General DeWitt's original mass exclusion orders were rescinded.

The War Department announced plans to form an all-Japanese American combat unit in January 1943, and called for volunteers. On February 1, 1943, the 442nd Regimental Combat Team was activated and in May three thousand volunteers from Hawaii and fifteen hundred from the U.S. mainland were assembled for training at Camp Shelby, Mississippi. The draft was reinstated for all Japanese Americans in January 1944.

In April 1944, the 442nd Regimental Combat Team, having completed their training at Camp Shelby, embarked on a 28-day voyage on flimsy Liberty ships bound for an unknown destination. The 100th Infantry Battalion had already undergone its "baptism of fire," experiencing nine months of bitter combat in Italy. By the time the 442nd RCT was ordered to join the thirteen hundred enlistees of the 100th Battalion, the unit had suffered nine hundred casualties!

Concurrently, in April 1944, while sons and brothers were fighting overseas, thousands of Japanese Americans incarcerated in ten detention camps continued to lead their drab, disenchanted lives. On the other hand, many others, especially Nisei adults, had already begun an exodus from camps to the outside—to work, to attend schools, to resume a more normal lifestyle. And many young, healthy males exchanged their just-vacated detention camp barracks for U.S. Army barracks—a perfect case of "jumping from frying pan into fire."

CHICAGO, A RELOCATION MAGNET

Chicago was a mecca for relocating detainees. They poured by droves into the Windy City from distant detention centers. From practically population zero in 1942, the number of Japanese Americans in Chicago increased sharply in four years to a peak of twenty-three thousand in 1946. The vigorous wartime economy and the military draft of able-bodied men created a shortage of labor which provided many job opportunities. It was also the time of massive northern migration of African Americans from the deep South. The city was jumpin' with hordes of servicemen on leave, newly-arrived migrants, and local citizens working and playing in a frenzy. Jazz clubs, theaters and bars were crowded with fun-seekers. The Oriental Theater on Randolph Street and the Chicago Theater on State Street in the Chicago Loop featured on stage celebrated big bands, star vocalists and novelty vaudeville acts. On the screen banal movies, often in a role secondary to stage attractions, provided diversification to satisfy audiences looking for a "complete show."

A happy memory of Chicago and jazz takes me back to the Downbeat Room in downtown Chicago. The Downbeat Room consisted of two floors. On street level in the center of the room, musicians performed on a small stage. I often stood just outside the entrance, peering into the darkness of the room, to catch gratis a few minutes of exciting jazz flavored with the combined reek of stale cigarette smoke and alcohol. What I remember clearly is Stuff Smith, his trim mustache and a huge smile, swinging away *madly* on his amplified violin, with Jimmy Jones comping lightly on piano on top of John Levy's moving bass-line.

Downstairs would be my favorite combo, Henry "Red" Allen and his great little band: Don Stovall on alto sax, Jay C. Higginbotham on trombone, and Red on trumpet on the front line, with Alvin Burroughs on drums and a piano man and bassist whose names I can't recall. "Whamp, whamp," Red would shout, stamping his foot on the carpeting, setting the tempo as he introduced the thematic melody on his horn. Red's trumpet and vocals were provocative, but it was Stovall's alto that evoked within the deepest sense of pure joy. Ellington's Johnny Hodges was sweet honey; Don Stovall was FIRE! Hot, dynamic, infused always with the blues…Stovall's sounds made my skin *crawl* with pleasure!

The South Side of Chicago in 1944 was, as it is today, the "colored" part of town—the Black Belt. There I discovered the Regal Theater on 47th and South Parkway, an exciting site of soul-stirring jazz. Seeking to hear Billy Eckstine sing "I'm Falling For You" and "Jelly, Jelly" backed by the irrepressible Earl Hines and his orchestra, I ventured one day to catch the show at the Regal.

Eckstine's vocals met all expectations. His baritone voice, drenched in throbbing vibrato, sounded just like his Bluebird recording. "Jelly, Jelly" is a slow, moaning blues which starts with a delightful Hines chorus on the piano followed by a marvelously mournful chorus on the alto sax. Then "Mr. B" comes on with his story—"Hello, Ba-bee. I had to call you on the phone; 'cuz I'm feelin' so lonesome and daddy wants his baby home…"

The surprise of the Earl Hines show, a happening I shall *never* forget, was the introduction of Hines's most recent discovery—a dark young lady in a light blue floor-length dress who had been inconspicuously playing piano opposite Earl Hines. It has been fifty long years, but I can still see her standing on the stage—so cool, singing "You Are My First Love" with elegance, delicacy and style. I was totally mesmerized by the purity of her voice, its extraordinary range, its rich timbre. Her phrasing, untainted jazz—natural, not self-conscious, free. She sang with impeccable time. She did swing! She was Sarah Vaughan, the quintessential jazz artist.

Another never-to-be-forgotten episode took place in White City, a ballroom also on the south side of Chicago. It was 1944, just before my induction into the U.S. Army. I worked at Warshawski's, a used auto parts reconditioning shop. It was a place where I rebuilt broken-down generators and starters which were encased in blankets of grease and dirt...ugh! There were a few other Nisei working there, some whites, several blacks. I became friends with James, one of the young black men working there. We both dug jazz.

Duke Ellington was in town. Duke was playing a dance at White City, an expansive wooden building which formerly had been a part of a huge amusement center.

Friend James says, "Hey, George...come on down to White City this Saturday night...Duke's in town."

Somewhat fearful about going to a dance in a strange hall in the middle of the Black Belt, I gave a feeble excuse: "I'd sure like to, but it's so far away, man. I live on the North Side. Crazy 'bout Duke's music...sure would like to go, but, you know."

Sensing my insecurity and reluctance, James persisted, "Hey, man, I'll be there...promise. I'll wait for you by the ticket office, meet you at 9 o'clock. We'll go in together, OK? Come on, man...it'll be all right!"

Still somewhat reluctant, I replied, "Well, OK. I'll meet you there...meet you at 9 o'clock...in the front. Don't forget." Dressed up in my four-button double-breasted blue serge suit, white shirt, a maroon tie with small white polka dots and a white kerchief in my breast pocket, I went that Saturday night to White City—caught the "el" on the North Side and transferred to a rickety, red streetcar in the South Side.

I bought my admission ticket (couldn't have been more than $2.50) and handed it to the man at the door, walked through the main entry where I was frisked by a giant with a don't-mess-with-me look. I didn't quite understand the search—was he looking for a pistol? A half-pint of Jack Daniels? Then I went through a wide opening into the spacious dance hall which was dark except for a few decorative light fixtures on walls. The immense stage was lit brightly, ready to receive Duke's band. Music stands with individual lamps were precisely lined up. Sonny Greer's massive assemblage of drums and accessories was set up high in the rear of the stage, every piece in its proper place, very much like a music store display. A glistening black, twelve-foot Steinway grand piano with its top raised high was positioned stage-right of the bandstand. No one was onstage. No sound of musicians warming up their instruments was heard from backstage. The bandstand looked lonely, uninviting.

The dance crowd was 98 percent black. Men and women waited patiently, flirting with each other. There was joking and laughter. A few people stood drinking cocktails at the bar. Small clusters of women smoked and chattered among themselves. Everyone appeared relaxed and anticipated good music and good dancing. My imaginary fears dissipated as I wandered around the hall looking for James. James had not waited for me by the ticket office as he had promised. Perhaps he was already inside.

Presently, the colored stage lights brightened and spots were activated. A tall, handsome gentleman walked elegantly to the grand piano. His hair was slicked back and his eyebrows and mustache were trimmed to perfection. He looked like a duke; he *was* the Duke.

Ellington sat gently…adjusted his shirt cuffs…paused briefly…then proceeded in his usual flamboyant, self-assured manner to lay down a series of rich, full chords accompanied by delicate, descending arpeggios. After several measures, Alvin Raglin, Jr., the bass player, walked on…carrying his huge, beautiful bass viol and joined Duke with a series of fat bass notes in playing the yet unannounced number. Then drummer Sonny Greer worked his way up to his throne and sat surrounded by his massive assemblage of drums, cymbals, gongs and chimes to contribute his indispensable rhythm. And Fred Guy, with his guitar, walked softly to his seat next to the piano to begin striking solid chords—"*chunk, chunk, chunk, chunk.*" The rhythm section is cookin'! Presently, the sax section and the brasses filed in to sit patiently with indiscernible emotion. A few more measures; then, with no apparent signal, except for a few tinkling sounds of familiar chords by Ellington, the entire band roared out precisely in unison…"A Train!"

Couples wearing warm smiles swiftly converged onto the smooth wooden floor to dance. The collective weight and rhythm of the dancers on the hardwood floor in synchronous sympathy with the infectious swing of Ellington's band produced an illusion that the whole building with its happy human content was bobbing up and down as an integrated unit in rhythm with itself. It was a *wonderful* feeling…truly a groovy experience. All was well with the world!

More sweet remembrances of Duke at White City: a distressed Johnny Hodges being harassed by a young, somewhat inebriated, female acquaintance; Hodges irritably spitting at her, "Get away, get away from me!" as colleagues laugh. Taft Jordan, a bit tardy from drinking with friends at the bar, running breathlessly onto the bandstand, just in time to pick up his trumpet for a solo. Sonny Greer, cool and supercilious, flipping his drumsticks into the air and pushing the band with powerful backbeats. Al Sears playing a thunderous Texas tenor, sending chills up and down my spine. Ray Nance's singing and swinging on his violin, eliciting a fat smile. Harry Carney in serious demeanor blowing a robust baritone saxophone, giving the band its bold, distinctive voice. And Lawrence Brown with warm marshmallow sounds flowing softly, smoothly from his trombone. Time obliterates fine details, but the rapture aroused by Ellington's music and the warm kinship I felt that night with the musicians onstage and with the dancing crowd remain undisturbed.

I never did locate James at the dance. But I forgive you, James, wherever you are…'cuz if you hadn't insisted that I go, I would have missed one of the *most joyful* evenings of my whole life. There *is* heaven on earth, yes!

NISEI SOCIAL LIFE IN THE WINDY CITY

Transplanted youthful Nisei, recently arrived from distant detention camps, eagerly sought each others' company. Crowds of Nisei in their "Sunday best" congregated on Saturday nights to dance the night away at the Trianon and the Aragon, elegant ballrooms on the Southside and the Northside. Social clubs were organized and dances for the Nisei community flourished in the ambience of a newly discovered freedom that had been denied for such a long time—a radical departure from the restrictive life in detention centers. Life on the "outside" was exhilarating. No more barbed wire fences, no more gun-toting sentries, no more waiting in tedious lines to eat dreadful, unappetizing meals in dreary mess halls, and, especially, no more critical, controlling parents to deal with.

Having acquired some polish to their social amenities, Nisei seriously became involved in Saturday night dates which evolved into complicated dating-game rituals. Where to go? What to wear? Who's taking whom? Who refused whom? Picky ladies postponing their responses to requests for dates, hoping for a better prospect. Phone calls, phone calls, phone calls. And grim problems for perpetual "lonesome wolves"—"Sad Sacks" who, fearful about dating, suffered frantic anxieties.

The *Heart Mountain Sentinel* reported on December 18, 1943:

> *NEW YEAR'S DANCE SLATED IN CHICAGO*
> *Nisei who have relocated to Chicago will enjoy dancing to the strains of an all-colored orchestra at the semi-formal New Year's Eve party sponsored by Mr. and Mrs. T. Mukoyama on the 22nd floor, Skyland Athletic Club, 188 W. Randolph Street. The dance is open to the public and a special invitation is being extended to all servicemen. A floor show will be the feature attraction. Tickets available at 4133 W. Madison Street or can be reserved by calling Kedgie 0806.*

Another dance:

CHICAGO 'Y' TO HOLD FIRST NISEI DANCE
Following in the footsteps of the YWCA which has opened its doors to the Nisei for socials in the past, the YMCA hostel is sponsoring an informal social on January 19 [1944] from 8:30 pm.

Several Nisei residents of the hostel are assisting in the plans for the gala social which is open to all Chicago Nisei and their friends.

Nisei servicemen have been invited to participate in the evening's festivities. It will mark the first social at the YMCA hostel, which has long been a popular residence for many relocatees.

Many Nisei, on their own for the first time in their lives, were experiencing unaccustomed freedom from social restraints of life in camps. Public dances, then, provided the outlet to test the newly discovered sense of self and sexuality. Furthermore, dances provided opportunities for networking. It was a time to meet new friends. Time to learn where the good jobs were. Time to locate better housing.

Imagine postadolescent Nisei preparing for an evening of dancing and, perhaps, romancing. Showers are taken, freshly ironed shirts are buttoned and bright ties are knotted. "Hey, Tak... remind me not to forget the corsage!" In another apartment, a brighter lipstick—"Sachi, do you like this shade of red? It's new, you know."

Meanwhile, twelve musicians gather early on the stage of the Midland Hotel Grand Ballroom. They've rehearsed religiously and it's time for their début. Anxiety shakes their confidence—"Hope they like our music." Hidé Kawano, formerly of Los Angeles via Poston Detention Camp, sits impassively behind his Slingerland drums. It's 8:30. Band members raise their horns up to their lips as leader Tad Yamamoto counts

Nisei Music Makers dance flyer. Chicago, Ill. 1944. Courtesy of George Yoshida.

CHAPTER FOUR   199

off the tempo for the first dance: "One, two, three, four." The rhythmic sound of Nisei Music Makers interrupts the gentle murmur of voices rising from patiently waiting dancers. The tune is a familiar one—"I Remember You." Yuki Miyamoto on his tenor saxophone solos the first chorus with much feeling. The Nisei Music Makers' earlier anxieties evaporate; settling down, they begin to enjoy the gig and soon fall into a comfortable groove. The lead trumpeter played great licks on his horn, especially on up-tempo Count Basie blues charts. The jitterbugs loved it!

The Nisei Music Makers. Chicago, Ill. 1944. Left to right: unknown, Hideo Kawano, Louis Sato. Roy Uno photo.

Just for a few hours, everything is all right. Never mind that just a few weeks ago they had received authorization to leave their respective camps—to leave family and friends for the liberty of living on the outside. For many young men, they will soon be wearing government-issue khakis and oiling their M-1 rifles. Uncle Sam is pointing his finger at Joe Nisei, ordering: "I want you!"

Two weeks later on the 15th, the Nisei Music Makers, emboldened by their earlier success, sponsored their own dance, this time at the Skyline Athletic Club Grand Ballroom at 188 West Randolph Street, 8:00 pm 'til 12:00—one hour less than the first gig. "Five hours is too much!" was the band's consensus. They played the same book with the same guys in the band. Since "All Proceeds Go to the Band" as stated in the pre-dance publicity, ladies were asked to pay $1.25 for admission and men paid twenty-five cents more than the first dance, $1.75. The second Music Makers dance was probably as well-attended and enjoyable as the first. None of the surviving band members remember, though...it was such a long time ago.

Yet all was not well within the emerging Japanese American social scene in Chicago. For many attendees, several dances had not been pleasant evenings of social interaction. Louise Suski reported from Chicago to the *Heart Mountain Sentinel:*

LACK OF MANNERS NOTED AT CHICAGO NISEI DANCE
The question whether the Nisei in Chicago really want all-Nisei dances or not was probably answered at the first large scale Nisei dance held here on November 20 [1943]. Some were of the opinion that the Nisei in this city were lonesome and didn't have anything to do in the evenings but to twiddle their thumbs and crave for big dances where they could meet a lot of other Nisei. Then there were those who opposed the large dances on the grounds that large gatherings would tend to make the Nisei conspicuous and may lead toward the segregation of the Japanese.

There was no doubt that a number of Nisei met friends whom they had not seen for several months. Addresses and telephone numbers were exchanged and the Nisei found new places to visit on the evenings they had nothing else to do.

The majority of the Nisei were of the opinion that somewhere between the Pacific Coast and Chicago many Nisei lost the good manners which they were known to have. This was evident at the dance which was held in the West Room of the Ashland Auditorium.

Many Nisei were surprised at the number of zoot suiters with "Pachuke" haircuts at this dance. The hall, which was really too small for the crowd, was filled with stags who occupied a greater portion of the floor. Tagging was prevalent during the entire evening since about 75 girls and some 250 men attended the dance.

One youth declared that he felt uncomfortable as he danced around the floor. He could see the sneers on the faces of the stags. He said, "I kept thinking all the time that I was dancing that I would get beaten up because I refused to let them cut in on my partner. Those fellows got very ugly about this and it was an experience that I never want to go through again."

More that one girl was disappointed at the people present and the crowd in general. One girl said, "I didn't like the crowd at all because it seemed cheap. The people I saw were mostly the rowdy type. I didn't see any fellow there that looked like he had any ambition. The dance didn't look nice at all."

It seems that many people went to this dance out of curiosity because it was the first big dance sponsored for the Nisei [in Chicago]. So many were disgusted that it is more than likely they will not attend the next dance if and when it is held. No one seems to know who sponsored this dance. In any event, the next dance will not be a success unless the dance is better planned and better managed and held in a larger hall with a good orchestra.

Where there is a will, there is a way. The clever organizers of Nisei social life put their heads together to formulate strategies for correcting dance disorders. Nisei gatherings needed to be "mellowed out." Louise Suski reported to the *Heart Mountain Sentinel* on December 9, 1944, about a year after her first disclosure of the shortcomings of Nisei behavior at public dances:

> CHICAGOANS FIND WAY TO KEEP ROWDY ELEMENT FROM SOCIALS
> *Profiting from previous mistakes, the three dances held here in the past few weeks can be termed a success. Two dances were held at Hotel Stevens and the third at the Loop YWCA. The two dances at the Stevens each drew more than 300 persons. One was sponsored by the employees of the huge hotel located on Michigan Avenue.*
>
> *The many dances of the past have been held in good locations, but have been failures in more ways than one. A Nisei youth has been quoted as saying, "I'd never take my girl friend to that dance, but I'm planning to go stag." There must be something wrong if such a comment is prevalent, although this is no reflection on the sponsors. The large number of stags that clutter up the dance floor and the conduct of some youth have resulted in the scarcity of girls at these dances.*
>
> *"I took a few steps with one friend," said one girl, "and a stranger cut in. I didn't know him and didn't want to dance with him and when my partner tried to continue dancing, the other boy threatened him. I didn't want to create a scene so I consented to dance with the stranger. I'm never going to another dance like that again." Several other girls have said the same thing.*
>
> *The recently organized girls' "Y" club which sponsored the benefit dance held at the Loop YWCA on November 11 is to be commended for sponsoring a successful dance. The committee in charge considered many important points regarding the dance. They selected a group of patrons and patronesses and their presence at the dance gave dignity to the event. Every member of the WRA [War Relocation Authority] office in Chicago was present.*
>
> *"One way to keep out the rowdy element is to sell tickets in advance and not sell any at the door," said one committee member who favored the advance sale method. On the evening of the dance some 100 persons were turned away due to the fact that no tickets were available. Any person who sought to crash the gate had another thought coming. Among those who helped to collect tickets at the door were Bert Lincoln of the Westside YWCA and Mrs. Bill McKee, advisor of the sponsoring club.*

(One wonders what kept the crashers out. Did the white authority figures at the door psychologically intimidate boisterous Nisei rowdies? Or could it be that Bert Lincoln was a *big* dude! Whatever actually happened, the Chicago Nisei social world did eventually brighten up and sponsors of dances breathed a bit more easily.)

HIDEO KAWANO

In the days prior to Pearl Harbor, **Hidé** was a precocious preadolescent who succumbed early to the spell of jazz and jazz drumming. This led to many hours of practice, sitting in with musician friends, and, of course, listening to as many jazz recordings as he possibly could. Soon, he was in great demand to perform in local talent shows where he gained much experience playing for live audiences. In Poston Camp #1, at age seventeen, he organized the Music Makers and led a well-disciplined dance band. When Hidé relocated in 1943 to Chicago, his career as a professional drummer slowly blossomed.

Hideo Kawano, Nisei Music Makers. Chicago, Ill. 1944. Roy Uno photo.

Lee Collins, a prominent New Orleans trumpeter, wrote in his autobiography, *Oh, Didn't He Ramble:*

I then went to work at the Casa Blanca on North Clark Street [Chicago]. This was 1941-42; the war was on for real now, and people had plenty of money to spend. This band had Little Brother Montgomery on piano, a white clarinet player from Detroit (I can't recall his name now), and a very nice Japanese kid called Joe on drums. Joe went for Chinese, though, because everyone was down on the Japanese because of the war. The Casa Blanca was a small place, so our four-piece band was just right for it. We decided to stay there as long as we made plenty of money.

As it turned out, "Joe Young" was Hideo Kawano, who played with Collins around 1944 (not '41 or '42, as Collins states above). Kawano moved to New York City after the Casa Blanca gig to live and learn among the jazz greats in the big city. He washed dishes in order to pay room rent and made every effort to meet musicians who represented the cutting edge—Charlie Parker, Ben Webster, Dizzy Gillespie—to talk to them, to listen, to learn. Experientially, the New York scene was fulfilling; professionally (playing gigs with prominent jazzmen), the city was just a hazy dream. Kawano returned home to Los Angeles, where he played drums in Phil Carreon's orchestra at the Avodon Ballroom in downtown Los Angeles. Subsequently, in August 1948, he toured the West Coast with Jimmy Zito and his dance band. Unfortunately, because of illness, he has had to accept premature closure to his early, obsessive ambition to make it as a jazz drummer.

Lee Collins Quartet. Club Casa Blanca, Chicago, Ill. 1944. Left to right, front row: Lee Collins, Hideo Kawano. Photo courtesy of George Yoshida.

Meanwhile, as the following report attests, Nisei were distinguishing themselves on the European war front:

The 442nd Regimental Combat Team's most well-known exploit was the relief of the 'lost' First Battalion, 141st Infantry Regiment of the 36th Division, which had been cut off by the enemy in the Vosges Mountains [France]. In three days of savage fighting, with close combat use of the grenade and bayonet, the Nisei broke through the enemy cordon. In gratitude, the men of the 36th Division launched a drive and had all members of the 442nd declared 'honorary Texans'...this Nisei unit sustained 814 battle casualties; e.g., Company K was down to seventeen riflemen; Company I, eight; there were no officers in either company the day after contact with the 'lost' battalion was made; sergeants were running the companies.

U.S. Congressional Record
November 1944
"Go For Broke"

THE MILITARY INTELLIGENCE SERVICE LANGUAGE SCHOOL
Ft. Snelling, Minnesota

November 1, 1991, marks the 50th anniversary of the founding of the Military Intelligence Service Language School (MISLS) at the Presidio of San Francisco. This once questionable experiment in military intelligence became the forerunner of the MISLS which trained over 6,000 Nisei (Japanese language) linguists who served in the Pacific war and in peace.

The direct impact of the MIS linguists on the outcome of the Pacific was considerable. Timely and accurate tactical intelligence obtained by the MIS Nisei through prisoners-of-war interrogations and document translations gave the American and Allied forces impressive advantage over enemy troops.

During the occupation of Japan, the MIS Nisei became the essential link between General MacArthur's general headquarters and the people of Japan. They made possible the smooth implementation of the Occupation policies.

—Clifford Uyeda, President
National Japanese American Historical Society, 1991.

The language school was first established at the Presidio of San Francisco, later moved to Camp Savage, Minnesota, and finally, in 1944, was relocated to Ft. Snelling, Minnesota. Because of the urgency and needs of the war in the Pacific arena, an extremely intensive Japanese language program was developed. Most Nisei who volunteered or were recruited for this program were limited in Japanese language skills; therefore, commitment, concentration and grinding memorization of a complicated language were necessary components of their daily lives. Classes were scheduled all day from 8:00 am to 6:00 pm with a dinner break, followed by several more hours of instruction.

Despite the excessive demands of study requirements, Nisei students managed to find time to rejuvenate the spirit through music. The **Eager Beavers,** a twelve-piece ensemble, was organized. This name had its origin in a medium-tempo swing tune made popular by Stan Kenton, whose advanced harmonic and rhythmic concepts set his band apart from the crowd. A photograph of the Eager Beavers discloses a host of men who earlier played in detention-center dance bands mentioned above—Poston, Gila River, Tule Lake, Minidoka, Heart Mountain and Topaz. The Eager Beavers, then, was a distillation of many scattered concentration camp dance bands—

The Eager Beavers. Ft. Snelling, Minn. 1945. Left to right, front row: Roy Endo, Harold Noguchi, Larry Tamanaha, George Yoshida, James Araki, Tom Sasaki, Tosh Makishima. Back row: Yosh Migaki, Tak Shindo, George Hara, Hiro Goto, Frank Suzuki, Yone Fukui, Shig Yamaki. Photo courtesy of George Yoshida.

a cohesive collection of mature Nisei musicians.[27]

George Hara, the trombone player in the 1945 Ft. Snelling band, recalls today: "I remember lugging my horn to evening language classes so that we could rehearse later in a nearby basement. We played a couple of dances at the Field House where many young Nisei and white girls from the St. Paul/Minneapolis USO (United Service Organizations) came to dance with language school students. I enjoyed playing in the band for these dances, but what I really wanted to do was to be on the floor dancing with one of those fine ladies. Instead, I was stuck up there on the stage! I envied those guys out there, and I don't think I was the only one."

James Araki, the band leader, played lead alto and I, playing second tenor, sat next to him in the sax section. Following my graduation from the language school in the latter part of 1945, I had absolutely no contact with Araki. The next time I met with him was forty-five years later in Honolulu in 1990. Jim came to the restaurant where my wife, Helen, and I had just enjoyed a delightful French dinner. We chatted a bit and then moved on to a nearby jazz club.

Jim, in quiet demeanor, spoke of his retirement from teaching Japanese literature at the University of Hawaii; spoke also of gigs with his alto at the Hyatt on Waikiki Beach. He handed me a cassette tape on which were selections recorded in 1958 and 1959. "Some things I did in Japan; it's medieval stuff, but the work contributed toward my Ph.D.," he said. The label on the tape identified several musicians: George Kawaguchi, drums; "Sleepy" Matsumoto, tenor; Sadao Watanabe, alto; and Hachidai Nakamura, piano—highly respected jazz pioneers of Japan.

Araki blew a great alto, but he was not one to blow his own horn. In my research I uncovered his special gifts in music and in Japanese literature—both disciplines requiring a sen-

James Araki. Zenda Ballroom, Los Angeles, Calif. ca. 1950. Photo courtesy of Janet Araki.

sitive aesthetic sense and creative energy. I discovered that he could arrange a harmonically and rhythmically complex jazz score for a seventeen-piece big band, whip up in a few minutes a bright arrangement for a drum and bugle corps, or compose a meditative Buddhist *gatha* (a hymn of thanksgiving).

Araki was a self-taught musician who could play the trumpet, saxophone, clarinet, piano and guitar. His favorites were the alto sax and the piano. I recall seeing him practicing the piano, all alone, on the huge stage of the Ft. Snelling Field House back in 1945. (He was probably memorizing chord changes to an Ellington tune.) Nobi Nakamura, while stationed at Ft. Snelling, wandered into a recreation room one night where a jukebox was blasting out a swinging jazz tune. To Nakamura's great surprise, he discovered a young Nisei cat comping on the piano—accompanying, with great energy and skill, the jazz streaming from the jukebox. It was Jim Araki. Nakamura couldn't believe his ears—"Araki's jazz piano knocked me out!"

After his discharge from the Army, Araki enrolled in the University of California, Los Angeles, to pursue studies in music. However, he soon abandoned his music curriculum because it contained much familiar subject matter. The culture of Japan—specifically, Japanese literature—then became his sole intellectual pursuit. Nevertheless, about this time, Araki was delighted to achieve an earlier goal. In 1955 he joined Lionel Hampton's sax section with his alto in a Norman Granz recording session; Buddy Rich was the guest drummer on that gig.

Despite his great love of jazz, academic interests took priority. Completing his studies and research in both the States and in Japan, Araki earned a Ph.D. in Japanese literature, taught at the University of California at Los Angeles for a short while, then was appointed in 1964 Professor of Japanese Literature at the University of Hawaii. Araki remained on its faculty until his retirement in 1988, when he assumed the title of Professor Emeritus.

Among a number of honors he received, the most impressive, perhaps, is a Japanese government decoration, the Order of the Rising Sun, 4th Class. It was awarded to Araki on November 3, 1991, for his contributions as an author and translator of Japanese literature and included recognition of his contributions in promoting jazz in Japan in the postwar period.

On a subsequent trip to Hawaii, I called Jim's number several times and was disappointed in not hearing a response. I discovered later that he had returned to Los Angeles; he was ill. On December 22, 1991, James Araki died of cancer at age sixty-six. In a 1992 obituary, Katsuhiko Takeda, Araki's colleague of Waseda University, Japan, wrote: "Jim's most scholarly work was 'The Ballad-Drama of Medieval Japan,' published in 1964. This was a study of *Kowaka mai* (ancient historical ballad-drama accompanied by music and dance), which the *Sengoku* (the Warring Period) warriors such as Nobunaga, Hideyoshi, and Ieyasu liked so much. Nobunaga was fond of *Atsumori* (another ballad-drama) and Jim transformed this work into beautiful English. Before setting out for the battle at Okehazama, Nobunaga chanted these famous words, 'People live for fifty years, but when life is compared to the things of this world, it is like a dream.' I wonder what Jim in the beyond now thinks about his life?"

"Paul Higaki Day." San Francisco, Calif. July 10, 1950. Left to right, front row: Tomi Takakura, Paul Higaki, Rose Moritomo. Back row: Florence Ohmura, Janet Ishida. Paul Higaki collection.

PAUL HIGAKI

They called him "Murphy." He did things others could not conceive of doing. On a Boy Scout camping trip, the guys took the usual hamburgers and hot dogs—Murphy took a rabbit to cook! Prewar San Francisco Nisei went to Commerce, Lowell or Poly High; Murphy chose Balboa. His friend, Kiyoshi Kawahata, sacrificed his love of music to pursue a stable profession; Murphy chose to become a trombone player in a swing band!

Paul Higaki was born in San Francisco on July 28, 1924. The teen years were exciting times for Paul. Starting with the soprano bugle in Troop 12 Boy Scout drum and bugle corps, he changed to baritone bugle as the corps developed into a crack ninety-nine-member ensemble. About this time, at John Swett Junior High School, he took up the trombone and his love affair with this instrument persisted for the rest of his relatively short life.

Tad Ishida, a teenage chum, was a fellow bugler who played trumpet and also enjoyed listening to swing bands. One Saturday morning about 9:00, Tad and Paul, in great anticipation, hurried down to the Golden Gate Theater on Market Street in San Francisco. The theater marquee shouted in bold block letters: **"ON STAGE—TOMMY DORSEY, THE SENTIMENTAL GENTLEMAN OF SWING AND HIS ORCHESTRA!"** Clutching their tickets, which cost "four bits" (50 cents), they rushed in to get the best seats—first row, center. Being Saturday, five live performances of the band, interspersed with an "action-packed" cowboy movie, news and a cartoon, were scheduled.

At the exact scheduled time, theater lights slowly dimmed and a mellifluous baritone voice flowed from the speakers: "Ladies and Gentlemen. The Golden Gate Theater proudly presents for your pleasure, Tommy Dorsey, the Sentimental Gentleman of Swing, and his Orchestra!" As the last word of the announcement escaped the speakers, Dorsey began to play on his trombone his theme song, "I'm Getting Sentimental Over You"—"ta ta ta ta taah…"

Spotlights hit the stage curtains which commence slowly to part, revealing the full band. At stage right, five saxes in front, with the bass viol and guitar behind the saxes and a piano on the side; Buddy Rich on drums on a riser in the center; at stage left, three trombones in line, with four trumpets behind the 'bones. Tommy Dorsey, standing front center completing the trombone section, splits the stage.

The mobile stage advances slowly toward the eager audience. The band joins Dorsey to complete the abbreviated intro of their theme song, then quickly jumps into their first number—a bright up-tempo Sy Oliver arrangement. Brass instruments sparkle in the flood of brilliant, colored stage lights. The collective sound of the big Dorsey band initially assaults the ears; then, the body whole!

Two adolescent Nisei, oblivious to the hundreds surrounding them, sit in awe and pure joy. The exciting live sounds of the great band, the engulfing presence of it, is too much! Paul, with super-intensity, concentrates, all ears, on Dorsey's trombone. He deeply digs the purity of the open horn, the variations of sound created by mutes, the phrasing of melodic lines, the smooth control of his rapid jazz lines. Paul to himself, "Damn, it sounds so fine…*gotta* play like that!"

Frank Sinatra is introduced. His sweet, youthful voice, gently backed by the Pied Pipers, laments, "I'll Never Smile Again." Connie Haines, petite and pert, sings; then Jo Stafford delivers her songs, coolly, with just a touch of vibrato. They all perform encores. Paul, of course, focuses on Dorsey. Tad likes Ziggy Elman's hot jazz solos on trumpet, but he really prefers Harry James.

As the notes of Dorsey's final number drift into the upper reaches of the balcony and the applause of the happy audience closes the curtains, the current Pathe newsreel in harsh black and white contrast, accompanied by the sound of loud martial music, flashes onto the movie screen—Hitler's Nazi Germany is top news. A short cartoon, "Porky, the Pig" is next. A class-B Western follows.

Paul: "Let's stay and catch Tommy's next show."
Tad: "OK."
So they get their kicks a second time.
After the second show Tad announces: "That was great stuff…let's cut out, Paul."
Paul: "Man, I'd like to stay for another show. Tommy will probably play some different tunes!"
Tad: "No, not me…I don't wanna'. Those movies were boring and I don't wanna' sit through them again. I'm goin'."
Paul: "Well, OK…if you gotta go, you gotta go. I wanna' catch the band again."
Tad: "OK, suit yourself. I gotta split, see you later."
Paul: "Later, man."

After the third stage appearance, a member of Dorsey's staff approaches Paul, who is still sitting in the same center seat. The man hands him an innocuous brown bag. Dorsey had observed that the same slight, bespectacled Asian lad sat through show after show in the same spot in the front row. Touched and amused by the lad's loyalty and enthusiasm for his music, Dorsey had sent Paul a hamburger and a Coke! If Paul had his way, he probably would have asked Dorsey to autograph the sandwich and had it encased as a shrine to be worshipped forever. Hunger forced the alternative. Paul stayed until the last show was over. (One wonders if he slept that night.)

In 1942 Higaki was interned with his family in Merced "Assembly" Center, where he organized his first dance band, the Stardusters. Subsequently, in the Amache Detention Camp, he was a member of the teaching staff of the Amache School music department and also directed a ten-piece dance band. In May 1943, Higaki volunteered for service in the U.S. Army and trained with the 442nd Regimental Combat Team at Camp Shelby, Mississippi. He was given a medical discharge five months later. Presumably, Higaki returned to Granada where his parents still resided. There he received the following Western Union telegram dated November 24 (ca.1943), originating in Omaha, Nebraska:

CLASS OF SERVICE
This is a full-rate Telegram or Cablegram unless its deferred character is indicated by a suitable symbol above or preceding the address.

WESTERN UNION

1204

SYMBOLS
DL=Day Letter
NT=Overnight Telegram
LC=Deferred Cable
NLT=Cable Night Letter
Ship Radiogram

A. N. WILLIAMS
PRESIDENT

NEWCOMB CARLTON
CHAIRMAN OF THE BOARD

J. C. WILLEVER
FIRST VICE-PRESIDENT

The filing time shown in the date line on telegrams and day letters is STANDARD TIME at point of origin. Time of receipt is STANDARD TIME at point of destination

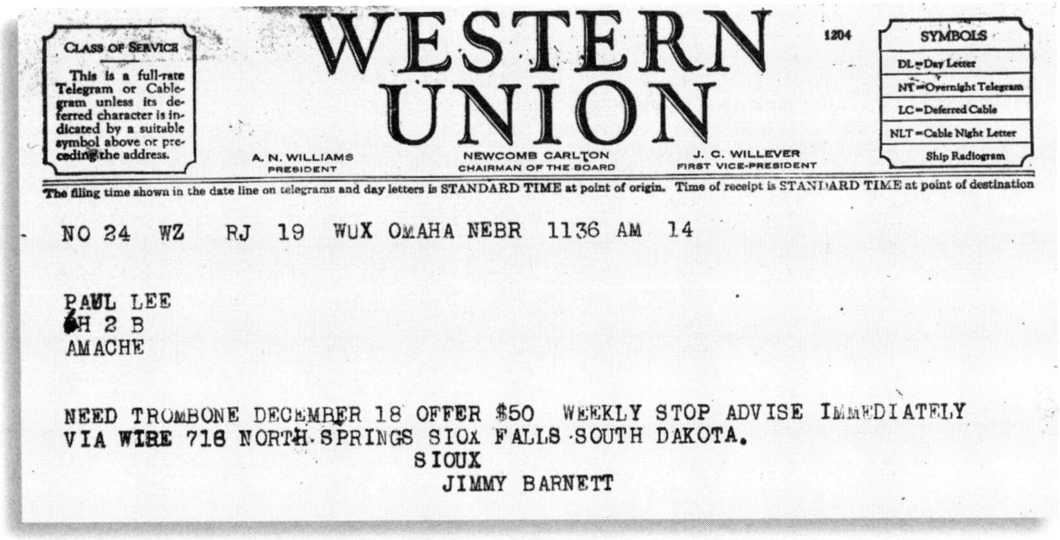

NO 24 WZ RJ 19 WUX OMAHA NEBR 1136 AM 14

PAUL LEE
8H 2 B
AMACHE

NEED TROMBONE DECEMBER 18 OFFER $50 WEEKLY STOP ADVISE IMMEDIATELY
VIA WIRE 718 NORTH SPRINGS SIOX FALLS SOUTH DAKOTA.
SIOUX
JIMMY BARNETT

Western Union Telegram. Job offer from Jimmy Barnett. November 24, 1943. Paul Higaki collection.

Barnett was the leader of a dance band operating in ballrooms and theaters in Midwest cities such as Riverside, Illinois; Milwaukee, Wisconsin; Indianapolis, Indiana; Calumet City, Indiana; Jackson, Tennessee. It is not clear whether Higaki accepted the job or not, but Higaki, nineteen years old, surely must have been extremely thrilled to receive an offer to work in a *real* dance band. To get paid for playing music he loved must have been too much. He was a *pro!*

Shortly after, on January 13, 1944, now professionally known as Paul "Murphy" Lee, Higaki became a member of the ten-piece Lee Williams Orchestra and played in leading cities of the Midwest until January 14, 1945. "It was a great band with some of the finest guys!" said Higaki, who was featured as soloist on trombone and as vocalist on novelty numbers.

The following letter was written by Joe Patrick Idé, who had relocated to Kansas City, Missouri. It was sent to "the boss," a columnist in the *PIONEER,* the Granada Center newspaper, and printed in the August 9, 1944, issue:

> *dear boss:*
> *this is a success story. two saturday nites ago we saw him at the popular plamor dance hall where 2,000 dancipated kansas citians joyously jigged to the 'stepping tone' music of lee williams and his orchestra.*

they called him murphy—murphy the irishman. he played a "fine" (his favorite expression) trombone and was spotlighted as a solo-man on 16 bars of "sugar blues." he vocalized…hep-cat style…he clowned, he mimicked, he was the life of the ork. the crowd went for him in a big way.

two years ago in the merced "assembly" center, he was the front man for the stardusters, a gang of amateur music-makers. perhaps you remember the star of the stardusters, the guy they now call murphy the irishman? he is frisco-reared, baby-faced PAUL HIGAKI.

incidentally, paul and 10 other fellow americans cover the middle west from denver to k.c. via sleeper bus playing one nite stands. occasionally they stop for a week or two weeks engagement. his life is a grind, he tells me, but he loves it! he was given a medical discharge from the u.s. army in december and joined lee williams in january.

take it from me, boss, he's doing all right—but he sure needs a haircut!

—*patrick*

Paul Higaki with members of Lee Williams Orchestra. Casino Royale. 1945. Paul Higaki collection.

Higaki's next job was with the Bob Cross band, which opened an engagement in the Empire Room of the Schroeder Hotel, Milwaukee, Wisconsin, on January 23, 1945. In the February 15, 1945, issue of the *Milwaukee Sentinel,* in the "Up and Down Amusement Row" column by Buck Herzog, was the following report: "There are four lads in the Bob Cross band at the Schroeder Hotel who have seen long service with Uncle Sam's warriors. One of them is a Chinese-Hawaiian, Paul Lee, who is affectionately referred to by his cohorts as "Murphy."[28]

The Billboard, a national periodical covering show-business news in general, reviewed the dance bands of Woody Herman, Gene Krupa, Bob Cross and Art Mooney in its "On The Stand" column of August 18, 1945. Of Bob Cross at the Melody Mill, Riverside, Illinois, the review noted: "Here's an 11-piece crew that's strictly a commercial crew. Arrangements are directed at the typical ballroom or hotel room dancer who likes a majority of sweet ditties with a smattering of sweet swing during his terping [dancing] hours. Cross wisely favors tunes which are coming up in popularity and those currently on the *Honor Roll of Hits.* Numbers such as 'One O'Clock Jump' and 'Take The A Train' are done with muted brass so that tonal quality rather than sheer blasting puts the number across..."[29]

Higaki's next move was a bit unusual. He joined up with the Allen Reed All-Girl Band which traveled the South. Higaki said at that time, when asked about the unique orchestra: "There was nothing wrong with playing with an all-girl band, except that women are too temperamental."[30] After his contract with Allen Reed was concluded, Higaki went home to San Francisco, where he organized his own band under the name of Paul Lee (ca. 1947). One of his earliest bands was composed of three white musicians and three black musicians and himself. Paul Lee and his Orchestra played dances for local Japanese American organizations—a Halloween Masque Ball for the San Francisco JACL, a Pre-Christmas Benefit Dance for the San Francisco Drakes, a New Year's Eve Dance for the JACL. These gigs were interspersed by casual jobs with orchestras of Henry King, Freddy Martin, Jimmie Lunceford and Lucky Millinder. These dance bands, white and black, exemplified the total spectrum of dance music—from sweet to hot.

In an early interview, when asked about his working with Jimmie Lunceford,[31] Higaki explained, "Oh, that was plain luck. Jimmie happened to be playing at the Trianon Ballroom here in town (San Francisco), and I thought I'd call him up for kicks. I didn't know him from Adam. I asked, 'You happen to need a trombone man?'" It happened that Lunceford did, so Paul went down for an audition and Lunceford liked him. The Lunceford band's next engagement after the Trianon was in New York City; since the Higakis were expecting their first child, Higaki declined to go and remained in San Francisco.

Kiyoshi Kawahata wrote: "While I was in high school, my father clearly opposed my electing music as a profession. A friend who actually did choose to become a working musician was Paul Higaki. Paul always had inborn artistic qualities and was a nonconformist. He was a gifted trombonist and my first encounter with him as a professional was when I heard his band play a dance at the San Francisco Buddhist Church, ca. 1947. He called himself, 'Paul Lee,' and had an interesting band featuring a trombone ensemble, no trumpets…somewhat similar to Kai Winding's band.

"While in Denver in 1949, he invited me to hear Hamp's band—Paul was a member. Paul's specialty with Hamp's band was to take the 'screecher' solos. We all know Maynard Ferguson, who played screaming trumpet solos with Stan Kenton, but there were not many trombone screechers."[32]

Higaki's crowning glory in terms of longevity with a single band and in receiving national recognition and prominence was his

Newspaper ad. Lionel Hampton Orchestra. Seattle, Wash. 1950. Paul Higaki collection.

'49-'50 two-year stint with Lionel Hampton. Hamp was the vehicle to Paul's success and tremendous self-satisfaction. His bountiful scrapbook collection of news articles, photos and advertisements of Hamp's appearances in theaters and ballrooms attests to his accomplishments and implies a sense of pride in his role as a member of the highly acclaimed swingin' jazz band.

A bit of trivia: How many ways can journalists spell "Higaki"? Answer: 15, at least! Count them—Higik, Hihik, Hagaki, Higiki, Higika, Hiyika, Higki, Hiyaki, Hijika, Hidin, Rigika, Hiagaki, Ligiki, Rigika and Higaki—all culled from news articles and dance-band advertisements in Higaki's scrapbook.

CROSSROADS, a Los Angeles Japanese American periodical, reported in its August 5, 1949, edition:

"This Hampton band is the movingest thing in the world," says Paul Lee (Higaki), newest member of the Lionel Hampton orchestra which played this week at the Million Dollar Theater.

The Million Dollar program moves to scorching heat in the last number, "Flying Home," and the house nearly comes down. While a frenzied sax is blowing off his head in front of the stage mike, Lionel Hampton, Paul Lee and the boys troop off the stage into the audience.

When the band opened last week, it used to go as far as the lobby during the "Flying Home" number. The police put a stop to that. The stomping in the balcony produced a major quake and threatened to bring the house down, but literally.

Paul plays the "bone." His job is to keep hitting the high notes, for which he's called the "Whistler." Lionel Hampton ("Hamp" to the boys) says that Paul plays the highest notes that he's ever heard played on the trombone.

Paul Lee joined the Hamp band about a month ago in San Francisco. "My 'bone' player was sick," recalls Lionel Hampton. "A friend in the Musicians Union who knew Paul's work in Jimmy Lunceford and Lucky Millinder's bands told me about him. He applied and I told him to come to rehearsal. I handed Paul our First Trombone book. That's hard because our 'whistler' has to play six tones higher than in other orchestras. He read the stuff fine. I consider Paul now one of the finest trombone players in the country today."

Gladys, Hamp's wife, is the composer of the tune that Paul is featured on at the Million Dollar. It's called "Gladys' Idea" and the super-high notes the number calls for has Paul kicking and squirming in front to the mike (he's a showman, too) to reach them. Paul stops the show with this number.

In a period of declining size of bands and fewer and fewer playing engagements, the Lionel Hampton band is still a healthy 19-man unit with not an idle night in sight. After Los Angeles, the band plays in

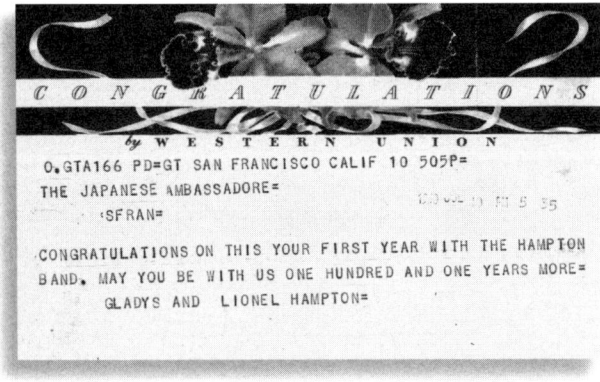

Western Union Telegram. Dated July 10, 1950. Paul Higaki collection.

Lionel Hampton and Paul Higaki. San Francisco. 1950. Paul Higaki collection.

San Francisco at the Barbary Coast, then back to Los Angeles to shoot a musical short at Universal Studios. Later in the year, Chicagoans can see the band at the Blue Note in the Loop.

July 10, 1950, was the celebration day to honor San Francisco's own Paul Higaki. He was feted as the "Japanese Ambassador of Jazz" on the stage of Golden Gate Theater. The occasion marked the first anniversary of the local trombonist's association with the orchestra, which he joined in San Francisco in 1949. Incidentally, the Golden Gate Theater schedule of band performances consisted of five seventy-five-minute shows daily—a grinding timetable which included television appearances and radio interviews with little time for rest and sustenance. (One wonders how musicians' chops held out with so much playing day after day.)

During the third show, Higaki was presented with a plaque from the Townsend Harris Post 438 of the American Legion—"For Outstanding Nisei Achievement in American Jazz." Telegrams of congratulations to Higaki from Walter Winchell, Lena Horne, Jackie Robinson, Ed Sullivan and Mr. and Mrs. Lionel Hampton were read. The celebration continued backstage with refreshments and drinks with Dr. and Mrs. Masuichi Higaki, parents of the musician, as hosts and assisted by Mrs. David Higaki.

Higaki enjoyed his association with Hamp for approximately another year. Their itinerary had included the South, which was a traumatic learning experience for Higaki; he and a white musician were the only two non-blacks in Hamp's band. In an interview backstage of the Golden Gate Theater following the public acknowledgment of Higaki on July 10, 1950, Marion Okagaki Tajiri, reporting for the *Pacific Citizen,* discussed with Higaki his concerns and experiences regarding dance bands and race relations in the South. Tajiri wrote:

The outstanding thing about Hampton's band, according to Higaki, is that it's precedent-breaking. Or, precedent-making. Higaki's first tour of the South had been with the Allen Reed outfit. "Things were real rough for Negroes then, but they're changing now," said Higaki.

Some of the changes—though they may be small—have been made by Hampton and his men. His was the first mixed band to play Memphis, Tennessee, even though Hampton did it in the face of a warning from Boss Crump that no mixed bands would play in his city. "We went in anyway," said Higaki. And down south, where minor customs relating to whites and Negroes are jealously maintained, Hampton has broken a few of them and gotten away with it fine. To the outsider some of the customs are pointless. In some southern cities where the band has played, whites and Negroes are allowed to attend at the same time. But the dance floor is partitioned with a rope or a line of chairs. (Yet, Higaki observed that social changes were taking place.) "In El Paso, Texas, we played the Coliseum and all the barriers were removed... there's a certain amount of intermingling now that you never saw before." Traveling with a Negro outfit, Higaki has seen his fellow-players suffer a lot of indignity in hotels, restaurants, and other places of public accommodation. "But, it's getting better all the time," he says.

Karie Shindo Aihara with Harry James Orchestra. Casino Gardens, Los Angeles, Calif. February 13, 1949. Toyo Miyatake photo, courtesy of Henry Aihara.

In the fall of 1950, the Los Angeles *Rafu Shimpo* reported that Higaki would appear with Hampton's band on October 30 at the famed Hollywood Palladium for the "Harvest Ball" being sponsored by the Beverly-Fairfax Jewish Community Center. According to the same article, also appearing was vocalist Karie Shindo, who had sung with Hamp on numerous occasions and had recently recorded "These Foolish Things" for Decca with Hamp.

Higaki's two-year association with Lionel Hampton ended around July 1951. The band was playing the Latin Casino in Cleveland and had been begrudgingly working overtime every night. In Gene Lees's book, *Waiting for Dizzy*, Al Grey explains:

This night we had been on overtime an hour and twenty minutes. And we hadn't even gone into "Flying Home" yet! And "Flying Home" meant another half an hour. Dinah Washington walked in and he [Hamp] was playing for her... I had a lady I was supposed to see back home, and now the last bus was about to leave. I got off the bandstand and the whole trombone section got off with me—Benny Powell, Al Hayes, Jimmy Cleveland, and a Japanese guy we had, Paul Hagaki [sic], from San Francisco, who could hit high notes on the trombone that I have not heard anybody else do to this day. Now Hamp don't even see this, he's doing a trio thing, and then he goes into "Flying Home" and he needs the band... and there's no trombone... and so [Gladys, Hamp's wife] fired me. Fired the whole trombone section!

Lionel Hampton Band. MCA Record #1315 album cover. 1980. Front row: Lionel Hampton, second from left. Paul Higaki, second from right. Courtesy of Tak Shirasawa.

Subsequently, an accord was reached between Hampton and the trombone section—three of them were rehired, Higaki and Al Grey were not. Higaki returned to San Francisco, his home base, to work local gigs.

Kawahata states: "I think he overdid himself; the next time I saw him was in Reno, Nevada, in the '70s. Paul told me he blew a hole in his stomach from playing [too much] and that he gigged only occasionally in local pit bands [for shows]. When not playing music, he worked the keno games at Club Nevada."

Sometime later, Kawahata met Higaki again. "The last time I saw Paul, he was somewhat sad because he played a wrong selection for his audition with the San Francisco Symphony Orchestra. He played a largo piece where the conductor was listening for something else. Who knows…if he had picked the right piece, today we would be listening to him with the S.F. Symphony. Paul was one who made it and enjoyed every bit of his musical career, just like all of us who enjoyed playing even though it never brought us fame or fortune."

Higaki met an untimely death by gunshot on December 20, 1973, in Reno, Nevada. His life spanned a tragically short forty-nine years, but he followed his heart and soul in search of goals most of us dared not seek. Paul Fumio Higaki took the other path—Robert Frost's "one less traveled"—and that made all the difference.

SUSUMU "TOTE" TAKAO

I would be remiss not to elaborate about **Susumu Takao,** who sang "My Foolish Heart," accompanied by Lionel Hampton on vibes and his orchestra at the special program honoring Paul Higaki in San Francisco. Apparently, Takao's association with Hamp preceded that of Higaki's. The November 16, 1946, "Vagaries" column in the *Pacific Citizen* quotes Dick Honma of the Los Angeles *Rafu Shimpo*: "Leland Young, the vocalist with Lionel Hampton's orchestra, is a Nisei, Leland Takao of San Francisco. Takao, a former University of California student, visited the famous Negro band leader backstage with a friend some time ago. He auditioned for Hampton and was given a contract on the spot although he had no professional experience."

A columnist in the *San Francisco Chronicle,* August 1949, wrote:

> *Music Dept: Lionel Hampton, the Negro band leader who'll put on a show at the Civic Auditorium Sunday night now has a completely "mixed" band. Along with Negro and white musicians, he will feature two S.F. Japanese Americans—a trombonist named Paul Higaki and a Nisei crooner named Leland Takawa [Takao]. Leland is the guy who makes the item. He is billed as "Tokyo Mose."*

According to Harold Murai of El Cerrito, California: "Tote was handsome and friendly. We were members of the Blazing Arrows, the Japanese YMCA club in San Francisco Japantown. I remember…when a bunch of us would walk down the street, Tote would always be singing or humming a popular song. He just loved to sing!"

Lily Oyama Sasaki recalls: "Susumu was a member of a high-school boys' choral group which came to Sacramento to entertain us. They performed at a beautiful Mexican church on Sixth Street which was the site for many local Japanese community events. Two of their selec-

Susumu Takao and Lionel Hampton, San Francisco. ca. 1946. Ray Whitten photo. Courtesy of Tak Shirasawa.

tions were 'Sylvia' and 'On The Road To Mandalay.' I clearly remember Susumu because he opened his mouth very wide when he sang. That struck us girls (we were very young and silly) as being so funny we doubled over with hardly suppressed laughter! He was naive, so cute...like a picture of a lovable, lightly-drooling baby with a big smile."

Takao's early vocal solos were performed at various San Francisco Japantown functions. His name appears on the program for the October 27, 1933, Benefit Entertainment of the Girls' Friendly Society of the Japanese Mission. He was accompanied this evening by Mary Tanaka on the piano. In August 1935, Leland Takao was the guest vocalist for the Japanese Cultural Broadcasting Society over Station KRKD in Los Angeles. Accompanied by Miss Shizuko Shirane, he sang "Auf Wiedersehen" and "Good Night Sweetheart." Leland Takao also performed on Los Angeles Radio Station KHJ broadcasts and was reported to have received many compliments for his singing.

In 1943 Takao was interned in Poston Camp #3, Arizona, where he sang with the Rhythmaires, the Camp #3 dance band. Returning to San Francisco after detention, he worked in a variety of jobs including that of selling custom-made silk pajamas on Grant Avenue in Chinatown. It was not long after his return that he met Lionel Hampton in 1946 and worked occasional gigs as Hamp's vocalist. Presently there is no evidence of his having recorded with the Lionel Hampton band.

YOSHIO TOMITA

Yoshio Tomita of Seattle, Washington, believes that his love for music was transferred to him by osmosis from his trumpet-playing brother, Kiyoshi, fourteen years his senior and a member of the '30s **Nisei Melodians.** Yoshio had gained facility on clarinet and tenor saxophone; he was introduced to swing band charts at Broadway High School in Seattle in the early '40s. Tomita subsequently became a charter member of the Koichi Hayashi dance band, the core group of the Mikados of Swing, which enjoyed much acclaim on their barnstorming tour of Oregon and California in the summer of 1941.

December 7, 1941, remains a bitter, lingering memory for Tomita: "I was enjoying the bright trumpet sounds of Louis Armstrong and his band onstage at the Palomar Theater in downtown Seattle. Suddenly, an announcement over the public address system interrupted the show: 'All military personnel will immediately report back to your bases!' At that moment, sitting in the theater, having a great time listening to Satchmo, I had no inkling as to the enormity of the situation. The theater audience was not told of the reason for the servicemen's emergency recall. I thought it was part of the stage show; I thought it was just a joke of some sort." Still uninformed, Tomita, unperturbed, enjoyed the balance of Armstrong's show and the movie. It was only after returning home in the afternoon that Tomita learned of the attack on the Pearl Harbor Naval Base. The thrill of seeing Armstrong and hearing his wonderful jazz quickly dissipated.

Soon after, with the eviction of Japanese Americans, Tomita played in the Harmonaires in Puyallup "Assembly" Center, Washington, and continued with the same band at Minidoka Detention Camp, Idaho.

Relocation from Minidoka found him in Denver, where he was enrolled in a technical

The Melodaires. Seattle, Wash. April 13, 1957. Left to right, front row: Richard Hirano, Yoshio Tomita, David Hirano. Back row: Masao Tomita, Billy Ishida. Photo courtesy of Yoshio Tomita.

school to become a machinist. It was not long before he discovered that Nisei were not being hired by the Curtis Wright Company, which manufactured aircraft engines for the U.S. Air Force. He dropped out posthaste, and in September of 1943, Tomita again relocated—this time to Omaha, where he worked in a hotel bakery and mastered the art of baking pies, cakes, rolls and bread. Says Tomita: "It was a lousy, hot job! The only consolation of life as a baker in Omaha was the opportunity to hear many topflight name bands that came to the city to play at the local theater. I went eagerly to see them all—Duke Ellington, Tony Pastor, Artie Shaw and even Guy Lombardo...at least it was live music."

Drafted into the Army in September 1944, he was stationed briefly at Ft. Meade, Maryland. Tomita lucked out. New York City was just a short haul away! All of the prominent big bands and jazz combos played the Big Apple. Tomita's biggest thrill then was catching Lester Young, the great tenor sax man, and his backup bass player and drummer. It was a small club—"*He* was just a few feet in front of me. Wow, what a *treat!*"

After completing a grueling Japanese language course at the Military Intelligence Service Language School in Ft. Snelling, Tomita was stationed at General Headquarters in Tokyo, where he toiled with many other Nisei in the translation section. He had many opportunities to play in a swing band made up of U.S. Army and Air Force personnel; Lt. James Araki was the leader. Tomita remembers being approached many times by local Japanese tenor sax players who wanted to buy his Otto Link saxophone mouthpiece. Link mouthpieces, a special design made of metal, were anxiously sought by young Japanese jazz aspirants who had a notion that Coleman Hawkins and Lester Young used them.

Following his discharge from the Army in November 1946, Tomita returned to Seattle, where he studied music for two years at the University of Washington. He had hopes of becoming a professional musician. "I realized that, despite my many years of experience playing dance band music, I was relatively an amateur when it came to music theory and legitimate playing technique. Because of the pressing responsibility of providing for a wife and children, I dropped out of school and obtained employment with the local utility company—worked thirty years and retired sometime ago."

Approaching his seventieth birthday, Tomita says brightly, "I still enjoy playing my flute and clarinet—not jazz or popular tunes, but classical music. I volunteer at the Keiro Nursing Home and also at my church. Last Sunday I played my flute for the morning worship service of the Japanese Baptist Church; I played "Ave Maria" accompanied by a guitar-playing friend of mine. Music has sustained me all of my life; it's given me great pleasure and satisfaction. Guess I'm just a lucky so-and-so."

HARRY KITANO

I've heard **Professor Kitano** lecture about his research findings on out-marriages of Japanese Americans and about his theories on the gradual dissolution of Japanese American culture/identity into mainstream America. A chance meeting provided an opportunity for us to talk informally about other matters.

The most revealing statement Kitano made during this exchange was the following: "I listen at least once a month to a record by Jay C. Higginbotham, my favorite trombone player. It's a fine, medium-tempo blues." These words reveal the spirituality of a man who is centered on jazz—Kitano's face reflected an inner sense of joy and satisfaction that jazz can produce. I cite this phenomenon because it is not an isolated case. It is a sublime condition I've observed in myself and in others. Music, good jazz, can induce a sort of hypnotic state; its potential is deep spiritual experience.

Harry Kitano. San Francisco, Calif. ca. 1946. Photo courtesy of Harry Kitano.

Kitano's initiation into instrumental music took place when he learned to play the bugle in San Francisco Boy Scout Troop 12 drum and bugle corps. Paul Higaki, a fellow bugler, introduced Kitano early, during their junior-high-school days as neophyte trombone players, to the incredible beauty of Jack Jenny's solo of "Star Dust." That did it—Kitano was drawn into the world of swing and jazz!

Another trombone idol was Tommy Dorsey, whose tone and phrasing captured the intense admiration of both Kitano and Higaki. Among Dorsey's hits was a swing version of Rimsky-Korsakov's "Song of India." The arrangement opens in medium-swing tempo with an introductory sixteen-bar unison sax solo accompanied solely by the drummer on the tom-tom. Then Dorsey introduces the melodic theme—a sixteen-bar legato trombone solo in the upper register. In the background is heard the staccato, syncopated riffs of saxophones that provide the swing. Dorsey played the melodic introduction beautifully and Kitano worked endlessly to duplicate the sound and the feel of the solo. Chizu, Harry's sister, remembers well this particular portion of Dorsey's hit Victor recording—the melody persists like an aching toothache that hangs on and on. How can she forget when Harry would practice those sixteen bars over and over and over again? "I didn't keep count, but he nearly drove us crazy!" she recalled. "India" is etched permanently in Chizu's memory.

The world of swing expanded for Kitano during the wartime eviction of Japanese Americans, when, at fifteen, he became the youngest member of the Starlight Serenaders, the Santa Anita "Assembly" Center dance band. Young Harry was awestruck in the presence of older, sophisticated Nisei—Francis Ikezoe, playing great jazz on the tenor; and Bob Kinoshita, suave, self-assured, crooning the latest pop hits.

A few months later, when the Kitano family was transferred to Topaz Detention Camp, Utah, Kitano advanced farther up the dance-band ladder playing in Tom Tsuji's Topaz Tooters. Innumerable rehearsals and public performances provided the opportunity for him to develop his trombone technique and to sharpen his reading of complex arrangements. He was having the time of his life. Becoming a professional dance-band musician became an obsessive goal.

Harry Kitano's subsequent experiences as he traveled from the camp to work as a trombone player on the Midwest dance-band circuit paralleled that of Paul Higaki. Harry Kitano was now "Harry Lee," as Paul Higaki was "Paul Lee." An interesting aspect of this name change was Kitano's response to my question, "Did other members of the all-white band know that "Lee" was not your real name…that you were Japanese and not Chinese?" Kitano answered, "No, they didn't…I just didn't discuss the name change with them because they were so racist! For example, there'd be very heated arguments about whether or not Harry James was Jewish. I was young and naive…I didn't want to get into it. They never suspected that I was Japanese…I never brought it up."

There was a bizarre payoff to Kitano's early efforts to emulate Dorsey. In 1945 Harry was traveling with a black dance band in the Midwest. On the job before his featured trombone solo, the band leader would announce: "Now, direct from India, here's Harry Lee playing the Song of India!" Kitano, with a hotel towel turban wrapped around his head—a "gen-u-wine" Indian—played Dorsey's solo, note for note, but one octave lower. Of course, the complex irony of a Japanese American under the guise of being Chinese, appearing as an Indian, and replicating a white trombonist's solo was lost on young Kitano.

In 1946 Kitano enrolled in the University of Minnesota. He had just completed a band tour, and in Minneapolis he made the decision to give up working as a full-time musician. Several reasons were given. First, Kitano did not feel comfortable, socially and psychologically, playing in a dance band. He explained: "If I had been either black or white, I might have continued with music and made it a career. Being Asian, it just didn't feel right." (Did the negative effects of Kitano's confinement in a detention camp have anything to do with this sense of insecurity?) Secondly, Kitano had become familiar with the unique, fresh sounds of Bill Harris, trombonist for Woody Herman's hot new jazz band of 1945-46. Robert Thiele, Director of Signature Records, wrote in 1945: "Bill Harris—here is a trombone style definitely new and different. Harris is exciting. One listens with anticipation for he is always playing the unexpected. His tone is a combination of brilliancy and warmth. Bill, who has a wonderful melodic sense, is capable of improvising melodies with perfect construction and continuity." Kitano continued: "When I heard Bill Harris blow his horn, I was convinced that I could never play that well…he was so-o good! Made me want to pack up my horn; another reason for my not pursuing music as a career. I decided to become an academic."

Transferring in 1946 to the University of California, Berkeley, Kitano, while pursuing his educational goals, gigged locally as a leader with his own all-black group—"Harry Lee and his Orchestra." Asked why he chose an all-black line-up, he replied, "I was a member of the San Francisco Musicians Union, Local #6, the white union; black musicians were members of Local #669, a segregated group. Nevertheless, I chose to play with black musicians because I felt more compatible with them." Kitano also worked with other black musicians for white dance audiences in San Francisco at the Fillmore Auditorium and in outlying cities of the Bay Area. Jerome Richardson, a Berkeley High School graduate, now a prominent alto sax player, was often the leader. Their gigs were booked by Ben Watkins, a black agent headquartered in New York City's Harlem.

Concurrently, Kitano was a member of the University of California marching band. The following incident in 1946 epitomizes the feelings that many Japanese Americans experienced after being incarcerated as "enemy aliens" in concentration camps. The California basketball team had won a hard-fought, frenetic game. The band, flushed with the hysteria of the win, spontaneously paraded en masse down Telegraph Avenue, the hub of the commercial section of the Berkeley campus. As a member of the trombone section, Kitano marched reluctantly in the front line. Being the only Japanese American in the group, and filled with feelings of self-effacing inadequacy and self-consciousness, Kitano, although surrounded by a mob of joyous fans, felt *alone*—he recalled thinking: "I'd like to die!" Such psychic scars remained in many former camp detainees. Ill at ease in the spotlight, they preferred the shadows.

Today Harry Kitano is a professor in the School of Social Welfare and Sociology Department of the University of California, Los Angeles, and has been on its faculty for thirty-five years. He is renowned for his research and publications on sociological aspects of the assimilation of Japanese Americans into American mainstream culture. In 1969, Kitano published a landmark book, *Japanese Americans: The Evolution of a Subculture.* His current book, *Generations and Identity: The Japanese American,* provides an apt summary of his personal experiences.

TADASHI TODD YAMAMOTO

I first met **Tad Yamamoto** in 1944 in Chicago, where he organized a band for a dance sponsored by the American Nisei Athletic Club. Three of us in the sax section were former members of the Poston Camp #1 dance band—Tug Tamaru and Yuki Miyamoto on tenor saxes and myself on the alto. Tad played first alto; sitting beside him, I played second alto. I knew then that Tad would eventually become a professional dance-band musician. He played a beautiful alto—his tone was true and full, his reading technique impeccable! Conversely, I was convinced that my future did not lie in the music profession. My saxophone skills were very much limited, hopeless. My prediction for Tad was not too far off-base.

Nisei Music Makers. Chicago, Ill. 1944. Left to right: Tug Tamaru, George Yoshida, Tad Yamamoto, Yuki Miyamoto. Roy Uno photo.

Although he did not become a full-time musician, Yamamoto experienced many hours of top-level dance-band performances—one-nighters with orchestras led by Tex Beneke, Xavier Cugat, Barrett Deems, Les Elgart and Skitch Henderson. He played in orchestras which provided accompaniment to illustrious vocal stars such as Carmen MacRae, the Carpenters and Engelbert Humperdinck. Attesting further to Yamamoto's outstanding musicianship are his professional contacts during innumerable casual gigs with members of the bands of Count Basie, Les Brown, Tommy Dorsey, Duke Ellington, Maynard Ferguson, Benny Goodman, Woody Herman, Harry James and Glenn Miller.

Yamamoto began his music education early. "Little did I realize that when my lips first touched the mouthpiece of a bugle in the fourth grade, this initial experience would pave the way to a lifelong love of music," says Yamamoto. Progressing rapidly on a borrowed trumpet, he became a member of a junior-high-school band in Santa Barbara. He also played in the Granada Theater Mickey Mouse Band, which entertained children prior to kiddie shows each Saturday morning.

In competition with two other school dance bands at Santa Barbara High School,

Yamamoto's band edged out the others to become the official school dance band which played for all dances, assemblies and other functions. A bonus benefit for their status was the privilege of receiving free band arrangements from the local radio station and opportunities to broadcast their music from the studio.

While matriculating in Santa Barbara State College, Yamamoto joined the brass choir which performed in many Southern California cities. When World War II commenced, he received governmental dispensation which exempted him from travel and curfew restrictions imposed on Japanese Americans. In the spring of 1942, the Yamamoto family was interned in Gila River Detention Camp, Arizona, where he organized a makeshift dance band and played clarinet, French horn, tuba or the baritone horn when concert music was requested.

Yuki Miyamoto. Chicago, Ill. 1944. Roy Uno photo.

In 1943 he left camp to enroll in Chicago Musical College. Yamamoto states: "At this stage of my music life, I switched to playing alto sax since I discovered that my trumpet chops were gone from too much experimentation with different mouthpieces, and I realized that good trumpet players were plentiful. I began practicing in earnest...taking sax lesson from Joe Sirola, an associate of the famed Santy Runyon.

"While attending music school in Chicago, I organized the Nisei Music Makers, which included a few white musicians—four saxes, three trumpets, two 'bones, piano, bass and drums. Eileen Nagatomo of North Dakota, a student also at Chicago Musical College, was the pianist. Other Nisei musicians included Yukio Miyamoto, Tug Tamaru and George Yoshida, saxes; Mas Tsuda, trumpet;[33] Hidé Kawano, drums; and Louis Sato, bass viol.

"My first professional break in Chicago came when I joined a band that played at an Irish-owned dance hall. When the promoter of the establishment saw my Asian face, he paid me on the spot for showing up and then asked me to leave. A year later, that same promoter who had secured a much larger dance hall hired me, personally apologized, and even bought me a drink...all three gestures I accepted gladly."

Realizing the difficulty for a full-time musician of enjoying a stable family life, Yamamoto resigned from school during his senior year after a short student teaching assignment which did not prove fulfilling. Yamamoto found employment in a motion-picture film processing lab and remained on the job until retirement in 1989. During his tenure in the film lab, he worked extensively as a musician in a variety of bands. He is currently playing with four different dance bands—some jazz-oriented, others more mainstream.

Yamamoto says today: "Being a musician, even on a part-time basis, has enriched my life beyond imagination. Music is, and will always be, a creative and energizing force, teaching me something new and different about myself every time I perform."

---

27 In 1946 the language school was relocated to the Presidio of Monterey, California. The war had ended, but language specialists were needed for occupation duties overseas. As at Ft. Snelling earlier, a dance band was organized by language school students in Monterey. Torao "Trucko" Kusaba, former trumpet-playing member of the Manzanar Jive Bombers, recalls, "We played many dances at the Presidio; one evening, more than a thousand guests crowded into the El Estero USO. We also traveled to San Francisco, Sacramento and Fresno to entertain dancers."

28 Higaki, as did many other Nisei in the entertainment world, used a Chinese pseudonym during World War II. Japanese American entertainers experienced great difficulty in obtaining employment because bookers would not hire anyone who had a Japanese name. It was easier for Paul to let on that he was Chinese Hawaiian than to explain his Japanese American origin. He was known professionally as Paul Lee for many years until he worked for Lionel Hampton, who induced him to use his real name.

Many "oriental" performers suddenly became exclusively "Chinese"; Japanese Americans did a magical disappearing act. Trombonist Harry Kitano became Harry Lee, drummer Hideo Kawano became Joe Young and Susumu Takao sang as Leland Young. Vocalists Yasuko Tani, Elsie Itashiki, Riki Matsufuji and Goro Suzuki became, respectively, Mary Tan Hai, Teal Joy, Dick Wong and Jack Soo. Helen and Dorothy Takahashi teamed with Paul Jew as the Three Mah-Jongs.

29 In review of Woody Herman's band at Cafe Rouge, Hotel Pennsylvania, New York: "Here's a band that without a doubt is the hottest commodity in the band biz today. Hottest is meant in a double sense, for the band (1) overflows with some of the warmest arrangements heard in a long time and (2) due to a couple of sensash [sensational] disks made for Columbia, the ork [orchestra] is cookin' toward the head of the pack..." Of Krupa at the Astor Roof, New York: "Gene Krupa's ork, sans strings, is a strictly commercial outfit in its present stage. Always the showman, GK is still king when it comes to putting on a drum show, and that he does all eve long. Rest of the band, sparked by Tommy Pederson, ace trombonist, is adequate in giving out both pops and specialties. Sensash singer Anita O'Day really knows how to handle a vocal. She's it,

but big. Gal knows what to do with her voice, hands, body, eyes, etc., when warbling, and don't think payees don't know it. Other singer, Buddy Stewart, is okay, but doesn't come close to Miss O'Day. One of the better features of the band is the jazz trio featuring Krupa, a pianist [Teddy Napoleon], and tenor sax man [Charlie Ventura]. They put on quite a show…"

30 Because of the demands of the military for young men, women filled shortages in dance bands. Several all-girl dance bands attained national prominence for a relatively short period during World War II.

31 The black band leader of a prototype swing band which gained nationwide fame with its hit recording, "Rhythm Is Our Business."

32 Kawahata grew up in San Francisco, played the bugle in Scout Troop 12 drum and bugle corps, the trumpet and French horn in high school. He enrolled in engineering at the University of California, Berkeley, where he played in the concert and marching bands. He was a trumpeter in the Topaz Tooters while interned in Topaz Detention Camp. After returning to Berkeley to complete his education, he moved to Denver, Colorado, where he became a member of a Nisei dance band (ca. 1947).

33 Early in 1945, just one day prior to the transfer of the 442nd Regimental Combat Team from France to Italy, the all-Nisei unit was entertained by the Glenn Miller orchestra led by Jack Leonard (Miller had been lost at sea). At the request of one of the Combat Team officers, Mas Tsuda was given the honor of playing solo "You Made Me Love You" accompanied by the Miller orchestra.

CHAPTER FOUR

Rehearsal for John F. Kennedy Presidential Inauguration Celebration. 1961. Left to right: Frank Sinatra, Pat Suzuki, Sammy Cahn. Mark Shaw photo. Photo courtesy of Pat Suzuki.

# CHAPTER 5

Establishing New Roots

POSTWAR MUSIC

"Starting all over again was painful. Anxiety attacks sapped my energy. I wanted to play my horn, but the desire was not compelling. There were so many other needs and, besides, I had already sold my sax some time ago. Eventually, as family and career goals evolved toward resolution, life began to settle down to a somewhat predictable routine. I thought it would be nice to play some blues again. I started looking at drum sets..."

—George Yoshida,
El Cerrito, Calif. ca. 1960

By December 1944, 35,000 of the 120,000 detainees had relocated out of camps to sites outside the Western Defense Command Area on the Pacific West Coast. The War Relocation Authority (WRA) worked toward an early closure of detention camps, and all but Tule Lake, which housed about 5,000 dissidents, were closed by January 1946. Throughout 1945, large groups of detainees returned home to the West Coast, not only from the camps, but also from interior states where they had resettled.

The termination of the wholesale detention of Japanese Americans did not spell the end of hardship for internees. It was a crucial, demanding time—a time to create new lives. It was time for the precious healing of the soul.

Meanwhile, the War Department announced: "Members of the 442nd Infantry Regiment, composed of American doughboys of Japanese descent, were in the vanguard of the Fifth Army's great offensive which has smashed the German army in northern Italy." Japanese Americans made "sensational gains of 76 miles in five days," as they took part in the capture of Genoa, Italy's largest seaport, on April 27, 1945. The 442nd then forged ahead to enter Turin, the last great city in the Po River Valley, on April 30. German troops were completely demoralized and were surrendering by the thousands. By May 2, 1945, the war was over in Italy. Soon after, on May 9, 1945, Germany unconditionally surrendered—the war was officially over in Europe!

> *"Fellas, the war which we fought, the war in which our [fellow soldiers] who slept with us and ate with us died…is over. You know, not one man cheered. I think most of them cried just thinking of their friends who wanted to see this day. You see people in New York…man, just cheering. I just couldn't see that, you know. [Among] the guys that went to the line, there was not one exhibition of cheering or jumping or anything. They just stood there at attention. You could see tears rolling down their eyes; I can't forget things like that. They never forgot the guys that lived with them and wanted to see that day, too."*
>
> A Nisei Infantryman
"GO FOR BROKE"
Chester Tanaka, Author

POSTWAR MUSIC

When the final resettlement of all incarcerated Japanese Americans was initiated, most camp musicians had to forego their previous involvement in music. For internees who were establishing new lives, there was no time for such luxuries. It was imperative that they plan for the future, find a job, enroll in college, start a business, pursue a profession, marry, establish a permanent, stable home. It was time to settle down…to live again in freedom.

The removal of detainees from detention camps during 1945 resulted in the dispersal of Nisei musician pools which had earlier been established by the concentration of Japanese Americans in centers. The closure of camps ensured the demise of camp bands and Japanese American dance bands in general. The rise and decline of Nisei dance-band activity coincided with the rise and decline of big bands on the "outside." At the conclusion of World War II, the entire country moved into a transitional period of adjusting to peacetime. Because of evolving changes in tastes of pop music consumers and the excessive costs of maintaining big band personnel, mainstream bands gradually downsized or totally disappeared.[34] The vibrant "Swing Era," which flourished roughly from 1935 to 1945, had come to a close.

Although a host of music makers deserted the ranks of Nisei dance bands, a few determined souls carried on during postwar years. Among the latter was **Paul Togawa,** who first tasted the exquisite flavor of jazz in Poston Detention Camp. The following résumé may be found in the 1960 edition of Leonard Feather's *The Encylopedia of Jazz*:

TOGAWA, PAUL, DRUMS, B. LOS ANGELES, CALIFORNIA, 9/3/32.
Studied drums in high school after taking a few trumpet lessons in a relocation center during World War II. Formed 10-piece orchestra after graduating high school; majored in music at East Los Angeles Junior College, then joined Lionel Hampton for a while. Has had own quartet and quintet on West Coast, appeared in movies and TV. Eddie Cano '59. Fav.[favorite drummer]: Philly Joe Jones. Own LP (Mode).

"I gave up gigging professionally around 1971—haven't played my drums at all except for my daughter's wedding reception and also for my son's reception not too long ago. You know, I hadn't really missed playing all these years until I played those two gigs for my kids. Somehow, I was turned on again. Maybe it was Andy Simpkins's swingin' bass or Larry Nash's funky piano or just the passage of time. Anyway, I feel like playing again…to jam again…lay down a funky beat...pick up some spare change on the side," said Togawa, 62, in 1994.

"As a full-time pro drummer, I prided myself in being an all-around drummer. I can play jazz, swing, country-western, society, rhythm 'n' blues and dixieland. I can play with a lot of speed, but I love slow, funky tempos. When I play, I always sing or hum the melody, even when I solo...helps me keep time. I also get my kicks accompanying singers.

"In looking back I feel fortunate that I've played with most of the top jazz guys that came through L.A. Someone once called me the 'white Art Blakey.' That was nice to hear 'cuz he was a monster, but I don't think I play my traps like Art does and I never intentionally

Paul Togawa. Poston Detention Camp #1, Ariz. 1942. Photo courtesy of Vincent Uyeda.

patterned my playing after his. Philly Joe Jones was the drummer I listened to the most. I really enjoyed his playing; he played with so much feeling, so much soul. Philly Joe influenced my drumming style very much, but I avoided copying his licks, even for just a bar. I admired Buddy Rich for big band work—he can really move bands. As for rock drummers today, there are so many young newcomers who sustain a bad, funky beat in their fusion sounds—great hand-foot coordination! I definitely respect them and marvel over their ability to lay down a beat somewhere in a medium groove that makes you wanna' dance...and I do like to dance in that groove.

"I was introduced to instrumental music in 1942 by a very kind priest of the Maryknoll Church in Poston Detention Camp #1, where I served as an altar boy for masses that were held daily. He lent me a trumpet and gave me lessons for about four months; I became fascinated with the horn and with music. Unfortunately, my mentor was transferred and I lost the chance to learn more about the trumpet. Sensing my disappointment, my father ordered through mail a pair of drumsticks for me. I didn't realize it then, but that was the opening of a new world for me—the beginning of my grand love affair with drums.

"From Poston I returned with my family to Boyle Heights in East Los Angeles in September 1945 and enrolled in the eighth grade at Hollenbeck Junior High School. Two years later I moved on to Roosevelt High School where I played snare drum in the ROTC marching band, the concert band and orchestra. In my senior year I played in the school dance band—enjoyed this experience very much. These were especially exciting times for me because I began to earn a few dollars playing gigs with my friends—dances, Chicano weddings and bar mitzvah celebrations. I also played Nisei Week Coronation Balls in '49 and '50.

"After graduating high school I enrolled in East Los Angeles Junior College, where I majored in business and chose music as a minor study. I learned a lot about harmony, picked up a bit of piano, studied solfège, played in the concert band and the dance band. In 1951, at nineteen, I dropped out of school to play congas and travel for a year with Hamp [Lionel Hampton] around the U.S.A., including the deep South. That was a kick…learned much about race relations and its complexities.

"In 1953 I reported to Camp Kilmer, where I completed basic training. I was then transferred to Ft. Lewis, Washington, where I played in parades and concerts with the Forty-fourth Division military band. I also played drums in an off-base jazz combo—mostly in black clubs in Seattle and Tacoma. At twenty-two, I was discharged at the Presidio of San Francisco and immediately got a gig with my trio at the Club Ginza in Los Angeles. For two years, six nights a week, we played quiet dinner music and did a show which featured Japanese dancers and singers. The last set each night was often a gas—usually just a few customers were left in the club, so we jammed. Friends came in after their gigs and sat in—imagine Hamp, Ornette Coleman, Eric Dolphy.

"In the late '50s, with Gabe Baltazar of Hawaii on alto, I organized a quartet which played straight jazz. We were invited to appear on ABC TV Network's 'Stars of Jazz' show several times. Three numbers from one of our telecasts were included in a Caliope Records LP album—'Split Kick,' 'Lover Man' and 'Love Me Or Leave Me.' This album, *Sessions Live*, also contained songs by Chris Connor, former Stan Kenton vocalist, and selections by Cal Tjader and his combo.

"With Dick Johnson on piano, Ben Tucker on

Record label. *SESSIONS LIVE.* Paul Togawa Quartet with Gabe Baltazar, alto sax, Caliope Records. 1957. Courtesy of Tak Shirasawa.

bass, Gabe on the alto and myself on drums, we recorded my first album in June 1957, for Mode Records Company. The album, *Paul Togawa/4,* featured three standards: 'Lover Man,' 'It's All Right With Me,' 'Love For Sale,' and three original tunes. To my surprise this album was reviewed in *Downbeat* magazine by a critic who gave it a two-and-a-half-star rating. In 1963, with Joe Sample on Hammond organ and Bill Plummer on string bass, I recorded Japanese and American favorites for Musifon Records—*The Paul Togawa International Jazz Trio.* This LP included six classical Japanese songs, including *'Kojo No Tsuki,' 'Hana,'* and *'Yerai Shan.'* Also some blues, of course, and a very up-tempo 'Cute,' a Neal Hefti tune long associated with Basie. In order to make it easier to get air time on radio, we kept our solos relatively short, but I can honestly say we *cooked* on this record!

"My most exciting and satisfying gigs took place in the late '50s and '60s with Hampton Hawes on piano—what a thrill that was. The guy was unreal! Other favorites were Art Pepper on alto, Joe Sample on piano and Bill McAfee playing those great rhythm 'n' blues sounds on the organ. In 1964 I dropped out of the local scene for the Far East—traveled and worked clubs for three years in the Philippines, Korea, Thailand and Japan. Made decent bucks playing and conducting dance bands accompanying American singers working in U.S. Army base clubs.

"As I explained earlier, I ended my musical career about twenty years ago—worked in automobile dealerships and later, in jewelry sales. I had become alienated with music; I didn't have time for rehearsals, gigs or jammin'. In retrospect, I devoted over two decades of my life to my first love, drums and jazz. I did get my kicks. And now I want a taste of it again, just a tiny taste."

GEORGE JUNICHI TAKAMOTO

George Takamoto of Monterey, California, a high-school junior at the time, began teaching himself to play the trumpet in Poston Camp #2 after Eugene Kodani lent him a horn sometime in 1943. Takamoto practiced diligently, learned from older musicians and listened with great intensity to dance bands of Camp #1 and Camp #2. With this modest introduction to the trumpet, he was motivated to pursue a career in music after completing his service requirements in the U.S. Air Force. Says Takamoto: "Getting drafted turned out to be not really a bad deal. I became a member of the base marching band which afforded me much time to practice and to perform on my horn. I also had opportunities to play big-band jazz arrangements and met many musicians who had plenty of experience in professional dance bands. My tenure in the Air Force was truly profitable. I had much time to sharpen my trumpet technique and my concepts regarding jazz and big-band music naturally expanded. As a matter of fact, I was so turned on to music, I enrolled in a conservatory in Chicago following my discharge to pursue seriously my goal to become a professional musician. I studied piano and trumpet and graduated with a substantial background in music composition, harmony and performance technique on both piano and trumpet."

After graduation, Takamoto played trumpet in the Midwest dance-band circuit. In time the stress of traveling from city to city, often night after night, along with the stormy winters, convinced Takamoto to make changes. He returned to the West Coast and settled permanently in San Francisco. As an experienced, professional musician, he worked steadily in orchestras playing for shows and dances. Concurrently, he rehearsed a seventeen-piece big band made up mostly of highly skilled professionals. In the band's book were several outstanding arrangements by Jim Araki, who was then a student at the University of California in Berkeley.

Joe Brattesani Orchestra with George Takamoto (left) and Kazu Maruoka, trumpets. San Francisco. ca. 1962. Photo courtesy of Kazu Maruoka.

In addition to his trumpet-playing, Takamoto provided piano accompaniment for female vocalists in Japanese restaurants and bars such as Bush Garden and Club Fuji in San Francisco. He taught voice and diction to Japanese vocalists and piano to children and adults. In the '60s he organized a quartet which at one time included himself on the piano; Lloyd "Gohan" Rice

George Takamoto and Augie Perez. The George Takamoto Quartet. San Francisco. 1956. George Yoshida photo.

on tenor or Kazu Maruoka on the vibes; Augie Perez, bass; and George Yoshida, drums. The George Takamoto Quartet played jazz sessions at Club Llama and dances at the Cathay House, both in San Francisco's Chinatown; it also played many dances for local Nisei organizations.

George Takamoto enjoyed a lengthy and varied career as a professional musician. His love of jazz and swing music sustained his longevity in the music business. He died in January 1996, in San Francisco.

Hayao Al Motoyama, a member of Takamoto's San Francisco big band, remembers: "I faithfully picked up George every Thursday to go to rehearsals. After practice, we'd share steamed crab cooked in black bean sauce in Chinatown. Neither of us talked while scarfing on the crab for fear that the other person will eat more than his share!" Motoyama earlier had played the alto and tenor sax in two different bands in Tule Lake Detention Camp—The Stardusters and Down Beats. He spent two-and-a-half years in the U.S. Air Force with much of the time in an Air Force dance band stationed in Panama. In the decade of the '50s, Motoyama lived in San Francisco; he now recalls fondly his association with Nisei musicians Takamoto, Kazu Maruoka and Yoné Fukui. Motoyama lives today in Lodi, California. He still works casual dance gigs with his tenor saxophone in company with a piano, bass and drums. "I wish I could play in a big band again," he says. "I really enjoyed playing swing music… I miss it very much."

San Francisco Examiner advertisement. December 15, 1956. Courtesy of George Yoshida

TETSU BESSHO

Tetsu Bessho was born on March 6, 1924, in Montebello, California. In a recent telephone interview he described his early beginnings in music: "I first played a harmonica when I was about eight years old; harmonicas were very popular then. In the third grade at Fremont Elementary

Tetsu Bessho and his Nisei Serenaders. Zenda Ballroom, Los Angeles. ca. 1950. Front row, left to right: James Araki, Joe Sakai, Haruo Fujisawa, George Ozumi, Tetsu Besso, Kay Noda, Gordon Sato. Back row: Walter Hayami, George Sumida, Bruce Kaji, George Shimizu, Roy Nakagawa. Photo courtesy of Haruo Fujisawa.

School, I was introduced to the clarinet. I took lessons and enjoyed playing very much. When I moved up to junior high school, I changed to alto sax and worked hard improving my technique on that horn through high school. There was no dance band at Montebello High School, so a few of my friends and I got together to form a pickup band. We played stock arrangements just for the fun of it…you know, tunes like 'I Can't Get Started' and 'Begin The Beguine.'

"About this time, my interest in jazz expanded and I began to listen to black jazz stars like [Charlie] Parker, Lester [Young], Coleman Hawkins, [Count] Basie and Duke [Ellington]. I also enjoyed the sounds of Artie Shaw and Glenn Miller. I used to catch live stage shows at the Paramount Theater in downtown Los Angeles. Even caught Sammy Kaye…Swing and Sway with Sammy Kaye…and what's-his-name, Ish Kabibble, yeah." Bessho's comments were accompanied by much raucous laughter—a signature mannerism.

"While in Heart Mountain Detention Camp, I had a chance to play in a fully staffed band which was led by veteran musician George Igawa. For a long time I had wanted to play in a big band and here was this chance. When Igawa left camp, I took over as the leader...that was a big thrill! Our vocalist was Yuki Mogi; our theme song, Glenn Miller's 'Moonlight Serenade.'

"In 1945 I played in the Koichi Hayashi band in Chicago. The following year, I lived in New York City where I took tenor saxophone lessons from Joe Thomas of Cab Calloway's band. Thomas was sharing a music studio with Cozy Cole, the outstanding black drummer. In New York, I hung out for a while with Hidé Kawano, who was in the big city getting on with his obsession in drumming and jazz on Fifty-second Street. He hung out with jazz musicians, learning from them and sitting in whenever he had the chance. Hidé introduced me to [Charlie] Parker and [Ben] Webster and other top jazz stars.

"Back in L.A. in the late '40s, I'd go to listen to jazz at the Normandie Club on Normandie and Adams Streets. Got to know Dexter Gordon, Teddy Edwards, Wardell Gray... all great tenor players. Even hired Billy Higgins, drummer, and Teddy Edwards for a few of my casual gigs. Daytime hours were spent at my parents' nursery where we grew carnations.

"I led my own big band, the Nisei Serenaders, for about three or four years around 1949. We played Nisei dances and high-school proms for Roosevelt, Belmont and Poly High Schools. Also did a little traveling up to Riverside and Fresno. Lane Nakano was our vocalist; Chickie Ishihara also sang with us. I remember getting about ten dollars a person for those gigs...thought the money was great.

"I'm still gigging casuals playing my tenor, alto, soprano saxophones, flute and the rare saxello, a B-flat reed instrument similar to a soprano sax. I always loved music... had an ear for it. I used to dream when I was young that I would like to play jazz. I've never stopped learning. I have no regrets. I'll continue playing the music I love...jazz!"

James Araki and Chickie White. Nisei Serenaders. Zenda Ballroom, Los Angeles. ca. 1950. Photo courtesy of Haruo Fujisawa.

SUE TAKIMOTO OKABE

Sue Takimoto must have been the envy of her high-school classmates while confined in Minidoka Detention Camp. At the tender age of ten, she had a very special gift—an unusually beautiful, clear singing voice. Not only that, her repertoire was purely classical; not the cute Shirley Temple stuff. She could sing "One Fine Day" from Puccini's opera, *Madame Butterfly!*

Let her explain the "envy" part: "Jerome Light, the principal of our high school, arranged for me to entertain on the outside—mostly in service clubs like the Rotary Club in Twin Falls, Blackfoot and Boise, Idaho. My sister, Michi, usually accompanied me on the piano. Once we went as a team with Masashi Hayashida on violin and Yosh Uchida, who sang basso, to enter a state-wide music competition. All three of us came home winning first place in our respective divisions! I guess these jaunts out of camp were for public relations, but the great treat of going outside was the food we were served. Camp food, mainly beef heart and mutton, was hard to take; in contrast, roast beef, gravy, mashed potatoes, fresh green salad and apple pie was heaven on earth! I'm sure my classmates in Hunt High School were envious of my trips out."

Relocation out of Minidoka Detention Camp presented opportunities for Sue to sing at the Denver USO for GIs, for U.S. War Bond rallies and for radio broadcast work on Station WGN in Chicago. On these occasions, she still sang tunes such as "Summertime," "Smoke Gets In Your Eyes" and "Begin The Beguine" in a classical mode.

Concurrently, Sue commuted to Lamont School of Music at the University of Denver, where she studied voice and opera, while she attended East High School; then the Los Angeles Conservatory of Music, while a senior at Belmont High School. She trained further in operatic singing at the University of Southern California and graduated with a B.A. in English.

Following her divorce in the late '50s, as Sue Joe (Joe—a bona fide Japanese family name), she made a radical change in her singing career. Due to financial need, she became a jazz singer—a complete turnabout from the past. Gershwin's "Summertime," which was written in slow tempo and with classical overtones, was now "Summertime" loosely phrased, subtly syncopated and effused with the blues!

"My heroes were now Ella [Fitzgerald], naturally, Billie [Holiday] and Dinah [Washington]. I sang in clubs with combos, but gravitated toward working solo, accompanying myself on the piano, or quite often accompanied by Clifford Fishback. For each gig, I could earn around $100.00 working solo, whereas I'd get only $10.00 to $20.00 singing with a group of musicians.

Sue Okabe, *Flower Drum Song.* Long Beach, Calif. 1963. Photo courtesy of Sue Okabe.

"For a spell I worked the Tai Ping [Restaurant] in the Los Angeles Crenshaw district; later, I moved to the Blue Lantern in Gardena for a couple of years. During the Lantern gig in '63, I experienced what I now consider the highlight of my career—playing 'Linda Low' in the Long Beach Civic Light Opera production of *Flower Drum Song*. The part was one of the lead roles, a challenging one. I sang 'I Enjoy Being A Girl' and 'Grant Avenue.' The audience response was great…I felt real good! Not only that, I was one of only three being paid and the money was fantastic. The owners of the Blue Lantern were kind enough to let me take time off for the three-week run of the show.

"Kyoto Sukiyaki Restaurant in Gardena was my next club engagement. It was a long gig…seven years! I was truly getting into jazz. Though some of the nights were long, I didn't mind too much because the singing style I was developing was a challenge and more attuned to my true self. Yet, I was sorry to drop the other stuff…I mean, classical music.

"In the spring of 1992, the Los Angeles JACCC (Japanese American Cultural and Community Center) invited me to sing with Tets Bessho and his combo at their special program commemorating the fiftieth anniversary of the wartime detention of Japanese Americans. Later in the year, I sang again with Tets for *Manzanar Canteen,* a stage production depicting diverse social aspects of detention-camp life.

"In August, 1993, I sang in the Nikkei Jazz Festival in Los Angeles. My backup was the Nunokawa brothers on piano and drums, Tets Bessho on sax and flute, and Jeff Takiguchi (who has played with Ray Charles) on bass. Some tunes I sang were: 'A Foggy Day,' 'Our Love Is Here to Stay,' 'How High The Moon', 'Star Dust', and 'Summertime.' It was a kick singing these tunes—the quartet swung nicely!

Bill Beadle (as Sammy Fong) and Sue Okabe (as Linda Low). *Flower Drum Song*. Long Beach, Calif. 1963. Photo courtesy of Sue Okabe.

"Both of my parents enjoy singing *utai*—classical songs of the Japanese Noh theater. I guess I inherited their affinity for music and, in turn, my mom picked up something from me.

CHAPTER FIVE 247

Let me explain. My public performance just prior to the Nikkei Jazz Festival was the San Fernando Valley United Methodist Church Benefit Jazz Concert. Larry Honda and his quartet backed me up then. After completing a set of my favorite standards, I dedicated my final selection to my eighty-eight-year-old mother who was in the audience—her favorite tune, 'Skylark.'"

Sue Okabe's busy schedule includes an occasional Afterhours Cabaret performance and much time teaching private voice lessons. Currently, she is enjoying the work of her daughter, Lisa Joe, a composer of contemporary songs and an accomplished flautist and pianist, who was the musical director of the Los Angeles-based East-West Players production, *29 1/2 DREAMS— Women Walking Through Walls.* Included in the cast of this musical montage were Marilyn Tokuda and Haruye Ioka, two of Okabe's students who have been studying voice for some time. Add a few hours of baby-sitting and you'll find a picture of a grandmother who is very much occupied, living a fulfilling, well-rounded life.

ETHEL AZAMA

"When I first heard **Ethel Azama** sing (or should I say "swing"), I was in awe of her extraordinary talent," observed Joy Teraoka. "Her phrasing, enunciation, tone quality and timing were perfect. She caressed a ballad or belted out an up-tempo tune with impeccable delivery and feeling. Her rapt audiences were drawn to experience her songs of joy and pain. Not only that, her personality sparkled in the light banter between songs—she seemed like everyone's friend. Ethel exuded self-confidence with an equal amount of grace."

Ethel was born in Honolulu on August 18, 1934. While a young girl, she learned Okinawan dances from her father who loved music and dance. Her mother encouraged her to sing. Imbued with this cultural heritage, enforced by the rhythmic beat of Okinawan music flowing in her blood, it is no wonder that Ethel became an outstanding singer and dancer.

Azama's career as an entertainer began modestly around 1955 as the emcee at the Oasis, a nightclub which featured musical revues from Japan. She may have sung a few songs, but prancing chorus girls and kabuki dancers were the featured entertainers. In the following year Azama's reputation as a pop singer expanded as band leaders began to hire her for gigs in military clubs in Honolulu. Paul Conrad, a professional pianist, provided Azama with valuable technical assistance to refine her vocal style and also wrote special arrangements to accompany her singing. In time, Azama was featured in Waikiki Beach night clubs, opening for big-name stars such as Herb Jeffries and Josh White.

Ethel Azama. *Cool Heat* album cover. 1958. Courtesy of Ken Yamada.

In 1958 Martin Denney produced *Exotic Dream,* a Liberty Records LP album, LRP 3104, which featured Azama singing several American standards such as "Speak Low" and "Autumn Leaves," a Japanese tune, and several Hawaiian Island-flavored songs arranged by Paul Conrad. This recording was ample evidence of the maturity of Ethel's vocal styling and it débuted about the same time as her first professional tour of the U.S. mainland.

Ethel Azama left Hawaii in 1958 to appear at Ye Little Club in Beverly Hills, California. That same year, upon the recommendation of Jimmie Rodgers, Liberty Records contracted Azama to record again. This time she was accompanied by Hollywood studio musicians under the direction of Marty Paich with his charts ranging from rich, classical strings to gentle, modern brasses—wonderful, swinging scores. This album, *Cool Heat,* Liberty 3142, "captures Azama's talent for posterity." Jimmie Rodgers wrote in the album liner notes: "Ethel has a way of doing extraordinary things with any material, sending little thrills chasing along your musical senses. Like the note she holds so-o-o long on 'My Ship'—the exciting vibrato you can almost feel on 'I'm Glad There Is You'—the sexy teasing of the kittenish invitation to 'Squeeze Me'— her feel for jazz on 'Daybreak'—the contrast between a tender 'Like Someone In Love' and a bouncing 'Johnny One Note.' When I walked into a Honolulu night club and first heard Ethel Azama singing, I flipped—I said to myself, 'Uh-oh…here's a talent!"

Azama worked clubs in New York City, Chicago and Los Angeles. She was billed with notable jazz singers such as Mel Tormé and the Four Freshmen in Las Vegas. Around 1960 she left for Australia, where she sang in many fine nightclubs and appeared on television and radio. In 1964 she and John Todd, her Australian pianist, were married. They traveled to Hong Kong, where she was booked into the stylish Eagle's Nest in the Hong Kong Hilton Hotel and other elegant clubs. Several years later the Todds traveled back to Hawaii where their two children were born. Ethel appeared in Waikiki Beach clubs both as a solo artist and as a partner in a duo with the popular Jimmy Borges, a local jazz singer who still performs in Honolulu supper clubs.

Ethel Azama suffered a cerebral aneurysm and died at forty-nine years in 1983 at the zenith of her career. Ironically, a gathering of top jazz musicians including Azama had been preparing a benefit performance for Punahou School. The concert was held as scheduled in memory of Ethel Azama, a superb artist.

ELSIE ITASHIKI, A.K.A. TEAL JOY

Elsie Itashiki was a show-stopper. Topaz Detention Camp high-school friends describe Elsie, at fifteen, as an energetic, outgoing teenager who possessed a charismatic personality which she projected when she sang. She was a crowd-pleaser who preferred singing medium and up-tempo, swinging tunes in her repertoire—"Chattanooga Choo Choo," "Basin Street Blues," "Ain't Misbehavin'." "Wacky" Sumimoto, a classmate, recalls: "Elsie was a real hep chick...different. She was usually unreserved...had a way of walking and stuff...wore makeup. She sang 'Cow Cow Boogie' and 'Mr. Five By Five'—more jazz, like Anita O'Day, than slow ballads."

Elsie Itashiki, a.k.a. Teal Joy. New York, N.Y. 1954. Photo courtesy of Robert Itashiki.

Elsie was born in Seattle in 1927. Later, the Itashiki family moved to San Francisco, where she attended Pacific Heights [Elementary] School. Her older sister Marie remembers taking Elsie to tap-dance lessons when Elsie was in the fourth and fifth grades. Adept in tap dance, she won top prizes in several local talent shows. At this time there was no hint of her future as a professional singer of pop songs.

The Itashikis were involuntarily removed in 1942 to Tanforan "Assembly" Center; then to Topaz Detention Camp. Because Mrs. Itashiki, Elsie's mother, had been a teacher of Japanese in a San Francisco school, she was forcibly separated from her family during their stay at Tanforan.

Mrs. Itashiki was transferred with other teachers to a site in Redwood City, where, isolated from her family, she tragically died of a heart attack. Leaving Topaz after a three-year stay, Elsie Itashiki traveled in 1944 by train to Chicago, where Marie had relocated. In 1946, at age nineteen, she left Chicago for New York to pursue seriously a career in show business. In the subsequent period up to 1950, Itashiki studied voice, worked casual gigs as "Teal Joy" and finally obtained steady booking as a singer and chorus-line dancer at the China Doll, a restaurant club in New York City. Other singing engagements took place at the Apollo Theater in New York City, Mr. Kelley's in Chicago, and television appearances on the Dick Clark and the Steve Allen shows. Foreign bookings resulted in travels to Cuba, Puerto Rico, Chile and Great Britain.

Brother Robert Itashiki is a jazz fanatic who digs the cool saxophone sounds of Paul Desmond and Stan Getz; Gerry Mulligan on the baritone is another favorite. Bob delights in tunes written by Matt Dennis—"Angel Eyes," "Everything Happens To Me," "Let's Get Away From It All," etc. Ahmad Jamal tops the list of piano players he admires. When asked what he remembers about Elsie, Bob replied: "When Elsie was a youngster, she took tap and ballet lessons. I clearly remember 'cause one day, out of curiosity, I tried on her ballet toe slippers to see how it would feel...just couldn't imagine anyone dancing on their toes. I found out it wasn't easy!

"In camp [Topaz] I used to think her singing sounded like Ella Mae Morse. Later, in Chicago, when Elsie got serious about singing professionally, I recall her being referred to as the 'Oriental Billie Holiday.' I also remember she really dug Johnny Hartman and Arthur Prysock—both outstanding black jazz vocalists. Gives you some idea about her taste in vocal styles and sounds.

"One of Elsie's overseas gigs was promoted by Sol Hurok, an influential impresario. She was asked to travel to South America with entertainers from Japan. Aside from singing, Elsie was given the responsibility of emceeing several shows. She was uncomfortable about the assignment because her Japanese language was limited—felt she couldn't adequately translate Japanese into English."

Itashiki recorded two LP albums. One, produced in 1969, is *Ted Steele Presents Miss Teal Joy*, a recording of twelve tunes in a variety of tempos and from a number of ethnic sources on the AAMCO label. Ted Steele, orchestra leader and arranger, is quoted on the album liner: "[I've] worked with giants like Perry Como and Frank Sinatra. I've worked likewise with newcomers... but, I have never been so positive of greatness as I am now. Miss Teal Joy. This young lady was singing in the Bamboo Club in Atlantic City, practically on the doorstep of the recording center of the world and virtually unnoticed, when I happened in. Now I am so grateful that I was the

Elsie Itashiki. a.k.a. Teal Joy. New York, N.Y. ca. 1960. Photo courtesy of Marie Nishimura.

one to come along and be completely stunned by her immeasurable talent and taste. I have now an opportunity to create with, what I consider, the greatest new voice in the last decade.

"Because of her amazing versatility I felt that we needed three distinctly different sounds to showcase Teal properly. Three different orchestras comprised of the outstanding names in the music world were called in to do this album. A complete 25-piece production orchestra was used on the 'Misirlou,' 'Sorrento,' 'Cumbanchero' and 'Let's Fall in Love' numbers. A 'wailing' jazz band for the up tunes and the simple sensitivity of lush strings, rhythm, woodwinds, horn and harp for the delicate ballads like 'Easy to Remember.'

Elsie Itashiki. *Miss Teal Joy* album cover. Bethlehem Records re-issue. ca. 1969. Courtesy of Ken Yamada.

"Listen to Teal Joy. You will discover, as I did, a 'once-in-a-lifetime' talent. This album is the first. You will hear Teal Joy many times again."

A publicity ad (ca. 1965) for the Cipango Club, a supper room in Dallas, Texas, exclaims: "TEAL JOY, the Oriental shyness of the Japanese 'blue blood'…she sings, she acts, she dances, she's cute, she's shy, she's subtle…savvy all the way."

Robert Itashiki adds: "Tony Callegari, Elsie's husband, is a jazz pianist, a graduate of the Julliard School. He and Elsie had moved to warmer St. Petersburg, Florida, to help Elsie's prolonged, debilitating rheumatoid arthritis. Eventually, her heart gave way. Elsie Itashiki, who brightened Topaz Camp talent shows as a teenager and achieved success as a professional singer, died in 1990 at age sixty-four. She is survived by her husband and a daughter, Teal."

Teal Callegari lives today in St. Petersburg. In a letter written on March 3, 1996, she wrote: "My father is semiretired, but still plays regular gigs here in St. Petersburg. As he puts it, 'It's the only thing I know how to do.' Unfortunately, I share very little of my parents' musical ability, aside from loving all types of music—this was instilled by my parents. The only [interesting] anecdote [about my mother] I can think of is when mom met Gene Kelly while auditioning for a play. She had trouble with her contact lenses and couldn't see very well. As she approached Mr. Kelly, she tripped and fell flat on her face in front of him! Mom said that Gene Kelly was very gracious.

"Mom always said how difficult it was being Japanese and in the entertainment business. The All-American look was always preferred regardless of talent. I think things have improved in the past ten years on that basis. She would have been glad."

GORO SUZUKI, A.K.A. JACK SOO

Goro Suzuki was reared in the West Oakland Japanese community where his father operated a tailor shop and his mother worked as a seamstress and taught sewing to young Nisei girls. Issei mothers made sure their daughters would become efficient housewives who could sew sensible clothing for themselves and their offspring without having to pay exorbitant store prices—the '30s were hard times.

Takako Tsuchiya Endo remembers to this day how, as a teenager, she looked forward to those sewing classes—not because of any great motivation to learn, but to be there to hear young Goro sing. Endo recalls: "Goro's household chore was, among others, cleaning the house, and while working the broom, he would break out very loudly in some popular tune of the day and all of us girls would swoon! We couldn't concentrate on our sewing—he had such a beautiful voice! And when he wasn't there, some of us would be very much disappointed. I wonder what was going on in Goro's mind as he sang without any inhibition while we labored nearby over our sewing projects. He probably was very much aware of the presence of us girls and his intention was, without doubt, to impress us. (That, he succeeded!) I also wonder if my mom ever thought it strange that I went so willingly for my lessons without complaints. I don't think I learned much about sewing, but it sure was fun taking lessons at the Suzuki Tailoring School."

Sachi Kajiwara has vivid memories of Goro because "he was such a clown and acted up all the time." Their families were members of the Oakland Japanese Methodist Episcopal Church. Kajiwara recalls: "Whenever the opportunity arose, Goro would offer his services as a vocalist. Weddings and receptions were common venues for his performances. He loved to imitate Bing Crosby and Perry Como, and did it well. My sister Michi used to accompany Goro on the piano. Several elaborate secular operettas were produced at the church as fund raisers; Goro assumed major roles in their success. He even took a cameo role in a Works Progress Administration (WPA) play at the Oakland Little Theater—ironically, he played the part of a butler."

Yoshio Kasai of San Leandro, California, now in his '80s, was a classmate of Goro Suzuki in 1935 at the University of California, Berkeley. Kasai sweated several seasons in an Alaskan salmon cannery in order to buy a car because the streetcar ride from East Oakland to the Berkeley campus made him ill. Kasai wrote: "Goro would wait for me to ride home on certain days when our classes ended around the same time. We both loved to sing the latest on the Hit Parade—memorized and sang many a song from song sheets on our way home from school.

"Goro and I were never serious students; we began to hang around together. On many occasions we double-dated. We must have attended almost every Bay Area dance—more often as stags, because it was cheaper. Goro was interested in dramatics while still in high school and had taken a few private lessons. He entered a Major Bowes amateur contest with a dramatic monologue and was very happy when he received honorable mention and not the gong.

"He then began in earnest to focus on vocals and studied voice. Even though the price of admission for dances was only fifty or seventy-five cents, Goro would tell the ticket-taker, 'I'm singing with the band,' so that he wouldn't have to pay. He then would approach a surprised piano player to rehearse a few bars of a song which he would sing during the intermission. I must say he had a lot of guts. He told me one day, 'I know people are making fun of me, but I don't care because I know I'm going to make it.' Perhaps, some may have called Goro a show-off, but I'm sure it was his determination that got him to where he was—a successful entertainer."

During the wartime eviction of the Japanese, the Suzuki family was ordered first into Tanforan "Assembly" Center and then to Topaz Detention Camp. In both of these camps young Goro became very much involved in providing entertainment for internees by organizing variety shows, singing and acting as master of ceremonies. Michi Kobi says, "In Tanforan, heading the talent shows, Goro lifted our spirits mightily with his humor and songs." Sadie Towata Tajima, a pianist, accompanied Goro in Tanforan and Topaz. She remembers: "'Ol' Man River' was a favorite of his fans—he must have sung it a hundred times! The tune starts out kinda low (in intensity), then builds and builds. Goro was a perfectionist. It was hard to play for him, he demanded a certain rhythm. But he had a lovely voice, so it was a pleasure [to play for Goro]. Everybody went crazy over him; there was always a full house when he performed in the mess halls! I was fortunate because I was designated as the official camp pianist and received $19.00 a month for my services as a member of the Recreation Department. That was fifty years ago! I still play—volunteering every Friday at a residence for seniors. They enjoy hearing popular music of the '30s and the '40s, and I love playing it!"

Goro Suzuki became "Jack Soo" before the war broke out. This was about the time he became the featured vocalist and emcee at the Sky Room and, later, the Forbidden City, both San Francisco Chinatown nightclubs. He explained to friend Yoshio Kasai: "I chose 'Jack Soo' because it could be taken as Korean or Chinese or Japanese—kinda like an all-inclusive Oriental name."

In 1943, when relocation out of detention camps became available for most internees, Suzuki went to Cleveland, Ohio. Having successfully worked clubs in San Francisco, he secured employment at Chin's, a Chinese restaurant and night club. Jazz fans, take note: Art Tatum, the remarkable jazz pianist, was a featured headline artist during Suzuki's stay at Chin's. One evening during Tatum's stint, Yosh Kasai's date, unable to appreciate Tatum's genius talent and bored with Tatum's piano offerings, urged Suzuki to ask Tatum to play a little boogie-woogie. Suzuki replied, "Art doesn't play that kinda trash; he plays real jazz…that's all!" Incidentally, Suzuki's day gig was slicing meat in the window of a hofbrau restaurant—he probably played the role to the hilt with great show-biz flair.

After auditioning in New York for a role in the stage musical *Flower Drum Song*, he was awarded the part of Sammy Fong, the proprietor of Celestial Gardens, a San Francisco Grant Avenue restaurant and night club. The show opened on December 1, 1958, with another Suzuki, Pat, who played the role of Linda Low. It is purported that Goro at that time wanted to change his stage name back to his legal name, Goro Suzuki, but the production management replied in the negative: "One Suzuki in the show is enough!" After a lengthy run on Broadway, Suzuki, with the original cast, enjoyed a successful tour of the musical stage circuit in the States.

A Hollywood movie version of *Flower Drum Song* followed; again, Suzuki played the part of Sammy Fong, the night club-owner. The film also starred Nancy Kwan, Miyoshi Umeki and James Shigeta. Subsequently, Suzuki was cast in a minor role in *Mr. Valentine,* a short-lived television sitcom, and later in the immensely popular *Barney Miller* television series. In the latter, he achieved prominence playing the part of Sergeant Nick Yamané, a droll, deadpan detective in an urban police department. In a tribute to Suzuki, upon his death from cancer, a special *Barney Miller* show consisting of clips from past segments and eulogies by fellow actors and production staff was produced to acknowledge Suzuki's valuable contributions to the success of this television series.

Goro Suzuki, a Nisei who grew up in the Japanese ghetto in Oakland, California, pitched a good hardball and sang at the drop of a hat, achieved precious success in gaining entrée into the mainstream entertainment world. As to his innumerable engagements as an entertainer in night clubs, Suzuki said, "I get a lot of gigs…like, I can work three hundred sixty-five days out of the year if I wanted to. You know why? *I work cheap!*" Goro Suzuki, unlike the stereotypical reticent Nisei male, was jocular, uninhibited and talented.

PAT CHIYOKO SUZUKI

Sometime ago I was enjoying a super veggie burrito in a funky Mexican restaurant in the San Francisco Mission district with Richard Wada, a Sansei photographer friend.

"Hey, Rich, have you heard of **Pat Suzuki**?" I knew that Rich liked music and I was checking him out to see if he was familiar with the Nisei vocalist who received national acclaim in the late '50s and the '60s.

Pat Suzuki. *Miss Pony Tail* album cover. 1958. Courtesy of Ken Yamada.

"Heard of Pat Suzuki? Are you kidding? I fell in love with her years ago! I looked all over for a record of hers. Finally found one… *Miss Ponytail*. It cost me fourteen big ones!" (Original retail price: $3.95.)

Rich had seen Hollywood's version of Neil Simon's *Biloxi Blues*. In one scene a young Army draftee, on a one-day pass from a Southern boot camp, visits the local USO to pass the time away. A party is in progress and the rookie soldier dances with a pretty young Southern belle—it's love at first sight. The young couple looks deeply into each other's eyes as they dance romantically. In the background a female vocalist backed by subtle Latin rhythms is heard singing very slowly, very seductively—"Somewhere there's music, how strange the tune, Somewhere there's heaven, how high the moon…"

"How High The Moon," sung with deep emotion by a mystery voice, jolted Rich's musical senses—"It knocked me out!" He was so turned on he could hardly wait for the credits to flash by at the end of the film. And, finally, there it was: "'How High The Moon.' Performed by Pat Suzuki. RCA Victor."

Pat Suzuki…a "sister." Wow! Rich was hooked!

I became acquainted with this talented Nisei singer's wonderful voice and style somewhat belatedly. I had heard of Pat Suzuki, but hadn't focused on her singing until I saw Wayne Wang's film, *Eat a Bowl of Tea*. Wang used "How High The Moon" in one of his scenes and it excited me then as much as it did Rich earlier. I had heard the tune played up-tempo many times in the past by jazz musicians, but not as a slow ballad as sung by Suzuki. I also discovered that many of my Nisei friends had purchased her LPs thirty years ago. Pat was a Nisei heroine—who among us had achieved such an inconceivably high place in show business as she?

Pat Suzuki. ca. 1961. Mark Shaw photo. Courtesy of Pat Suzuki.

Today Pat Suzuki lives in New York City in semiretirement. "What do I do everyday? Well, I get up in the morning, eat a simple breakfast while I read my mail. I read books...I read a lot. As a matter of fact I recently joined a club where we discuss novels and poetry. I've enjoyed these stimulating, thoughtful gatherings; I also spend some time painting. The visual arts have had great appeal to me since my days in college. And I love to travel. Paris and Europe were great, but my favorite spot is Japan. I worked with Sammy Davis, Jr. in the American Pavilion during the 1970 World's Fair in Tokyo—enjoyed meeting with Japanese show-biz folks then. On another trip sponsored by the U.S. Government, I sang for U.S. Army personnel and did several Tokyo club dates. Several years ago, I spent some time getting acquainted with gracious relatives in Toyohashi, located not too far from Nagoya...that was nice. Kyoto is a bit too cluttered and crowded for me; Nara was less hectic, more amiable. I also loved strolling through secluded, cypress tree-covered hills in the vicinity of the handsome bronze Buddha of Kamakura. It was a trip gawking at ancient wooden sculptures of *oni,* those fierce-looking devils that guard entrances to the grounds of finely crafted shrines. I have fond memories of lovely walks in quiet, verdant forests of Japan."

Pat Suzuki, the youngest of four Suzuki children, was born on September 23, 1930, in the vicinity of the central California town of Cressey. She was named after her father, but young Chiyoko became "Pat" when a local grocer had difficulty pronouncing "Chiyoko." Chiyoko grew up in the quiet, somewhat isolated world of a hundred-acre ranch which produced almonds, grapes and peaches. She spent her childhood days studying in a two-room schoolhouse, riding horses bareback, swimming in the irrigation canals and attending Sunday school at the Japanese Methodist Church. Music provided solace for Pat from an otherwise dull routine of life on the farm; the family phonograph was a source of abundant pleasure. And Pat loved to sing; she displayed a precocious talent in song at age five. In time, accompanied by her sister Mary on the piano, she was invited to sing for wedding ceremonies and other community gatherings.

In 1942, in compliance with Executive Order 9066 shortly after the Japanese attack on Pearl Harbor, eleven-year-old Pat was interned with her family with thousands of other Japanese Americans in Amache Detention Camp, Colorado. Ironically, she had sung a moving "God Bless America" during one of her last public performances, just prior to her family's forced move to the inland camp. Interned in Amache for three years, the Suzuki family relocated at the end of the war to a farm in Colorado where they raised sugar beets for about a year. In 1946 they returned to their California ranch in Cressey.

Time spent in Livingston High School was a tedious, lingering pain for Pat. Academia had no appeal. After graduation, Pat enrolled in a series of schools—Mills College, Modesto Junior College and San Francisco State College. The latter was an eye-opener. The school offered an entrée into an exciting new world of contemporary music, dance and theater—life, thought Pat, did have some possibilities. With a new perspective and friends of like predilection, Pat spent pleasurable days making the scene in a fresh, creative setting. But in time, parental "wisdom and guidance" forced Pat to think about a career. She then matriculated in art at San Jose State University, graduated in 1954 and did postgraduate work in education. Perhaps she would teach, she thought.

Pat Suzuki. *Looking at You* album cover. 1961. Courtesy of Ken Yamada.

During her senior year at San Jose State, Pat began singing in earnest, delivering pop and standard jazz tunes with style and sophistication. "My vocal heroes then were Billie [Holiday], Peggy Lee and Teddi King; the Hi-Lo's [a male vocal jazz quartet] was another favorite. My first paid gig took place in a small club in nearby Mountain View. I was accompanied by a quartet. Earned $30.00 that night!" It was an exhilarating experience. Singing in an intimate setting with a swinging backup *felt good;* it afforded a sense of satisfaction and direction in her life.

After achieving her academic goals at San Jose State College, Pat moved to New York City, where she worked at Macy's with plans to go to Europe—her doting father promised her a trip. On a lark, she auditioned for a walk-on part in a play, *Teahouse of the August Moon.* To her surprise, she was hired for the national touring company. Pat embarked with the troupe on a circuit of cities which led to Seattle, Washington, where the company was booked for a three-week engagement at the Moore Theater.

John Voorhees, a writer for the *Seattle Post-Intelligencer,* wrote in the June 17, 1955, issue:

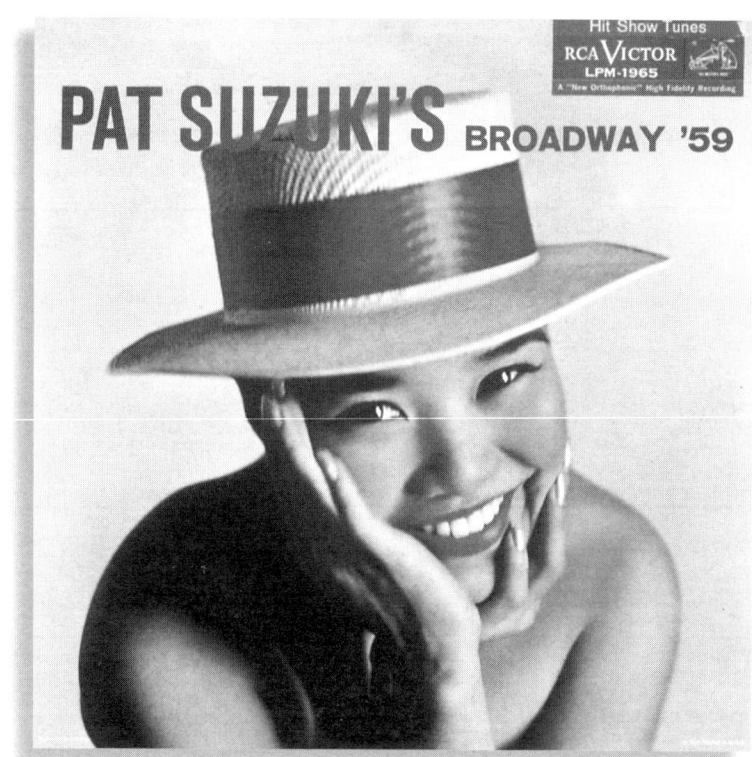

Pat Suzuki. *Broadway '59* album cover. 1959. Courtesy of Ken Yamada.

> ...and there's another member of the cast who'd much rather sing than act—pretty Pat Suzuki. Pat has only a small role in "Teahouse," but the theater is not her cup of tea. She'd rather sing. In every town that "Teahouse" has played, Pat has sought out little clubs with combos, sometimes sang a few choruses just for fun. In Seattle Pat did just that at the Colony where many of the cast go after each show. To make a long story short, Pat had trouble leaving the

bandstand because the crowd kept insisting on more songs. Now every time she returns to the Colony, everyone who has heard her sing won't let her leave without singing again. This reviewer heard Pat the other night and really believes she's got a future. Pat has a soothing, warm voice with a real feeling for the kind of standards and pop tunes she sings. Pat does that thing that divides the singers from the mere noisemakers—she understands the lyrics and makes them mean something. This listener got the same kind of feeling from Pat's singing as from that of Ella Fitzgerald or Jeri Southern. Let's hope many Seattleites who like the kind of singing Pat does so ably will be lucky enough to hear Pat before she moves on to charm the ears of listeners in some other city.

Voorhees's column proved to be a harbinger. Norm Bobrow, the Colony Club's owner, offered Pat a contract to sing that summer of 1955. A long-term association with the club followed. It was time for Pat to direct her energies into her true love—time to pay her dues as a cabaret singer.

George Tsuchiya remembers going to the Colony Club with his wife, his brother-in-law Shiro Yamaguchi and his wife. It was a quiet weeknight—just a few couples on the town. Upon completion of a bright first set, Pat invited the audience to dance to the music of her backup band which was playing an up-tempo tune. The Tsuchiya party remained seated, not dancing. Pat approached them with her bubbly self and greeted them. A brief exchange of impersonal chitchat followed: "What's your name?" "Where are you from?" etc. Again, Pat invited them to dance. The Nisei couples apologized for their restraint, "The music is just a little bit too fast for us, Pat."

Pat directed the band to "play something schmaltzy for my friends here." It did; whereupon the Nisei couples moved onto the small dance floor. The irony of this situation was that Yamaguchi, a veteran of the Japanese American 100th Infantry Battalion, had lost a leg in combat in Italy. He was still unsteady on his feet with an artificial leg, and therefore refrained from dancing to the livelier up-tempo tune.

It was in the Colony Club, in the summer of 1957, that Bing Crosby first heard Pat sing. Crosby was so charmed that he returned three times. He wrote the following notes for Pat's first record album produced by Vik Records—*The Many Sides of Pat Suzuki with Henri René and his Orchestra:*

Halfway between the chatter and the chateaubriand, the lights dimmed in their traditional theatrical fashion, the pianist played an arpeggio and a voice came zooming out of a half-pint gamin like a great locomotive chase. It roared up the trestle against the walls—and I surrendered. Pat sings anything from jazz to light opera. Great bet for the big time. I really mean that. The summer of '57 was the time the voice of Pat Suzuki happened to me. May this be the time Pat Suzuki happens to you.

[Signed] Bing Crosby

Pat Suzuki. *The Many Sides of Pat Suzuki* album cover. 1957. Courtesy of Ken Yamada.

After three years and more than two thousand consecutive appearances at the Colony Club, opportunities for other gigs opened up. Suzuki accepted engagements at the Arctic Club in Vancouver, the Fairmont Hotel in San Francisco, the Flamingo in Las Vegas and the Black Orchid in Chicago. She was the well-deserved winner of the Downbeat Magazine National Disc Jockey Poll as "America's best new female singer of 1958."

On opening night, December 1, 1958, at the Saint James Theater in New York, Pat, playing the part of Linda Low in the original Rodgers and Hammerstein musical *Flower Drum Song,* brought down the house singing "I Enjoy Being A Girl."[35] Working under the direction of Gene Kelly, Pat delighted audiences in the show, which successfully ran for no less than six hundred performances. During the *Flower Drum* run in New York City, Pat acquired another "feather in her cap" in July 1959—she sang her spirited vocals at the prestigious Newport Jazz Festival. Jimmy Jones, the highly respected African American jazz pianist, generously stocked with swingin' big band charts, accompanied Pat.[36]

During the 1960s, after *Flower Drum Song* closed, Suzuki performed in the drama/comedy play *Owl and the Pussycat.* This road company toured Chicago, St. Louis and several Canadian cities—a successful engagement which continued for seven months. Another stage production touring Canadian cities followed, with Suzuki playing the lead in *Irma La Douce.*

Also, prior to *Flower Drum,* Pat Suzuki had "burst upon the nation's television audiences with phenomenal impact" on the *Jack Paar Show,* the *Ed Sullivan Show,* the *Pat Boone Show* and the *George Gobel Show.* One of the bigger, unforgettable events in Pat's career took place during the celebration commemorating John F. Kennedy's 1961 presidential inauguration. She appeared in a major production headlined by Frank Sinatra with eminent guests such as the acclaimed Nat "King" Cole and prolific lyricist Sammy Cahn.

During the time she performed in clubs and in musicals, Pat Suzuki recorded for RCA Victor several successful albums: *Miss Pony Tail,* 1958; *Broadway '59,* 1958-59 and *Looking at You,* 1961. These recordings included great American standards, of course: "Star Dust," "As Time Goes By," "I'll Never Smile Again," "Solitude," "My Funny Valentine," etc.

In 1974 Pat Suzuki played a dramatic role in Chinese American playwright Frank Chin's *Year of the Dragon,* a story about the disintegration of a Chinese family in San Francisco. It opened at the American Place Theater in New York City on May 22, 1974. Suzuki enacted the part of Hyacinth Eng, a youngish Chinese American mother in her middle '50s—"maniacally efficient, practical and irrational." The stage production was followed by a PBS television version of the *Year of the Dragon,* featuring George Takei in the lead. Suzuki repeated her "Ma" role in this production.

Fast forward to June 7, 1994—Pat Suzuki sings in the Long Beach Civic Light Opera Company production of *South Pacific.* Nisei fans flock to see the show—to witness, not so much the romanticized musical itself but the "resurrection" of Pat Suzuki. And they were rewarded with absolute satisfaction.

Somewhat apprehensive that her voice might not fulfill the rigid requirements of a live performance on stage, Suzuki nevertheless con-

Flower Drum Song Playbill. December, 1958. Courtesy of Pat Suzuki.

Pat Suzuki. Rehearsal for John F. Kennedy Presidential Inauguration. 1961. Photo courtesy of Pat Suzuki.

sented to the role of Bloody Mary following a successful audition with musical director Jack Lee, who had worked with her in 1956 in the Kansas City production of *The Wizard of Oz.* She reportedly took the gig because the site of the production was a relatively small city and the term of the production run was limited. She needn't have been concerned.

When Pat appeared on stage, the audience greeted her with loud cheers. Her solos were a moving "Bali Hai" and a bright, light-hearted "Happy Talk." Two excitable showgoers who had heard Pat sing many years ago in *Flower Drum* exclaimed, "Pat carried the show! She sang just two songs, but stole all her scenes. Her acting and stage presence were great…much better than the lead. Pat's voice is still incredible—clear and full. We were thrilled!" *South Pacific* ran from May 5 through May 22, 1994, at the Long Beach Terrace Theater.

In a telephone interview five months following her appearance in *South Pacific,* I asked Suzuki how she felt in retrospect about her recent stage appearance in Long Beach. "It was regional," she replied. When pressed to explain what she meant by that, she implied that it was "nothing to write home about"—no big deal. But she did discover that "if I don't abuse my voice, it still will do what I want it to do. It's like an automobile engine; you keep it well-maintained, oiled, and you won't blow a gasket or something."

Would she want to resume singing professionally? "What I really want to do now is work in some job that involves art. I've enjoyed painting for a number of years and it would be great to be in the art business, whatever that may be. One thing I know is that I don't want to sit in an art gallery waiting for customers to come in. You go to church, don't you, George…say a little prayer for me."

Fast forward again, this time to March 8, 1997: Alcazar Theater, San Francisco. A benefit concert for Nihonmachi Legal Outreach—*PAT SUZUKI RETURNS!* About four hundred, mostly Nisei, gather to hear the Japanese American musical icon. They're curious to see how well Pat had weathered the effects of time. Can she still sing? How does she look? Local citizens had no inkling of her current status as a vocalist. She lives in New York City, isolated from the West Coast community, and hadn't performed in years in the San Francisco area. Furthermore, according to advance publicity, she had not appeared anywhere in solo concert in twenty-five years!

A swingin' thirty-minute set of big-band charts by the J-Town Jazz Ensemble opened the show. Pat followed in a well-modulated singing voice unmarked by time, moving freely and confidently onstage. She was backed ably by Barry Levitte, her pianist-arranger; with Richard Girard playing lyrical string bass; and tasteful drums by David Rokeach. Overcoming initial technical problems in sound, Pat Suzuki sang a diverse program of charming standards, novelty songs and, of course, her signature song, a jazzed-up version of "I Enjoy Being A Girl" from *Flower Drum Song*. People in wonderment asked: "How does Pat manage to retain such a powerful, emotive voice…after all these years? And she looks great!" The standing ovation and calls for encores were ample evidence of the audience's elated response to Pat's return. They had not been disappointed.

Many years ago, Michi Kobi, Nisei writer, a resident of New York City, declared: "Pat Suzuki was obviously our first comet to soar on the theatrical-musical stage!"

Addendum, March 8, 1997: The comet returns, burning brightly!

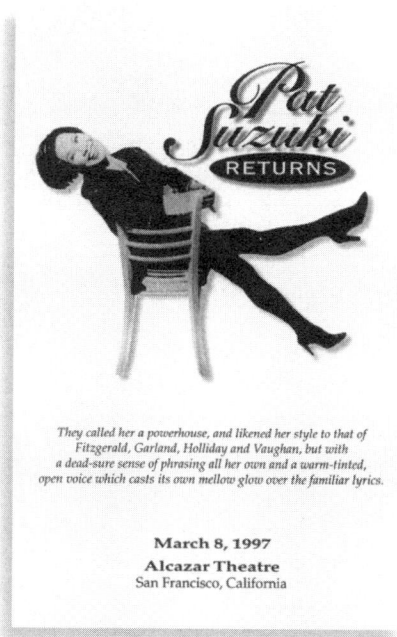

Pat Suzuki Returns concert program cover. San Francisco. 1997. Alberto Rizzo photo. Courtesy of Nihonmachi Legal Outreach.

---

34 Big bands under the leadership of Lionel Hampton, Count Basie and Duke Ellington were the few exceptions.

35 *Flower Drum* was not her musical stage début. In 1957 she had played the part of Dorothy in *The Wizard of Oz* at the Starlite Theater in Kansas City.

36 Jimmy Jones was reputedly Sarah Vaughan's favorite accompanist in the '50s.

George Yoshida. San Francisco. 1995. Michelle Deng photo

CHAPTER 6

Reflections on the Beat

I dance the only dance—life.
I move in time with all of life's rhythms that
permeate my body, my soul—
sometimes awkward, sometimes flowing, sometimes in despair…
But I shall dance through the curtain
mostly with joy!

—GEORGE YOSHIDA, 1982

As I gathered material for this book, collecting the fragile remembrances of Nisei music makers, I uncovered a few stories that didn't fit neatly into a historical framework but seemed too important to lose. Much of our love of the music is tied to our vision as Nisei, to our unique culture, to our spirituality—a reaction to our personal histories growing up in America as Americans. What follows are vignettes that provide some insight into the music makers of my generation—men and women who relished playing and singing pop songs of the swing era. Jazz whispered in my ear as I wrote this book, and here is a look "inside" three Nisei jazz enthusiasts. Reflections on how the love of jazz is ageless; once bitten, the passion is with you forever.

GEORGE "YAMI" YAMASAKI

Ask any Nisei, "Do you know Yami?" The answer, probably, would be, "Yeah, but which one?" You see, there's a mess of "Yamis" out there. For some reason, among the Nisei, nicknames were quite common—often derived from contractions of Japanese names. Anyway, the Yami I'm talking about, **George Yamasaki,** lives in San Francisco—about seventy-two years old. Don't know much about his family, but I do know he worked in the Postal Service and is retired. Yami first played clarinet in Commerce High School. He played in the So-Nichi Marching Band in 1939 and, just for a short while, in a dance band about the same time. He insists, "I'm not a musician! I was just a body; they needed guys and I was forced to play…just a body."

Not so. Yamasaki is, I insist, a *true* musician. He grew up absorbing the sounds of his time—jazz and swing, combos and big-band music—and he loved it all deeply. His heroes were black saxophone players: Coleman Hawkins, Lester Young, Johnny Hodges and Willie Smith.

While stationed at Camp Lee, Virginia, Yami befriended an ex-Benny Goodman sideman—call him Frank—who had played the Second Alto Sax chair. Frank and Yami were among several hundred GIs who gathered to hear Woody Herman's Herd, considered then in 1945 to be the hottest jazz band around, featuring Ralph Burns, piano; Flip Phillips, tenor; Pete Condoli, trumpet; Chubby Jackson, bass and Dave Tough, drums—all prominent jazz stars. Frank had urged Yami earlier, "Come on, man…we gotta catch Woody doin' Dizzy's kick!" (Yami explained that "Dizzy's kick" was in reference to Dizzy Gillespie's role as a pioneer proponent of bebop.)

It was the first time Yami heard a big band playing bebop—"Apple Honey" and "Northwest Passage." Says Yami, "Woody knocked me out…it was so good. I could really dig that stuff!" After the concert, behind the makeshift Army camp stage, Frank introduced Yami to Dave Tough, Woody Herman's drummer. Tough was smoking a joint. He offered Yami a taste. Yami took a light drag. (He hadn't tried it before and didn't want to offend the great drummer.) Yami says, "It doesn't do a thing for me." Frank suggests, "Pull in a lot of air when you inhale." Yami takes a couple more deep drags on the joint. In a short while, Yami goes, *"Gawd da-am!* Everything looks *beau-ti-ful!*—everything's *so gre-een!"*…so much for Yami's "Dave Tough story."

Postwar San Francisco jazz was great for Yami. He hung out at Jimbo's Bop City, the Town Club, Jack's Tavern and Club Alabam—all black joints in the Fillmore, where he joyfully caught many, many sessions featuring local musicians.

For a while, Yami with a few of his friends took ukulele lessons from Sho Ikemi, a genius on the ukulele from Hawaii, who also played upright bass and guitar. This group eventually formed a Hawaiian music ensemble and enjoyed making music and playing happy tunes for their many friends who were truly impressed with the band's enthusiasm. Moreover, Yami learned about chords—their significance in music, especially in jazz improvisations. He learned about the circle of fifths in musical chord progressions. Says Yami, "Now I understand jazz…how important it is to study music. I can really appreciate good musicians now."

Yamasaki's interest in music, especially jazz, is deep-seated—"I like music I can stamp my feet to!" He was curious about music and his curiosity has not diminished in the least in all these years. He listens to music; he keeps up with jazz—the old classics and the contemporary. George Yamasaki is a true musician.

And I suspect there are quite a few other "Yamis" still out there!

KAZU MARUOKA

Sometime ago I asked my soul brother **Kazu Maruoka** to write a few words about what music means to him. Before I describe his response, I need to explain the "soul brother" bit. You see, he and I share with equal intensity a common set of values and interests. Neither of us are sports fanatics—not adept at playing or interested in "who won the game." We shed tears rather easily; have grave concerns about the many injustices on this planet. We enjoy reading books and appreciate good jokes. We are close to being obsessed with jazz—the beautiful swing of Count Basie's band sends us into overpowering ecstasy!

Back to Kazu. He started his lengthy career in music on clarinet in the Roosevelt Junior High School orchestra, San Francisco. He remembers his excitement playing pieces such as "Come Back to Erin" and the "Russian Sailor's Dance." World War II put a stop to this newfound diversion, but Kazu's initial musical experiences and radio broadcasts of groups such as Lu Watters and the Yerba Buena Jazz Band provided the catalyst for him to maintain his interest in music. Although there was no music activity for Kazu in Tanforan "Assembly" Center, his eventual relocation to Topaz Detention Camp presented opportunities to experiment and to indulge in music. He discovered the jazz of Louis Armstrong, Coleman Hawkins and Bunny Berigan. He marveled at Harry James's trumpet playing; the trumpet became the focus for his budding aspirations. Playing gigs with the Jivesters and the Rhythm Kings enabled him to develop both in technique and musical concepts.

Upon his return in 1946 to San Francisco after a three-year detention in Topaz, Maruoka enrolled in San Francisco State College and earned a teaching credential in elementary education. In 1950 he began his outstanding career in education—the first native San Francisco Nisei to teach in the San Francisco Unified School District.[37]

As time went by, Maruoka's interest in jazz continued at a high pitch. In subsequent years, he experimented with different instruments—the trumpet, valve-trombone, vibraphone, upright bass and electric bass. It's been years since I last heard Kaz play trumpet, valve-trombone or vibes, but I do remember how well he played.

On the job, Maruoka could play any tune, any tempo, called by the leader. I have never heard him complain; he was truly a professional. Our association during the past few years when he played the bass and I the drums next to him has been pure joy—he swings!

Today, Maruoka rarely picks up any instruments; instead, he indulges in a great deal of listening. He also composes love songs and marches on the computer. As to what music means to him today, he says, "I never have considered myself to be a musician nor have I felt comfortable being referred to as one. Although the spirit [of a musician] is contained in me, the discomfort arises from feelings that have to do with questions about my self-esteem, self-confidence and absence of formal training [in music].

"I must express my gratitude to people who knowingly or inadvertently helped me through some difficult times via music. Not being athletically inclined as a teenager in Topaz, I sought relief from my adolescent angst and discovered my righteous path—playing jazz. I thank those who organized music ensembles and invited me to join them. I thank skilled and experienced musicians who helped to whet my skills in instrumental technique and in conceptualizing the essence of jazz.

"The '70s were my most productive years as far as playing regularly from week to week—played bass in a combo led by Peter Damante. We played engagements in private homes, clubs, major hotels, restaurants—vantage points from which I indulged myself in observing people and places, from the ordinary to the elegant.

"I used to play one-hour gigs at the West Berkeley YMCA for their quarterly senior citizens birthday lunches. I drove all the way into Berkeley from Sonoma (sixty miles one way) for those gigs…got $30.00 or so. Obviously, money was not the attraction. In retrospect I feel that I endured the tedious and time-consuming automobile journey because the gig provided me with the opportunity to play jazz with Vernell 'Mad Genius' Glenn, a two-fisted black piano player who was born in New Orleans back in June of 1917. 'Genius' can play beautiful ballads with poetic phrases…can make you cry. He could, as well, swing madly—approaching the climax of a tune, he'd go into a series of syncopated riffs that just wouldn't quit. It was pure jazz…pure pleasure!

"So there you are. From the time of my unstable adolescence in Topaz—when I felt as if I were falling through the cracks—into young adulthood, I was fortunate that along the way were supportive Nisei who helped me by encouraging my interest in music, even to this day. Music helped me to reach outward, to establish contact with people of all races and ethnicity. Specifically, playing jazz with Vernell or Gladys Palmer or John Marabuto, jazz pianist extraordinaire, was wonderful; but just being with them evoked a sense of love which transcended the music we played. The person became important… music enhanced the relationship. Music leads me into the soul of others. It is a hub which radiates and fosters love."

Late one December evening in 1996, several years after the above interview, I talked with Kazu on the phone. I found him in an excited state, full of renewed energy. He'd started playing music again. "I think it was Bernard Shaw who said: 'We don't stop

Kazu Maruoka and Vernell Glenn (foreground). Berkeley, Calif. 1996. Photo courtesy of Kazu Maruoka.

playing because we get old; we grow old because we stop playing,'" explained Kazu. "I really believe in Shaw's concept about aging. Since last spring, when I met a friend who plays classical cello, I've been biz-zeeeee. Together with her, a fine guitarist and my upright bass, we've been rehearsing jazz standards in the fashion of a supper club trio. The musical interplay among us is mainly experimental, with many exciting avenues to explore. I've also resumed playing my valve trombone—weekly rehearsals for concerts and parades with the Sonoma Home Town Band. We sound very much like a high-school band, but that's OK…I get a kick out of playing and hanging out with some great people. What else…oh yeah, I'm back to playing casuals…playing old favorites in convalescent homes, senior residences and fraternal lodges. These are volunteer jobs for very appreciative audiences. Gigs at San Francisco hotels and restaurants are few, but always a gas. One more thing…I've enrolled in a Music Improvisation class at Santa Rosa J.C., three days a week plus lots of woodshedding.

"George, I'm two years shy of seventy years, but I'm staying young, deeply immersed more than ever in music…and meeting new folks, enjoying their company. Hope my chops don't give out."

ABOUT CUTTING OFF ONE'S ARM

Tad Ishida, a San Francisco Nisei in his 70s, would now rather discuss cardiology than music. His trumpet playing began in junior high school when he was required to join either the choir or the band. "I tried the choir for a few days, but too many girls; so I joined the band. I was given a trumpet, and through the encouragement of an excellent teacher, developed a lifelong appreciation of the trumpet and big-band sounds. I still have my old King [trumpet] I played in dance bands years ago. It's tucked away somewhere down in the basement. I still can finger 'In the Mood' on the valves of my trumpet, but I can't play it anymore…and I don't."

When asked why he keeps his horn, he replied, somewhat wistfully, "I'm afraid to throw it away."

Afraid? Why this element of fear? Might it lie in the fact that his trumpet symbolically embodies a very significant phase of his life—his unfettered youth, good times, a period of creative energy and spiritual growth?

Many other Nisei have their own "dusty old King" sitting around somewhere—if not a trumpet, a dried-out clarinet reed, a pair of splintered drum sticks, a favorite '40s melody floating around in their subconscious. And they can't let go! Would you cut off your arm? Just goes to show you that once stung by the jazz bug, you're gone. It's a life sentence! And, moreover, who knows, *up there,* there just might be a jazz harp to mess with and some great sessions to dig.

In the early '50s, I assembled a makeshift drum kit from assorted sources and took a few lessons from amiable jazz drummer Earl Watkins. In 1956 I became a member of San Francisco Musicians Union Local #669, a black union, which convened mandatory monthly meetings on Sundays at the Union Hall. These were cordial social gatherings—friendly handshakes and much laughter—which led to delightful associations with seasoned jazz players such as Gladys Palmer and Vernell Glenn, piano; David Lott and Charlie Oden, bass; Ike Bell, trombone; George Fleming, trumpet; and Pee Wee Claybrook, tenor. Unfortunately, #669 meetings were discontinued when Local #669 and Local #6, the white union, were merged by mutual consent on April 1, 1960.

Musicians' Union card. 1957. Courtesy of George Yoshida.

In 1952, upon graduation from the University of California, Berkeley, I began my teaching career at Washington Elementary School in Berkeley. In the mid-'60s Principal Herb Wong, a jazz advocate/journalist, initiated and developed an innovative, stimulating jazz education program for the youngsters at Washington. Through Wong's efforts, a series of concerts in the school auditorium introduced pupils to the stirring sounds of live jazz. Dig: the Oscar Peterson Trio; the Roland Kirk Quartet; Phil Woods on alto sax; Vi Redd on alto sax and vocals; and the Washington Wailers, a.k.a. the New Deal Society Orchestra. The latter was the Washington School faculty jazz ensemble which included teachers Manny Funk, Richard Hadlock and Bob Houlehan, saxes; Phil Hardymon, trumpet; Dick Whittington, piano; myself on drums; and augmented by musician friends.

Topping the above performances was the friendly visit on October 16, 1969, of Duke Ellington to the Washington School playground as children excitedly waved placards and shouted:

Left: Gladys Palmer. Berkeley, Calif. 1987. Photo courtesy of George Yoshida.

"We dig the Duke!" This event was the culmination of several days of preparation for Ellington's arrival. His classic recordings were played in classrooms; his orchestra, its members and instrumentation, and simple elements of jazz were discussed. Children drew water colors of what jazz meant to them. A multimedia presentation conceived by Phyllis Richmond of Washington School incorporated the pupils' art and was utilized as the stage backdrop for the Ellington Festival scheduled for that evening at the Berkeley Community Theater. The concept of the festival, "The Magic of the Duke and Berkeley's Children," was initiated by Principal Wong in commemoration of the complete racial integration of Berkeley schools. The presence and majestic sounds of Ellington's gifted entourage (Cootie Williams, Cat Anderson, Lawrence Brown, Paul Gonsalves, Johnny Hodges, Harry Carney, Rufus Jones, et al.) that evening was a rare privilege. We dug the Duke; we loved him madly! In his book, *Music is My Mistress*, Ellington recalls that "the whole day really got to me."

The concert of pianist Oscar Peterson with Sam Jones on bass and Louis Hayes, drums, took place on October 27, 1966. In addition to the trio's playing their standard repertoire, Peterson patiently explained to youngsters the rudiments of jazz rhythms and demonstrated theme and variations by playing "Twinkle, Twinkle Little Star," the simple children's tune—playing it "straight" at first, and then swinging and improvising the melody for several choruses. After their performance in the school auditorium, back in the classroom, I asked my 4th/5th graders to

Oscar Peterson Trio. Washington School, Berkeley, Calif. October 27, 1996. Left to right: Louis Hayes, Sam Jones, Oscar Peterson. Photo courtesy of George Yoshida.

CHAPTER SIX   275

Oscar Peterson. Washington School, Berkeley, Calif. October 27, 1966. Photo courtesy of George Yoshida.

write, either in prose or poetry, how they felt listening to the music.

Karen Barrett wrote:

Oscar, move your fingers faster and faster,
Oscar, play chromatic scales in tunes,
Oscar, play that jazzie jazz!
Oscar, play before boss soul bosses--
Play like you're the boss.
Oscar, Oscar, play the piano,
Play as never before!

Claire Brown's response:

We were going to the auditorium to listen to the Oscar Peterson trio perform. I felt real excited... it sent a shiver of excitement down my back when they started. The piano sounded like a chorus of birds singing variations of tunes and the bass like the slow thumping of some heavy animals' footsteps. The drums sounded like a housewife working. I noticed that every once in a while they would bring out their handkerchiefs to wipe their brows. I looked over toward Louis Hayes, the drummer. He sat there expressionless and still, and seemed to be almost mad at O.P. [Oscar Peterson] for having to make them perform for "those awful kids"... [yet] he played with ease and hardly looked at what he was doing. He usually had to play the softest of all and just keep the beat. I think he was about the best in the group.

Children listening to the Oscar Peterson Trio. Washington School, Berkeley, Calif. October 27, 1966. George Yoshida photo.

David Miyasaki, 4th grade, wrote:

The Drummer
Louis, Louis, go and play,
Go and play the swingingest jazz around.
Play, I say, play that wild jazz,
Go play those drums!
Make them sound like cannons,
Like the roaring sea, like thunder!
"Boom, bang! Boom, bang!"
"Clang, bash! Clang, bash!"
Louis, Louis, go and play,
Go and play the swingingest jazz around!

Susan Shinagawa. San Rafael, Calif. 1986. George Yoshida photo.

Randy Senzaki. Oakland, Calif. May 1984. Photo courtesy of George Yoshida.

Many, many Nisei in their retirement years discovered to their delight the joys of ballroom dancing. No longer having the responsibilities of child-rearing, they plunged into this new diversion with a vengeance. Nisei dance clubs flourished. Anticipating and attending parties with other organizations in nearby towns resurrected pleasant emotions associated with earlier, youthful days of social interaction—it was fun, once again, "to dress up" and "to party." In response to this dance craze, I organized sometime around 1975 "Sentimental Journey," a quartet, with Randy Senzaki, tenor; James Leiby, piano; Bill Carpender, bass; and myself on drums. Susan Shinagawa soon came aboard with her free-wheeling jazz vocals. This was the beginning of many pleasant evenings of standard ballads, light swing and a bit of cha-cha-cha.

A few years ago an acquaintance who plays the piano asked, "Hey, George, why do you play the drums? You can't play musical notes on the drums—no melody, no harmony—and you're never in the spotlight. No one really watches or listens to you; you're always hidden in the back. And you repeat and repeat the same old beat all

J-Town Jazz Ensemble, conceived and directed by George Yoshida. San Francisco. February 1995. Left to right, front row: George Yamasaki, Clay Yoshida, Paul Yonemura, George Nobori, Ron Fujie, David Uyeno, Jan Yonemoto, John Kiyasu. Second row: Tony Vella, Vernon Miyata, David Umemoto, Andrew Luey. Third row: Bob Henderson, Gene Ravaglioli, Mack Horton, Yone Fukui. Andy Nozaka photo. Courtesy of George Yoshida.

night long. What a boring instrument! Why in the world do you play drums?"

To be honest, I've asked myself "Why?" many times in the past. Often, I felt like giving it up. Especially when the gig was over and the others had packed up and left the hall to stop off somewhere for a late snack. All alone, I would take down and pack up my drum set—cymbals, snare drum, tom-toms, bass drum, cymbal and drum stands, drum seat, drumsticks and wire brushes. All to be hauled to my pickup truck. And, then, home where the unloading commences again. It's exhausting work and the load gets increasingly heavier each year! Unlike merchandise inventory which is "first in-first out," for drummers, it's "first in-*last out*." (Lester Young, the immortal tenor sax player, was purported to have given up drums for a tenor sax because all the good-looking chicks left early with horn players while he was still packing up.) So why in the world do I want to play drums?

Junius Courtney Orchestra. Oakland, Calif. ca. 1970. Left to right: David Lott, George Yoshida, Alan Hoeshen, Junius Courtney.

I feel a drummer's basic responsibilities are to keep consistent time, to lead the band, and to listen to other members of the group in order to enhance the musicality of the ensemble and of soloists. Another more subtle, but equally important function, if not the most important factor in jazz drumming, I believe, is creating and sustaining the element of swing.[38] Fortunate are those who can feel it in their bones—and it is *in the bones*. Moreover, implicit in the word "swing" is physical movement. Swing invites you, urges you to move—to snap your fingers, to nod your head, to rock your shoulders, to tap your toes, to loosen your knees, to shake your "bootie"—to dance!

It is truly difficult to describe the emotional and physical gratification I experience when making music with others who embrace very similar, if not identical, concepts in jazz—people I can groove with. The joy comes from a magical chemistry that occurs when like human beings join together to listen and play in concert with each other. It is often an occasion of serendipity; there is no assurance of its happening each time musicians converge. Emotionally, it can be a sensation of undiluted rapture. Physically, the rhythm and sounds of the music *naturally* move you. Behind the drum set I become a dancer moving synchronously with the music. Being in the groove means that there is movement in my center, my hands and arms, feet and legs, my shoulder and back, my bobbing head balanced atop a supple neck. Deep down inside, the soul dances, too!

Most cultures have their drum and dance—for celebration, for joy, for healing. I embrace that basic humanness. *Drum/dance, drum/dance, drum/dance, drum/dance*—the life beat flows magnificently in us all. And that's why I drum (and suffer the indignities of setting up and breaking down my drum set).

MY SPIRITUALITY IS...

About twenty years ago, Bill Miller, who was the pastor of the Lake Park United Methodist Church in Oakland, California, approached me and said: "George, tell me about your spirituality." I don't recall what my response was at the time, but if I were asked today, I would explain to Bill that my spirituality lies somewhere in the realm of music—in jazz.

I define "spirit" as the catalyst which activates a person's life—the force which animates human matter and its body systems. The presence of spirit or the lack of it determines who is or is not alive.

My personal spirit is embodied in the divine swing of Count Basie's band, in the provocative sounds of Duke Ellington's jazz, in Jimmy Witherspoon's soulful blues shout propelled fiercely by Ben Webster's goading tenor sax and in Mahalia Jackson's sweet crooning of "Silent Night" in three-quarter time. This, then, is my spirituality from which energy flows to whomever I meet and whatever I do.

At seventy-five, I do not feel any age—"There is no age in spirit."

A PILGRIMAGE

In June of 1993, four hundred anxious Americans of Japanese ancestry embarked on a pilgrimage to the long-unoccupied site of the Topaz Detention Camp in Utah. In the dusty, desolate brushland, former citizens of Topaz, their offspring and friends spent time in remembrance of the brutal ordeal. They uncovered archeological evidence of the past in pieces of broken crockery, rusty nails and barbed wire. But the musical strains of saxophones and muted trumpets of camp dance bands past were sweet sounds forever lost—diffused into the dry, hot winds of the forlorn Utah prairie.

Anthony Brown's African-EurAsian Eclipse. San Francisco. February 1997. Left to right: Liu Qi-Chao, Wayne Wallace, Mark Izu, Francis Wong, Anthony Brown. Brian Akizuki photo.

Yet popular music of Japanese Americans has endured. Pioneer Nisei music—a humble, barely passable replication of professional dance bands and jazz soloists—has evolved into a '90s model of Pan Asian/African American jazz. Contemporary Asian American artists express in their compositions and performances musical concepts in harmony with unflappable ethnic pride, integrity and exceptional skill—an extension of the original '20s thread that has turned silken as it continues to unravel.

The beat goes on...

* * * * *

37 Because of racial discrimination in the hiring policy of many public school districts, Japanese Americans earlier found difficulty in obtaining employment as public school teachers.

38 Defining "swing" is difficult. Swing involves the ear, instinct and soul. It has to do with intuitive feeling and behavior. For drummers, it has to do, in part, with the left foot pumping the pedal of the sock or high-hat cymbals to create "chick sounds" to accent the second and fourth beats in each 4/4 measure. It also has to do with the way in which the large ride cymbals or the high-hats are repeatedly struck with drum sticks or the snare drum stroked with wire brushes in sustained, propelling rhythmic sequences.

CHAPTER SIX

DANCE BANDS & PERSONNEL

Note: Dance-band personnel frequently change during the life of the band. In each group below, there may be more names listed than actual members constituting the ensemble at any specified period of time. These listings are by no means complete for all bands. Some names were not included because of lack of information. Abbreviations are as follows: **ba**=string bass, **bj**=banjo, **d**=drums, **g**=guitar, **l**=leader, **p**=piano, **s**=saxophone and/or clarinet, **sp**=sousaphone, **t**=trumpet, **tb**=trombone, **vi**=violin, **vo**=vocals.

BERKELEY YMWBA ORCHESTRA, Berkeley, California, 1927—Willie Ito (l); Charles Kaneko, Al Kosakura, Shigeru Nakamura, Hisashi Kaneko, Shigeo Kawakami, Mr. Miyamoto, Masaki Tono, Martin Akiyama (s); Dick Fujii (tuba); Takahashi sisters, Mitsue Matsuda, Takeo Fujii (vi); Dick Mansho (p); Taihei Tsuda (d); Hatsuko Muramoto Hoshi, Tomiko Harano Kosakura (vo).

CLUB HARMONY ORCHESTRA, a.k.a. LOS ANGELES MELODIANS, Los Angeles, California, 1933—Akira Ohno (l, g); George Saito, Mits Aiso, Mas Manbo, George Abe, Sus Chikami, George Igawa (s); Ernie Arima, Hajimu Masuda (t); George Sasaki (tb); Mary Kato (p); George Kitahara (bj); Joe Shimada (d), Joe Sakai (vi, ba).

DENSONEERS, a.k.a. D-ELEVENS, Jerome Detention Center, Arkansas, 1942—Frank Tashima (l,s); Mackay Yoshimura, Sonny Nishimoto, Tom Nakamichi (s); Buddy Hirasuna, Yasu Chono, Jimmy Hirasuna (t); Terry Chono (tb); George Nakatani, Fred Harada (vi); Haru Yoshikawa Goya (p); Sam Seno (g); Hank Yoshikawa (d); Misa Hatakeda Asakawa, Eddie Funahashi, Bill Nikaido (vo).

DOWN BEATS, Tule Lake Detention Camp, California, 1942—Woody Ichihashi (l); George Nakao, Tosh Makishima, Hayao Motoyama, Al Nitta (s); Frank Suzuki, Norman Ishimoto (t); Sam Himoto (tb); Richard Muraoka (g); Sam Mayeda (d); Don Johnson (ba); Riki Matsufuji (l, ba, vo); Mabel Sugiyama Eto (p).

EAGER BEAVERS, Ft. Snelling, Minneapolis, Minnesota, 1945—James Araki (l, s); Tosh Makishima, Tom Sasaki, George Yoshida (s); George Hara (tb); Hiro Goto, Frank Suzuki, Yone Fukui, Shig Yamaki (t); Roy Endo (p); Larry Tamanaha (g); Yosh Migaki (d); Harold Noguchi (l,vo); Tak Shindo (mgr).

GEORGE IGAWA BAND, Heart Mountain Detention Camp, Wyoming, 1943—George Igawa (l, s); George Azuma, Susumu Chikami, Tetsu Bessho, James Toyama, Harry Takamura, Kenneth Oku (s); Yoneo Fukui, Frank Hirahara, Max Koga, Tomo Fukui, Walt Hayami (t); Yutaka Yamamoto, Tami Hirashiki (tb); Eiko Watanabe, Haruko Satow (p); Alfred Tanaka (ba); Joy Takéshita, Takako Kunimatsu, June Yoshino (vo).

HARMONAIRES, Puyallup "Assembly" Center, Washington, & Minidoka Detention Camp, Idaho, 1942-43—Art Koichi Hayashi (l); Thomas Sasaki, George Ogata, Yoshio Tomita, Kaoru Kitayama, Tosh Hori (s); Terry Kumagai, Masao Tomita, Henry Suzuki (t); Roy Yoshitomi (tb); Joe Owaki (d); Yoichi Ito (g); Louis Sato (p); Chickie Ishihara White (vo).

J-TOWN JAZZ ENSEMBLE, San Francisco, 1997—George Yoshida, (l,d); Yoné Fukui, Bob Henderson, Mack Horton, Stuart Yasaki (t); Andrew Luey, Vernon Miyata, David Umemoto, Tony Vella (tb); Ron Fujie, John Kiyasu, George Nobori, David Uyeno, Jan Yonemoto (s); George Yamasaki (p); Clay Yoshida (b); Michael Sasaki (g); Paul Yonemura (d).

JAPANESE SANDMEN, Los Angeles, California, 1933—Charles Izumi (l,p); Mitsuya Yamaguchi, Hajimu Masuda (t); George Abe, Susumu Chikami (s); George Kitahara (bj); Tsuneo Tajima (sp); Joe Fullert (g); Joe Shimada (d, v); Mariko Takasu (v).

JIVE BOMBERS, Manzanar Detention Camp, California, 1943—Bill Wakatsuki (l,t); Bruce Kaji, Torao Kusaba (t); Henry Onishi, Yoshiteru Murakami, Yoshindo Shibuya, Gordon Sato (s); Roy Nakagawa, George Maeda (tb); Zush Matoba, Bob Honda (d); Kiyo Nishi Tanaka (p); Joe Sakai (ba); Joe Shikami (g); Kazuko Nagai, Lillian Uyemura, Machiko Sasaki, Junko Yoshimoto, Lillian Wakatsuki (vo).

JIVESTERS, Topaz Detention Camp, Utah, 1944—Takeshi Enomoto (l,s); Yutaka Yoshida, Ike Nakamura, Kazu Maruoka (t); I. Matsuhara (s); Ichiro Sasaki (d); Sadie Towata Tajima (p).

LOS ANGELES MELODIANS, 1933—See: CLUB HARMONY ORCHESTRA.

MIKADOS, Sacramento, California, 1926—See RICHARD'S ORIGINAL SYNCOPATERS.

MIKADOS OF SWING, Seattle, Washington, 1939-41—Art Koichi Hayashi (l); Thomas Sasaki, George Ogata, Yoshio Tomita, Satoshi Shiota, Kaoru Kitayama, Tosh Hori (s); Terry Kumagai, Masao Tomita, Henry Suzuki (t); Roy Yoshitomi (tb); Kenny Nelson, Louis Sato (p); Joe Owaki (d); Katsuro Yamamoto (g); Chickie Ishihara (vo); Davis Hirahara (business agent).

MUSIC MAKERS, Amache Detention Camp, Granada, Colorado, 1943—Nob Kuwatani (l, s), Tad Kuwatani, Yutaka Kuwatani, Sherman Kishi, George Murakami (s); Joe Shiro, Leland Nakamura, Satoshi Tom Hirano (t); Yas Hirano, Bob Shiro (tb); Kitty Hirai (p); George Honda (d).

MUSIC MAKERS, Gila River Butte Detention Camp, Arizona, 1943—Tad Yamamoto (l,t); Hiroshi Goto, Ichiro Ino, Jack Kusaba, George Kikuchi, Paul Suzuki, Mas Tsuda (t); George Hara, Yosh Araki, Yoshio Migaki (tb); Haruo Hayashi, Tak Ogino, Ben Tamaki, James Araki, Joe Kobara (s); Suzi Tamura Ochi (p); Yosh Tsukahara, Mitsugi Kawamoto (d).

MUSIC MAKERS, Poston Detention Camp #1, Arizona, 1943—Hideo Kawano (l,t); Tom Murakami, Raymond Sunada (t); Shig Aramaki (tb); Yukio Miyamoto, Tug Tamaru, Paul Matsuda, George Yoshida (s); Frank Oshima (g); Jack Wada (p); Haruo Fujisawa (d).

NIGHT HAWKS, Sacramento, California, 1926—See RICHARD'S ORIGINAL SYNCOPATERS.

NISEI MELODIANS, Seattle, Washington, 1926—Sam Amano (l,d); Kelly Yamada, Shungi Kashiwagi, George Okada (s); Kiyoshi Tomita, Alex Jue (t); Fred Kaneko (tb); Kimi Takayoshi, Yurino Takayoshi, Shizue Takakoshi Hoshide (p); Frank Berkenkotter, Hatsuo Takahashi (bj); Hannah Kosaka (vi and vo).

NISEI MUSIC MAKERS, Chicago, Illinois, 1944—Tadashi Todd Yamamoto (l,s); Yuki Miyamoto, Tug Tamaru, George Yoshida (s); Mas Tsuda (t); Hideo Kawano (d); Louis Sato (ba); Eileen Nagatomo (p). [Incomplete: unnamed are 2 (t) and 2 (tb).]

NISEI SERENADERS, Los Angeles, California, 1950—Tetsu Bessho (l,s); Bruce Kaji, Walter Hayami, George Sumida (t); Roy Nakagawa, George Shimizu (tb); George Ozumi, Kay Noda, Gordon Sato (s); Joe Sakai (ba); James Araki, Mary Minato (p); Haruo Fujisawa (d); Lane Nakano (vo).

OAKLAND SONS AND DAUGHTERS ORCHESTRA, Oakland, California, 1926—Etchie Utsumi (l, bj); Hachiro Yuasa (s); Setsu Kitamura Akaba (v); Mary Ikeda (p); Noboru Idé (d).

OAKLAND YMWBA ORCHESTRA, Oakland, California, 1927—Willie Ito (l); Tony Yokomizo, Ikaru Mitoma, John Koyama, Mits Nakashima, Kenji Nakahara, Tad Tani, Shigenobu Kuramoto, Mitsuteru Nakashima (s); Fujio Okawa (t); Tad Hirota, George Nobori, John Kido, Iwajiro Hosano, Hajime Kawazoe (vi); Roy Akiyoshi (d); Maki Koyama Takahashi, Nobue Tani Yokomizo, Fumi Matsuda Kawamura, Mary Nobori Fujimoto (p).

POMONANS, Pomona "Assembly" Center, California, 1942—George Igawa (l,s); Tetsu Bessho, Toyo Niitake, Kenneth Oku (s); Yoneo Fukui, Tomo Fukui, Tom Hirashiki, Harry Niitake, Bill Furukawa (t); Frank Hayami (g); Eiko Watanabe (p); Jimmie Akiya (d); June Yoshino, Beverly Kawata, Mary Watanabe, Margaret Takaki, Tomiko Tsubochi (vo).

POSTON CAMP #2 BAND, Arizona, 1943—Helen Okamoto Iwanaga (l); Ben Tada, Tom Murakami, Raymond Sunada (t); Shig Aramaki (tb); Jimmy Izumizaki (s); John Kado (d); Harumi Nagase (p).

PRESIDIO DANCE BAND, Monterey, California, 1946—Yoshiteru Murakami (l), Torao Kusaba (t) 3 saxes, 2 trumpets, guitar, bass, piano, drums.

RHYTHM KINGS, Topaz Detention Camp, Utah, 1945—Ichiro Sasaki (l,g); Kazu Maruoka (t,s); Al Noda (tb); Hid Sakashita (ba); Tak Nakayama (d); Mrs. Maas (p).

RHYTHMAIRES, Poston Detention Camp #3, Arizona, 1943—Hiratsuka (l,s); Tom Koga, Sho Miyamoto, Nobi Nakamura (s); Sam Kitano, Joe Tsuchiyama, Miyamoto (t); Tom Miwa (tb); Kei Nakamura (d); Grace Tsuchiyama (p); Susumu Takao (vo).

RICHARD'S ORIGINAL SYNCOPATERS ORCHESTRA, a.k.a. MIKADOS, a.k.a. NIGHT HAWKS, Sacramento, California, 1926—Richard Okumoto (l, s); Richard Hamada (sp); Wesley Oyama (tb), Clem Oyama (t); Henry Tanaka, (d); Henry Onishi, Elizabeth Kozono (s); Raymond Okumoto (bj); "Smoky" Kumamoto (p); Bill Nikaido (vo).

ROSEBUD ORCHESTRA, San Francisco, California, 1926—Charlie Kikugawa (l, d, vo); Willie Ito, Paul Kato (s); Henry Ishihara (t,vi); George Mukai (bj); Yuki Morikawa Saka (p).

SAN FRANCISCO DANCE BAND, San Francisco, California, 1941—Mike Aoki, Al Kimoto (l); Louis Hirakawa, Matao Shigio, George Inouye (t); Mike Aoki, Dick Otsubo, Paul Higaki (tb); David Higaki, Jimmy Hiraoka, Al Kimoto, George Yamasaki (s); Jimmie Akiya (sp); Tad Sugiyama (p); Jimmy Kikugawa (d).

SAN FRANCISCO JAZZ BAND, San Francisco, California, 1934—Tamotsu Kikugawa (d); Harry Yasuda (t); Dick Motoyoshi, Ted Yasukawa, Toshi Suzuki (s); Yuki Morikawa (p), Pasa Suzuki (vo).

SAN FRANCISCO "SECOND GENERATION" ORCHESTRA, San Francisco, California, 1932—Willie Ito (l); Akira Omoto (t); M. Suzuki, Tom Matsuda (cl); Ted Yasukawa, Joe Morisuye (s); Willie Ito (tb); Tsuneo Fukushima (p); Tamotsu Kikugawa (d).

SAVOY FOUR, Topaz Detention Camp, Utah, 1944—Mabel Sugiyama Eto (p); Tom Nakashige (s); Frank Suzuki (t); Jimmy Kikugawa (d).

SHO TOKYANS, Los Angeles, California, 1936—George Igawa (l,s); Hajimu Masuda, Ernest Arima (t), Mas Manbo, Susumu Chikami (s); Joe Sakai (ba); Sachi Amano (p); Tamotsu Kikugawa (d), Aki Ohno, Tadashi Kamayatsu (g), Chiye Tawa (vo), Clara Suski, Louise Suski, Kimi Sakai (vo trio); Dolly Fujioka (vo in Japan); Hicky Noma (d, mgr.).

STARDUSTERS, Denver, Colorado, 1948—George Kobayashi (l); Frank Yama, Walt Moriya, Dick Motoyoshi (s); Sam Sato (c); Albert Noda, Kiyoshi Kawahata (t); Jiro Shoji (p); George Matsumonji (b); Bob Sakata (d); Eddie So (g).

STARDUSTERS, Merced "Assembly" Center, California, 1942—Paul Higaki (l,tb); Dave Higaki, Paul Sakuma, Henry Wada, Leo Kikuchi, Nob Kuwatani (s); Satoshi Hirano, Ben Kuruya (t); Miyo Mizutani (vi); Sumi Kawamura (vo).

STARLIGHT SERENADERS, Gila River Canal Detention Camp, Arizona, 1942—Tom Ishii (l, d); Danny Kawahara (t); Frank Onishi, Sak Yamashita, Ted Iseri (s); Roy Teranishi (vi); Mary Oino Shibata (vo).

STARLIGHT SERENADERS, Santa Anita "Assembly" Center, California, 1942—Yukio Miyamoto (l, s); Francis Ikezoye, Glenn Jiobu, Susumu Chikami (s); Ernie Arima, Roy Nishimura, Jim Nakanishi (t); Nob Okuno, Harry Kitano (tb); Akira Ohno (g); Eddie Inouye (d); Dorothy Takii (p); Yoshiko Iwashika, Bob Kinoshita (vo).

STARLIGHTERS, a.k.a. STARDUSTERS, Tule Lake Detention Camp, California, 1942—Mickey Tanaka (l,s); Tadashi Funakoshi, Americk Ishikawa, Hayao Motoyama, Richard Hamada, Tom Sasaki (s); Norman Ishimoto, Roy Hatamiya, George Sumida (t); Yutaka Hamamoto, Tets Ito (tb); Bryan Maeda (d); George Yamamoto (g); Haruko Sato (p); Art Kozono, Patricia Kitazumi Kyono, Lois Kitazumi Yamaguchi (vo).

TANFORAN TOOTERS & TOPAZ TOOTERS, Tanforan "Assembly" Center, California & Topaz Detention Camp, Utah, 1942-43—Tom Tsuji (l); Hoagy Ogawa, Yoneo Kawakita, Tom Nakashige (s); Frank Ono, Tad Ishida, Kiyoshi Kawahata (t); Sawai Ichisaka, Paul Higaki, Harry Kitano (tb); Hisashi Tani (baritone horn); Mark Bando, Jimmy Kikugawa (d); Itaya Kurita (p); Katsuso Arima (g).

WATSONVILLE YBA ORCHESTRA, Watsonville, California, 1940-56—Helen Iwananga (l); Kenji Torigoe, Walter Moriya, John Sakamoto, Art Izumizaki, Mutsu Iwanaga, Susumu Matano, Mits Nishihara, Mitsuru Hashimoto, Terry Waki (s); George Takamoto, Ken Muronaka, Tom Murakami, Donald Shiraichi (t); Henry Taniguchi, Shig Aramaki, Ben Tada, Kensaku Kitamura (tb); Gus Nakagawa, Tony Matsuda (vi); Harumi Nagase (p); John Kado (d).

GLOSSARY

A-A-B-A: Many popular American songs consist of four eight-measure phrases, thirty-two measures in total. The first two and the fourth eight-measure phrases are melodically nearly identical; the third eight-measure phrase, the bridge, is different from the others. Thus, an A-A-B-A pattern.

"assembly" center: a temporary collection site for Japanese Americans who were incarcerated in camps by Executive Order 9066 during World War II.

ax: slang: any musical instrument.

bad: slang: very good, excellent.

ballad: a popular romantic or sentimental song, usually performed in slow tempo.

band's book: musical arrangements comprising the dance band's music library.

bata-kusai: [Japanese] literally, reeking of butter. Connotation: very Western, un-Japanese. Not pejorative.

Big Apple: New York City.

blow: to blow—a colloquial expression in jazz to de-note the playing of any kind of musical instrument.

bone: contraction of trombone.

bootie: slang: buttocks.

Buddhahead: colloquial: a Japanese American male. Origin: Hawaiian pidgin.

cat: slang: a player or a devotee of jazz; a male person.

chicken: slang: afraid to do something.

chops: slang: technical mastery of a musical instrument.

cold turkey: complete and abrupt cessation of an addictive behavior or drug.

cook: slang: play well with fervor.

commercial: used in reference to a popular song or musical presentation of average or inferior quality produced for quick market success.

comp: [contraction of "accompany"] to play rhythmic jazz accompaniment—usually block-chords on the piano—while another person solos.

crack a nut: colloquial: to break through [a barrier] so as to gain recognition or acceptance.

crasher: slang: uninvited guests to a party.

cut the rug: colloquial: to dance; generally, to swing music.

detention camp: a permanent site for the incarceration of persons of Japanese ancestry during World War II.

dig: to understand, appreciate, admire, like.

dixieland: jazz music marked by two beats or multiples of two beats per measure; played by a small band and characterized by ensemble and solo improvisation.

ear: sensitivity to musical tone and pitch.

el: elevated railroad.

Fillmore: a street in San Francisco; an area in the African American section of the city where jazz clubs existed during World War II and in the postwar era.

fuddy-duddy: one who is old-fashioned, pompous, unimaginative or concerned by trifles.

gas: slang: a happening that has a great appeal.

gig: a job; especially a musician's engagement for a specified time.

grease the palm: to bribe.

groove: to enjoy oneself intensely or to interact harmoniously.

groovy: marvelous, wonderful, excellent.

hip: [alteration of hep, of unknown origin] characterized by a keen informed awareness or interest in the newest developments.

hi-hat: a percussion instrument used by the drummer—two cymbals on a stand designed to strike each other with the action of the drummer's foot.

hot: loud, lively and rhythmic.

jam: to improvise on a musical instrument a melody from an original musical composition.

jam session: an impromptu performance engaged in by a group of jazz musicians and characterized by solo and group improvisations.

jerk sodas: to mix and dispense carbonated drinks and ice cream at a soda fountain.

jitterbug: a person who dances in time to up-beat swing music, e.g., the Lindy Hop, in which couples swing and twirl in standardized patterns and often with vigorous acrobatics.

jive: swing music or the dancing performed to it. Deceptive or foolish talk.

joint: slang: a marijuana cigarette.

jumpin': [contraction of jumping] moving energetically, bustling with activity.

karaoké: [Japanese] literally, without an orchestra [kara=without, oké=contraction of orchestra]. Singing accompanied by recordings in which the lead vocal voice is omitted.

kazoo: a toy musical instrument consisting of a tube with a membrane which vibrates when one sings or hums into it.

Keio boy: a student or graduate of Keio University, which was considered to be culturally liberal.

Kibei: [Japanese] an American of Japanese heritage who acquired part of his/her elementary/secondary education in Japan and then returned to the United States.

knocked out: slang: to be emotionally affected by something that is sensational and attractive.

licorice stick: slang: clarinet.

mean: slang: musically exciting, excellent.

moldy fig: slang: out of fashion, antiquated.

monster: slang: technically proficient, excellent.

name band: a popular, well-known band.

New Orleans jazz: music originating in New Orleans characterized by four beats per measure with accent on the second and fourth beats; played by small ensembles which feature improvisations by individual musicians.

Nikkei: [Japanese] people of Japanese heritage.

ninth wave: an exceptionally high wave in a series of moderate waves. The height of popularity of an object or activity.

Nisei: [Japanese] literally, second generation; offspring of Japanese immigrants.

ol′ man: slang: father.

one-nighter: a dance-band engagement for just one night in a specific site.

pay one's dues: to work diligently to achieve a specified goal.

pit band: orchestra or band situated in a recessed portion of a theater just in front of the stage for the purpose of accompanying singers and other performers on stage.

platter: phonograph record.

Sansei: [Japanese] literally, third generation; offspring of Nisei.

scarf: slang: to eat.

schmaltz: [Yiddish] literally, rendered fat; sentimental or excessively flowery music or art.

sideman: a member of a dance band.

sister: a woman related to another person by a common tie (e.g., same ethnicity) or interest.

sit in: to play with other musicians.

skins: a dance-band drum set.

smack-dab: exactly, squarely.

smoothie: a young man who is polished, suave and worldly.

stag: a man who attends a party or a dance unaccompanied by a woman.

stagette: a woman who attends a party or dance unaccompanied by a man.

stock arrangement: a commercially prepared dance-band arrangement of a popular tune.

swan song: a person's last act or piece of work.

swing: to sing or play an instrument with a lively, compelling rhythm.

tag: to cut in; to interrupt a dancing couple and take one as one's partner.

tickle the ivories: to play the piano in a light, pleasant manner.

Tin Pan Alley: a district in New York City that was the center for composers and publishers of popular music.

too much: excessively good.

traps: [contraction of "contraptions"] a dance band drum set generally consisting of a bass drum, snare drum, tom-toms, cymbals and hi-hat.

two-fisted: marked by energy; virile.

unreal: slang: unbelievably good.

vaudeville: live stage entertainment consisting of various unrelated acts (acrobats, singers, dancers, comedians, etc.)

wail: slang: to play an instrument or sing with exceptional vigor and skill.

woodshed: slang: to practice on a musical instrument. [Probably from the former use of woodsheds for private practicing.]

WRA: War Relocation Authority, a U.S. government agency responsible for the care and movement of Japanese and Japanese American internees during World War II.

yogoré: [Japanese] literally, soiled; slang: juvenile delinquent.

INDEX

Abbey, Roy, 17
Abe, George, 30, 32, 284, 285
Abe, Yutaka, 65
African EurAsian Eclipse, 281
Aihara, Karie Shindo, 219
Aiso, Mits, 32, 284
Akaba, Setsu Kitamura, 23, 24, 286
Akimoto, George 125, 148, 156, 183
Akiya, Jimmie, 153, 159, 161, 286
Akiyama, Martin, 18, 284
Akiyoshi, Roy, 19, 20, 286
Al King Band, 48
Allen Reed All-Girl Orchestra, 214
Allen, Bob, 126
Allen, Henry "Red", 195
Aloha Hawaiians, 78, 90
Aloha Serenaders, Pomona, 152
Amache Camp Music Program, 172
Amache Detention Camp, 170-173
Amakusa, Midori, 85
Amano, Sachi, 35, 38, 101, 135, 287
Amano, Sam, 8, 35, 285
Amber Saints Orchestra, 151
Anchovies, Los Angeles, 32
Aoki, Mike, 286
Araki, James, 109, 112-115, 135, 145, 146, 147, 206, 207, 208, 224, 244, 284, 285, 286
Araki, Yoshimura, 145, 146, 285
Aramaki, Shig, 131, 132, 135, 285, 286, 287
Aratani, Shig, 34
Arima, Ernest, 34, 35, 38, 101, 129, 284, 287
Arima, Katsuso, 180, 287
Arishita, Johnny, 171
Armstrong, Louis, 71, 95, 223
Asakawa, Misa Hatakeda, 284
Ashida, Mitsuru, 82
Ashizawa, Roy, 94
"Assembly" Centers: Merced County Fair Grounds, 168; Pomona Fair Grounds, 152, 158; Salinas Fair Grounds, 139; Santa Anita Racetrack, 123; Tanforan Racetrack, 123, 180-183; Washington State Fair Grounds, 142
Atsumo, George, 86, 87, 135
Awaya, Noriko, 48, 59, 74, 85
Azama, Ethel, 248-250
Azuma, George, 153, 284
Babbit, Harry, 126
Baker, Bonnie, 125
Ballet Tabarin, 38, 101, 102, 103, 105
Baltazar, Gabe, 240
Bando, Mark, 180, 287
Barney Miller Show, 256
Barrett, Karen, 276
Basie, Bill "Count," X, 29, 71, 98, 176, 280
Bechet, Sidney, 71
Bell, Ike, 274
Beppu, Taft, 8, 9, 45, 46, 79, 82
Berigan, Bunny, 46
Berkeley Buddhist Temple, 19
Berkeley Nihonjin Kai Hall, 19
Berkeley Nisei Club, 19
Berkeley YMBA Orchestra, 18, 19
Berkenkotter, Frank, 285
Berry, Chu, 176
Bert LaMar Orchestra, l43
Bessho, Tetsu, 67, 135, 152, 153, 158, 160, 163, 243-245, 247, 284, 286
Betty Boop, Japanese, 45
Big Apple, 71
Black Bottom, 71
Blakey, Art, 239
Blue Knights, Kikugawa's, 58
Bobrow, Norman, Colony Club, 261
Boogie-Woogie, 115
Borges, Jim, 250
Boswell, Connie, 9, 71
Bow, Clara, 71
Brattesani, Joe, 242
Brown Anthony, 281
Brown, Claire, 276
Brown, Lawrence, 197
Brown, Sidney, 153
Buddhahead Blues, 120
Buddhist Church of Seattle, 10
Burke, Ed and Betty, 6,7
Burroughs, Alvin, 195
Busby, Mariah Masako, III
Cahn, Sammy, 234, 263
Callegari, Teal, 253
Callegari, Tony, 253
Calloway, Cab, 176
Carle, Frankie, 126
Carney, Harry, 197
Casa Loma Orchestra, 30, 63, 115
Chante Clare, 38, 101, 102
Charleston, 71
Chicago Nisei social scene, 198
Chicago, Ill., relocation magnet, 194
Chikami, Susumu, 30, 33, 34, 35, 38, 101, 102, 129, 153, 284, 285, 287
Chin, Frank, 263
China Doll, 251
Chono, Terry, 284
Chono, Yasu, 284
Christian Church, Los Angeles, 32
Claybrook, Pee Wee, 274
Cleveland, Jimmy, 219
Club Alabam, 270
Club Harmony Orchestra, a.k.a. Melodians, 31, 35
Cole, Cozy, 46, 245
Cole, Nat "King," 263
Coleman, Wayne, band, 48
Collins, Lee, 203
Columbia Rhythm Boys, Japan, 45
Conrad, Paul, 248
Corcoran, Corky, 125, 141
Courtney, Junius, 279
Crane, Barton, 63, 115
Crawford, Joan, 71
Criterion Theater, T.C. Talley's, Los Angeles, 31
Crosby, Bing, 261

Cruz, 102, 105
Damante, Pete, 271
Dance Halls, Japan, Florida, 47, 48, 93, 80, 94, 110, 126; Ginza, 126; Marigold, 97; Shinbashi, 86, 126
Davis, Miles, X
Davis, Sammy Jr., 108, 258
Densoneers, a.k.a. D-Elevens, 149-151
Depression, 1930s, XI, 6, 43
Detention Camp, closure, 188
Detention Camp, relocation out of, 193
Detention Camps, 118-188: Amache, 170-173; Gila River Butte Camp, 144-148; Gila River Canal Camp, 143-144; Heart Mountain, 152-163; Jerome, 149-151; Manzanar, 163-167; Minidoka, 142-143; Poston Camp #1, 123, 131-136; Poston Camp #2, 137-140; Poston Camp #3, 140-142; Rohwer, 148; Topaz, 120, 182-188; Tule Lake, 174-179
Domoto, Takiji, 52, 53, 55
Domoto, Toichi, 53
Domoto, Yoshiko, 53
Domoto, Yukiko, 53
Doro, 102, 105
Dorsey, Jimmy, 71
Dorsey, Tommy, 32, 71, 168, 209, 226
Down Beats, Tule Lake, 174, 175
Downbeat Room, Chicago, 194
Duchin, Eddie, 32, 126
Eager Beavers, 205
Eckstine, Billy, 195
Ellington, Edward Kennedy, "Duke," 29, 196, 197, 224, 274, 280
Elman, Ziggy, 30, 210
Endo, Roy, 206, 284
Endo, Takako Tsuchiya, 254
Enomoto, Tak, 210, 182, 183, 185, 285
Eto, Amy Morizono, 24, 186
Eto, Mabel Sugiyama, 161, 175, 177, 184, 186, 284, 287
Etting, Ruth, 71
Executive Order 9066, 123
Fields, Shep, 126

Fishback, Clifford, 246
Fleming, George, 274
Florida (Dance Hall), Tokyo, 47, 48, 73, 80, 94, 110, 126
Flower Drum Song, Pat Suzuki, Goro Suzuki, 247, 256, 262
Flower Drum Song, Sue Okabe, 247
Forrest, Helen, 125
Four Freshmen, 249
442nd Regimental Combat Team, 10, 141, 168, 171, 188, 194, 204, 237
Frank Skinner Co., 46
Fujie, Ron, 278, 285
Fujii, Takeo, 18, 284
Fujii, Wataru Dick, 18, 284
Fujioka, Dolly, a.k.a. Dolly Lee, 49, 101-104, 287
Fujisawa, Haruo "Foozie," 107, 131, 132, 134, 135, 136, 244, 285, 286
Fujiyama, Ichiro, 88
Fukui, Tomo, 153, 284, 286
Fukui, Yoné, 152, 153, 158, 160, 206, 243, 273, 284, 285, 286
Fukushima, Tsuneo, 21, 286
Fukuyama, Miyoko, 154
Funahashi, Eddy, 286
Fullert, Joe, 30, 285
Funakoshi, Tadashi, 174, 287
Funk, Manny, 274
Furukawa, Bill, 152, 286
Furuya Bank, Seattle, 8
Furuya, Masajiro, 6
Futaba Band, 67
Fuyumi, John, 146
Garber, Jan, 22, 32
Gay Quintet, 114
Gila River Butte Camp, 144-148
Gila River Canal Camp, 143
Gill, Eric, 69
Gillespie, Dizzy, X
Ginza Dance Hall, 126
Girard, Richard, 265
Glenn, Vernell, 272, 274
Goodman, Benny, 24, 30, 32, 33, 71, 125
Gordon, Dexter, 245

Goto, Hiro, 206, 284, 285
Goto, T.R., 13
Goya, Haru Yoshikawa, 149, 284
Grant, Archie, 107
Granz, Norman, 208
Gray, Wardell, 245
Greer, Sonny, 197
Grew, Joseph, 128
Grey, Al, 219
Guy, Fred, 197
Hada, "Joker," 184
Hadlock, Richard, VI, IX, 274
Haines, Connie, 210
Hamada, Dorothy, 155
Hamada, Richard, II, 26, 29, 174, 286, 287
Hamamoto, Yutaka, 174, 287
Hampton, Gladys, 216, 219
Hampton, Lionel, 14, 190, 208
Hara, George, 144, 206, 207, 284, 285
Harada, Fred, 284
Harada, Jimmy, 60
Harano, Mary, 69
Hardymon, Phil, 274
Harmonaires, 142
Harris, Bill, 227
Hashimoto, Mitsuru, 287
Haskell, Tad, 172
Hata, Bill, 180
Hatamiya, Roy, 174, 287
Hattori, Ryoichi, 43, 44, 86
Hawaiian Surf Riders, 67
Hawaiian-Negro Band, 107
Hawes, Hampton, 241
Hawkins, Coleman, 33, 186
Hayakawa, Sessue, 65
Hayama, Peggy, 111
Hayami, Frank, 152, 286
Hayami, Miyo, 155
Hayami, Walter, 153, 244, 284, 286
Hayashi, Art Koichi, 11, 13, 135, 150, 245, 284, 285
Hayashi, Haruo, 145, 146, 147, 285
Hayashida, Masashi, 246
Hayes, Al, 219
Hayes, Louis, 275

Heart Mountain Detention Camp, Wyoming, 104, 152-163
Heidt, Horace, 126
Henderson, Bob, 278, 285
Herman, Woody, X, 32, 98, 231
Hewitt Street School, Los Angeles, 36
Hibino, Yoshiko, 163
Higaki, David, 169, 286, 287
Higaki, Mrs. David, 190, 218,
Higaki, Paul, a.k.a. Paul Lee, 14, 168, 169, 173, 190, 209-221, 226, 286, 287
Higginbotham, Jay C, 195, 225
Higgins, Billy, 245
Hilo Hawaiians, a.k.a. Hilo Collegians, 74, 89
Himoto, Sam, 175, 177, 286
Hines, Earl, 195
Hirahara, Davis, 12, 285
Hirahara, Frank, 153, 284
Hirai, Kitty, 285
Hirakawa, Louis, 286
Hirano, Satoshi, 169, 285, 287
Hirano, Yas, 285
Hiraoka, Jimmy, 286
Hirasawa, Jimmy, 149
Hirashiki, Tami, 153, 284
Hirashiki, Tom, 286
Hirasuna, Buddy, 284
Hirasuna, Jimmy, 284
Hiroshima (Fusion band), X
Hirota, Tad, 12, 14, 20, 79, 286
Hiura, Margaret, 155
Hoare, Bill, 107
Hodges, Johnny, 195, 197
Hodo No Sasayaki, Betty Inada film, 75
Hoeschen, Alan, 279
Holman, Libby, 31
Honda, Bob, 283
Honda, George, 285
Honda, Helen Yukiko, 45, 61, 75, 91, 92
Honda, Larry, 248
Honma, Dick, 221
Hori, Tosh, 13, 284, 285
Horton, Mack, 278, 285

Hosano, Iwajiro, 286
Hoshi, Hatsuko Muramoto, 18, 284
Hoshide, Shizuko Takakoshi, 9, 285
Hosokawa, Shuhei, 90
Hosono, Iwajiro, 20
Hot Club of Japan, 114
Houlehan, Bob, 274
Hurok, Sol, 251
Hyakumannin No Gasho, Helen Sumida film, 88
Hyotan Orchestra, 44
Ichihashi, Woodrow, 174, 175, 176, 284
Ichisaka, Sawai, 180, 287
Idé, Joe, 212
Idé, Noboru, 23, 24, 286
Igawa, George, 33-37, 101, 102, 103, 107, 152, 158, 244, 284, 286, 287
Iijima, Takeru, 39
Iino, Fumitaka, 86
Iiyama, Chizu Kitano, 226
Ikeda, Mary, 23, 24, 286
Ikemi, Sho, 270
Ikezoe, "Chick," 152
Ikezoye, Francis, 129, 287
Iki, George, 5
Inada, Betty, 45, 48, 61, 64, 67-78, 126
Inada, Lawson, back cover
Inada, Sadie Sadako, 68
Ino, Ichiro, 145, 146, 283
Inouye, Eddie, 129, 287
Inouye, George, 286
Ioka, Haruye, 248
Irie, Takako, 91
Irma La Douce, 262
Iseri, Ted, 287
Iseri, Tom, 143
Ishida, Tad, 180, 183, 209, 273, 287
Ishihara, "Chickie," see White, Florence
Ishihara, Henry, 2, 55, 286
Ishii, Tom, 143, 287
Ishii, Yoshiko, 98, 116
Ishikawa, Amerik, 174, 287
Ishimoto, Norman, 174, 175, 177, 284, 287

Itashiki, Elsie, a.k.a. Teal Joy, 150, 184, 250-254
Itashiki, Marie, 250
Itashiki, Robert, 251, 253
Ito, Michio, 71, 88
Ito, Tets, 174, 287
Ito, Willie, 2, 17-22, 55, 284, 286
Ito, Yoichi, 13, 284
Itoi, Henry, 84
Iwanaga, Frank, 180
Iwanaga, Helen Okamoto, 137, 286, 287
Iwanaga, Mutsu, 287
Iwashika, Yoshiko, 129, 287
Izu, Mark, X, XI, 281
Izumi, Charles, 30, 31, 285
Izumida, Lois, 33
Izumizaki, Arthur, 137, 287
Izumizaki, Jimmy, 286
J-Town Jazz Ensemble, 99, 154, 265, 278, 280
Jackson, Mahalia, 280
James, Harry, 30, 125
Jampel, David, 110
Japanese American Citizens League, JACL, Seattle, 9
Japanese American Courier, 5, 115
Japanese Baptist Church, Seattle, 7
Japanese Sandmen, 30, 31
Jeffries, Herb, 248
Jenkins, Gordon, 98
Jenny, Jack, 226
Jerome Detention Camp, 128, 129, 149-151
Jimbo's Bop City, 270
Jiobu, Glenn, 129, 287
Jive Bombers, 104, 163-167
Jivesters, Topaz, 120, 182, 183-186
Jo, Lisa, 248
Jo, Sue, see Okabe, Sue
Johnson, Dick, 240
Johnson, Don, 175, 177, 178, 284
Jones, Philly Joe, 239
Jones, Sam, 275
Jordan, Taft, 197
Joy, Teal, see Itashiki, Elsie

Jue, Alex, 285
Juliet and Romeo, 33
Kado, John, 137, 286, 287
Kadona, Shinta, 163
Kaga, Shiro, 77
Kaji, Bruce, 165, 166, 244, 285, 286
Kajiwara, Sachi, 254
Kamayatsu, Hiroshi, 111
Kamayatsu, Tadashi "Tib," 34, 36, 37, 38, 94, 101, 102, 103, 109-112, 287
Kameoka, Tak, 171
Kami, Kyosuke, 83
Kaneko, Charles, 18, 19, 284
Kaneko, Fred "Mack," 9, 10, 285
Kaneko, Hisashi, 18, 284
Karisome no Kuchibeni, Helen Honda film, 91
Kariya, Kaz, 180
Kasagi, Shizuko, 44
Kasai, Yo, 181, 254
Kashiwagi, Shungi "Shang," 5, 9, 285
Kato, Mary, 32, 33, 284
Kato, Paul, 2, 54, 55, 286
Kato, Tatsuo, 73
Katsutaro, 88
Kawabata, Fumiko, 40, 45, 46, 48, 60-67, 68 87, 88, 92
Kawada, Haruhisa, 190
Kawaguchi, George, 114, 207
Kawahara, Danny, 287
Kawahata, Kiyoshi, 180, 209, 215, 220, 232, 287
Kawakami, Ritsuko, 135
Kawakami, Shigeo, 18, 284
Kawakita, Yoneo, 180, 287
Kawamoto, Mitsugi, 145, 146, 285
Kawamura, Fumi Matsuda, 286
Kawamura, Sumi, 168, 169, 287
Kawata, Beverly, 153, 286
Kawano, Hideo, 131, 136, 199, 203, 230, 245, 285
Kawazoe, Hajime, 20, 286
Kaye, Sammy, 125
kei ongaku (light music), 97
Keio University, 53
Kelly, Gene, 253, 262

Kemp, Hal, 126
Kent, Wash., 9
Kido, John, 20, 286
Kikuchi, George, 145, 146, 284
Kikuchi, Leo, 169, 287
Kikugawa, Charlie, X, XI, 2, 20, 21, 22, 40, 43, 46, 49, 55-60, 107, 286
Kikugawa, Jimmy, 186, 286, 287
Kikugawa, Mari, 2, 49, 58
Kikugawa, Tamotsu "Tomate," X, XI, 20, 21, 22, 38, 101, 286, 287
Kikumoto, Yo, 85
Kimoto, Al, 97, 286
Kinoshita, Bob, 129, 287
Kirk, Roland, 274
Kishi, Sherman, 285
Kitahara, George, 30, 31, 32, 167, 284, 285
Kitamura, Kensaku, 287
Kitano, Harry, 129, 225-228, 287
Kitano, Sam, 286
Kitayama, Kaoru, 11, 13, 284, 285
Kiyasu, John, 278, 285
Kobara, Joe, 285
Kobayashi, George, 287
Kobi, Michi, 16, 255, 265
Kodani, Eugene, 241
Koga, Max, 153, 284
Koga, Tom, 286
Koichi Hayashi Band, see Mikados of Swing, 10-14
Koike, Joe, 31
Kokugo Gakko, Seattle Japanese School, 7, 10
Komatsu, Fukiko, 163
Kono, Keora, 31
Kono-san, see Takeuchi, Kono
Konomi, Jin, VI, 47
Kosaka, Hannah, 285
Kosakura, Al Shigeru, 18, 284
Kosakura, Tomiko Harano, 18, 284
Koseki, Roy, 57
Kosugi, Isamu, 40
Koyama, John, 20, 286
Koyama, Maki, 19, 20, 286
Kozono, Art, 174, 287

Kozuma, Teddy, 21, 56, 57
Krupa, Gene, 71, 125, 135, 231
Kubota, George, 173
Kudo, Susumu, 58
Kumagai, Teruo, 11, 13, 284, 285
Kumamoto, "Smoky," II, 129, 286
Kunimatsu, Takako, 153, 154, 284
Kuramoto, Shigenobu, 20
Kuraya, Ben, 169, 287
Kurita, Itaya, 180, 287
Kusaba, Jack, 144, 285
Kusaba, Torao, 163, 166, 231, 285, 286
Kusama, Henry, 16
Kuwahara, Danny, 143
Kuwatani, Tad, 285
Kuwatani, Nobuo, 168, 169, 171, 285, 287
Kuwatani, Yutaka, 285
Kwan, Nancy, 256
Kyono, Patricia Kitazumi, 287
Kyser, Kay, 126
Lapham's Sakura, 46
Lapham's, Nisei Hollywood Romance, 47
Lapham, Claude, 46
Lee Williams Orchestra, 212
Legrand, Michel, 99
Levitte, Barry, 265
Lewis, Ted, 4, 29, 71
Li'l Osaka, San Francisco Japantown, X, 14
Li'l Tokyo Players, 33
Lindsay, Mrs. H., 39
Lindy Hop, 71
Liu Qi-Chao, 281
Lombardo, Guy, 22, 32, 224
Los Angeles JACL, 37; Nisei Week, 19, 33, 37, 48, 66; Talent Shows, 33, 36, 37, 38
Los Angeles Melodaires, 33
Los Angeles Musicians Union, Local #47, 39, 164
Los Angeles, prewar, 30-39
Lott, David, 274, 279
Luey, Andrew, 278, 285
Lunceford, Jimmie, 82, 151, 214

M Street Cafe, Sacramento, 25, 29
Maas, Mrs., 187, 286
Maeda, Bryan, 287
Maeda, George, 285
Magara, Kana, 155
Makashima, Tosh, 175, 177, 206, 284
Manbo, Masao, VI, 32, 35, 37, 38, 47, 97, 101, 102, 103, 105, 107-109, 112, 284, 287
Manny Harom's Orchestra, 131
Mansho, Dick, 18, 284
Manzanar Canteen, 247
Manzanar Detention Camp, 104, 163-167
Marabuto, John, 272
Marigold Dance Hall, 97
Marsala, Joe, 46
Maruoka, Kazu, 44, 120, 182-185, 187, 243, 270-273, 285, 286
Masuda, Albert, 9
Masuda, Fumi, 20
Masuda, Hajimu "Hy," 30, 33, 35, 101, 102, 103, 105-107, 109, 284, 285, 287
Masunaga, Ernest Michio, 120
Matano, Susumu, 287
Matoba, "Zush," 165, 166, 285
Matsuda, Mitsuye, 18, 284
Matsuda, Paul, 131-134, 285
Matsuda, Tom, 21, 286, 287
Matsufuji, Riki, 175, 177, 286
Matsumonji, George, 287
Matsuhara, I., 120, 182, 183, 285
Matsumoto, "Buddy," 31, 32
Matsumoto, Nobu, 58
Matsumoto, Shin, 63, 73, 85, 86, 104, 110
Matsumoto, "Sleepy," 207
Matsumura, Tsuyuko, 34
Matsuno, Flora, 31
Matsuoka, Jack, 138
Mayeda, Bryan, 174
Mayeda, Harry, 174
Mayeda, Sam, 175, 176, 177, 284
McAffee, Bill, 241
McCoy, Clyde, 30, 33, 126

McKee, Rose, 61, 77, 88, 91
McShann, Jay, 71
Melodaires, a.k.a. Club Harmony Orchestra, 31, 35
Merced County Fair Grounds "Assembly Center," 168-169
Migaki, Yosh, 206, 284
Migaki, Yoshio, 145, 146, 285
Mikados of Swing, Seattle, Wash., 10-14, 142
Mikados, Sacramento, Calif., 25-29
Military Intelligence Service & Language School, 141, 148, 166, 188, 205
Miller, Bill, 280
Miller, Glenn, 24, 135, 127
Millinder, Lucky, 214
Mimbu, Bill, 5
Miné, Dick, 45, 48, 49, 64, 75, 77, 78, 90,
Minidoka Detention Camp, l42
Misora, Hibari, 190
Missman, Thomas, 62
Mitani, Shunzo, 163
Mitoma, Ikaru, 20, 286
Miura, Tamaki, 96
Miwa, Tom, 286
Miyagawa, Chizuko, a.k.a. Harumi Miyagawa, 45, 49, 84-87
Miyagawa, Fumiye, 87
Miyagawa, Shinichiro, 45, 46, 49, 81-83, 85
Miyakawa, George, 78
Miyamoto, Sho, 286
Miyamoto, Yukio, 129, 131, 132, 133, 200, 229, 283, 287
Miyasaki, David, 277
Miyashita, Shisui, 7
Miyata, Vernon, 278, 285
Miyatake, Toyo, 68, 78
Mizutani, Miyo, 129, 285
Moana Glee Club, 75
Mogi, Yuki, 245
Morgan, Helen, 31
Morisuye, Joe, 21, 286

Morita, Fumiko, 6
Moriya, Walter, 137, 287
Moriyama, Hisashi, 20, 46, 82, 85, 92-99, 100, 110, 126
Moriyama, Iwao, 98
Moriyama, Ryoko, 98, 100
Morizono, Mike, 180
Moten, Bennie, 71
Motoyama, Hayao Al, 174, 177, 243, 284, 287
Motoyoshi, Dick, 22, 99, 284, 287
Moulin Rouge Band, 48
Mr. Valentine, 256
Mukai, Arlene, 155
Mukai, George, 2, 54, 55, 286
Murakami, George, 285
Murakami, Tom, 131, 136, 137, 285, 286, 287
Murakami, Yoshiteru, 164, 166, 285, 286
Muraoka, Richard, 175, 177, 284
Murata, Elizabeth Kozono, 28, 29, 93, 286
Muronaka, Ken, 287
Murata, Goro, 88, 91
Music Makers, Amache Detention Camp, 170
Music Makers, Gila River Butte Camp, 144-148
Music Makers, Poston Camp #1, 124, 131-137
Music Makers, San Francisco, 171
"My Trumpet," 116
Nagai, Kazuko, 285
Nagai, Ralph, 47
Nagakura, Margaret, 152
Nagase, Harumi, 287
Nagano, Florence, 184
Nagase, Harumi, 137, 284
Nagatomo, Eileen, 230, 285
Najar, Sam, 102, 102
Nakagawa, Gus, 287
Nakagawa, Roy, 285, 286
Nakagawa, Saburo, 75, 85
Nakahara, Kengo, 20
Nakai, Clem, 184

Nakama, Roy, 163
Nakamichi, Tom, 149, 284
Nakamura, Dorothy, 12
Nakamura, Hachidai, 207
Nakamura, Ike, 120, 182, 183, 285
Nakamura, Jobo, 174
Nakamura, Kei, 286
Nakamura, Leland, 285
Nakamura, Noboru "Nobi," 140, 208, 286
Nakamura, Shigeru, 18, 19, 284
Nakanishi, Jim, 127, 287
Nakano, Lane, 155, 286
Nakano, Lyle, 153, 155
Nakao, George, 175, 176, 177, 284
Nakaoka, Konichi, 66
Nakashige, Tom, 161, 180, 181, 186, 287
Nakashima, Mits, 20, 286
Nakatani, George, 149, 284
Nakayama, Katsumi, 16
Nakayama, Tak, 187, 286
Nako, Joyce, 36
Nance, Ray, 197
Nanri, Fumio, 45, 58, 87
Napoleon, Teddy, 231
Nash, Larry, 238
Nelson, Kenny, 285
National Japanese American Historical Society, VI
Neville, Kathy Iino, 87
New Deal Society Orchestra, 274
New Pacific Orchestra, Japan, 98, 110
Newport Jazz Festival, 262
Nichols, Red, 29, 71
Night Hawks, II, 25-29
Nihonmachi Legal Outreach, 265
Niitake, Harry, 286
Niitake, Toyo, 152, 286
Nikaido, Bill, 29, 126-129, 149, 284, 286
Nikaido, Roy, 76
Niki, Takeo, 72, 73, 80, 82
Nippon Kan, Seattle, 5-7, 81, 84
Nisei Club, Tokyo, 128
Nisei Hollywood Romance, Claude Lapham, 47

Nisei Melodians, Seattle, 7-10, 79
Nisei Music Makers, Chicago, Ill, 199, 229, 230
Nisei Serenaders, Los Angeles, 166, 244, 245
Nishimoto, Sonny, 284
Nishimura, Roy, 129, 287
Nitta, Al, 175, 176, 177, 284
Noble, Ray, 104
Nobori, George, Jr., 278, 285
Nobori, George, Sr., 19, 286
Nobori, Mary, 20, 286
Noda, Al, 187, 286, 287
Noda, Kay, 244, 286
Noguchi, Harold, 206, 284
Noma, "Hickey," 38, 287
Nunokawa brothers, 247
O'Day, Anita, 231
Oakland Buddhist Church, 19
Oakland Methodist Episcopal Church, 14, 24
Oakland Sons and Daughters Orchestra, 23
Obana, Roy, 107
Obata, Masuo, 63
Obata, Mitsuyuki, 73
Obata, Shigenori, 74
Ochi, Suzi Tamura, 146, 285
Oden, Charlie, 274
Odori, 1934, 63, 64
Odoriko no Nikki, Betty Inada film, 77
Ogata, George, 11, 13, 284, 285
Ogawa, Hoagy, 180, 287
Ogino, Tak, 145, 146, 285
Ogura, Mineko, 85
Ohara, Reiko, 155
Ohno, Akira, 32, 33, 34, 129, 284, 287
Ohtaki, Pete, 125
Ohye, Mitzi, 47
Oino, Yumiko, 143
Oishi, 107
Okabe, Sue Takimoto, 67, 245-248
Okada, George, 5, 9, 285
Okada, Hito, 5
Okami, Kiyonao, 74, 89, 90, 97, 104
Okami, Naoyuki, 38, 74, 101

Okawa, Fujio Walter, 19, 20, 286
Oku, Kenneth, 284, 286
Okumoto, Raymond, II, 21, 26, 29, 67, 286
Okumoto, Richard, II, 21, 25, 29, 56, 57, 174, 286
Okuno, Nob, 129, 287
Old Boys, Jimmy Harada's, 60
Oliver Club, 31, 36, 37, 101, 111
Oliver, Nellie, 31, 36
Omoto, Akira, 286
Oliver, Sy, 210
Omoto, Shigeru "Shinglin," 20, 21, 56, 57
100th Infantry Battalion, U.S. Army, 194
ongaku imon dan (music consolation corps, Japan), 90, 197
Onishi, Frank, 143, 287
Onishi, Henry, II, 21, 27, 29, 163, 164, 285, 286
Ono, Frank, 180, 287
Ono, Mitsuru, 114
Oshidari, Tom, 98, 99, 100
Oshima, Frank, 131, 132, 133, 135, 285
Osuga, May, 155
Ota, Mark, 161
Otsubo, Dick, 286
Owaki Bakery, Seattle, 10
Owaki, Joe, 11, 13, 284, 285
Owl and the Pussycat, 262
Oyama, George Clem, II, 29, 33, 286
Oyama, Hideo, 59
Oyama, Iwao, 165
Oyama, Wesley, II, 29, 286
Ozumi, George, 244, 286
Pacific Citizen, 109, 111
Pacific Dance Hall, Yokohama, 58, 107
Paich, Marty, 249
Palmer, Gladys, 272, 274
Parker, Charlie, 245
Pastor, Tony, 224
Paul Gerson School of Dramatics, 88
Peabody, Eddie, 24
Pearl Harbor, Japanese attack on, 6, 105

Pederson, Tommy, 231
Pepper, Art, 241
Perez, Augie, 243
Peterson, Oscar, 274, 275, 276
Pilan, Pete, 101
Pine Methodist Episcopal Church, San Francisco, 29
Planton, Lauro, 39, 101
Plummer, Bill, 241
Pollock, Ben, 33
Pomona "Assembly" Center, 152, 158
Pomonans, 152
Pope, Edgar, 58
Poston Camp #1, Ariz., X, XI, 131
Poston Camp #2 Band, 137-140
Poston Camp #3 Rhythmaires, 140-142
Powell, Benny, 219
Puyallup Fair Grounds "Assembly" Center, 6, 142
Raglin, Alvin, Jr., 197
Ravaglioli, Gene, 278
Red and Blue Stompers Jazz Band, Keio University, 53
Redd, Vi, 274
Regal Theater, Chicago, 195
Reid, Rufus, 19
Rey, Alvino, 33
Rhythm Kings, Topaz Detention Camp, 187
Rhythmaires, Poston Camp #3, 140
Rice, Lloyd, 242
Rich, Buddy, 134, 208
Richard's Original Syncopaters Orchestra, a.k.a. Mikados, a.k.a. Night Hawks, 25-29, 67
Richards, Larry, 87
Richardson, Jerome, 228
Richmond, Phyllis, 275
Roaring Twenties, XI
Rodgers, Jimmie, 249
Rohwer Detention Camp, Arkansas, 148, 149, 151
Rokeach, David, 265
Rosebud Orchestra, 2, 55
Roxie Theater, New York City, 31
Sacramento, California, 25-30

Saito, George, 32, 284
Saito, Ty, 151
Saka, Yuki Morikawa, 2, 22, 55, 286
Sakai, Joe, 22, 32, 38, 39, 101, 102, 103, 104, 105, 107, 135, 164, 166, 167, 244, 284, 285, 286, 287
Sakai, Kimi, 287
Sakamoto, John, 287
Sakashita, Hid, 187, 286
Sakata, Bob, 287
Sakuma, Paul, 169, 287
Salinas Dance Band, 20
Salinas Fair Grounds "Assembly" Center, 139
Sample, Joe, 241
San Francisco Chinatown, 43
San Francisco Musicians Union, Local #6, 13, 57, 228, 275
San Francisco Musicians Union, Local #669, 228, 275
San Francisco Japantown, 14
Santa Anita "Assembly" Center, 129, 132
Santa Maria, Calif., 38
Santiago, Chiori, VI
Sasaki, George, 32, 34, 284
Sasaki, Ichiro, 120, 182, 183, 187, 285, 286
Sasaki, Lily Oyama, 4, 29, 36, 37, 71, 78, 93, 221
Sasaki, Machiko, 164, 285
Sasaki, Michael, 285
Sasaki, Tom, 174, 206, 284, 285, 287
Sato, David, 37
Sato, Gordon, 166, 244, 285, 286
Sato, Haruko, 174, 287
Sato, Louis, 200, 230, 284, 285
Sato, Sam, 287
Satow, Haruko, 153, 284
Savoy Four, 186
Sears, Al, 197
Seattle Broadway High School, 8, 9, 10
Seattle Japanese American Citizens League, 9
Seattle Japanese Baptist Church, 7, 8, 9
Seattle Nippon Kan, 5

Seattle Symphony Orchestra, 7
Seattle Washington Hall, 9
Seattle: Collins Field House, Olympic Hotel, Queen Anne Field House, 8
Seno, Sam, 36, 149, 151, 284
Senzaki, Randy, 277
Shanghai Filipino Musicians Union, 106
Shibata, Mary Oino, 143, 287
Shibata, Welly, 6, 89, 91
Shibuya, Yoshindo, 166, 285
Shigeta, James, 246
Shigio, Matao, 286
Shigio, Shig, 20
Shikami, Joe, 285
Shimada, Joe, 30, 31, 32, 129, 284, 285
Shimanouchi, Midori, 180
Shimizu, George, 244, 286
Shimizu, Mits, 154
Shimoto, Harry, 153
Shinagawa, Susan, 277
Shinbashi Dance Hall, 86, 126
Shindo, Tak, 135, 206, 284
Shinta, Pauline, 155
Shiota, Satoru, 11, 13, 285
Shiota, Takashi, 285
Shiraichi, Donald, 287
Shirakata, Buckie, 78, 89, 90, 111
Shirane, Shizuko, 223
Shiro, Bob, 285
Shiro, Joe, 170, 285
Shitama, Kaz, 13
Sho Tokyans, Los Angeles, 22, 33, 34, 35, 37, 38, 39, 101-112
Sho Wa Lo, San Francisco, 21, 55
Shoji, Jiro, 287
Shusho, Stan, 184
Silva, Cecil, 78
Simpkins, Andy, 238
Sims Family, John "Zoot" and Ray, 167
Sinatra, Frank, 210, 234, 263
"Sing, Sing, Sing," 86, 115
Sirola, Joe, 230
Smith, "Pine Top," 147
So, Eddie, 287
Soo, Jack, see Suzuki, Goro

Sotelo, Frank, 16
South Pacific, 263
Stafford, Jo, 210
Stanicci, George, 167
Stardusters, Japan, 77
Stardusters, Merced "Assembly" Center, 168
Starlight Serenaders, Gila Canal Detention Camp, 143
Starlight Serenaders, Santa Anita "Assembly" Center, 129, 130, 226
Starlighters, Tule Lake, 174
Starr, Judy, 126
Steele, Ted, 251
Stewart, Buddy, 231
Stockton, Calif., 38, 39
Stovall, Don, 195
Sudderth, Claire, 15 5
Suenaga, Jiro, 180
Sugi, Kyoji, 40
Sugi-Machi, Miyoshi, 46
Sugimachi, Yaesu, 147
Sugiura, June, 154
Sugiyama, Tad, 286
Sumida, George, 174, 244, 286, 287
Sumida, Helen, 45, 49, 61, 63, 87-89, 126
Sumimoto, Charles "Wacky," 250
Sumimoto, Yo Ikeda, 184, 185
Sunada, Raymond, 131, 136 285, 286
Surf Riders, 159
Suski, Clara, 36, 287
Suski, Louise, 36, 200, 202, 287
Suzuki, Denmei, 64
Suzuki, Frank, 175, 176, 177, 186, 206, 284, 287
Suzuki, Goro, a.k.a. Jack Soo, 254-256
Suzuki, Henry, 11, 284, 285
Suzuki, M., 21, 286
Suzuki, Pasa, 22, 286
Suzuki, Pat, 257-265
Suzuki, Paul, 145, 285
Suzuki, Toshio, 20, 22, 284
T & D Theater, Oakland, Calif., 24
Tachibana, Fumiye, see Kawabata, Fumiko

Tada, Ben, 137, 286, 287
Tai, Tamiko, 84
Taiheiyo Band, Los Angeles, 104, 107
Tajima, Sadie Towata, 120, 182, 183, 184, 255, 285
Tajima, Tsuneo, 30, 285
Tajiri, Marion Okagaki, 218
Tajitsu, Mrs., Seattle Japanese School, 10
Takagi, Ayako, 154
Takahashi, George, 99
Takahashi, Hats, 9, 285
Takahashi, Helen and Dorothy, 31, 109
Takahashi, Masako, 18, 284
Takaki, Margaret, 286
Takamoto, George, 241, 243, 287
Takamura, Harry, 153, 284
Takao, Susumu, a.k.a. Leland Young, 221-223, 286
Takasu, Mariko, 30, 285
Takasuka, Fochy, 180
Takayama, Florence, 39
Takayoshi, Kimi, 6, 285
Takayoshi, Mary, 6, 39
Takayoshi, Taiji, 6
Takayoshi, Tomeu, 6, 8
Takayoshi, Yurino, 6, 285
Takeda, Bean, 66
Takeda, Katsuhiko, 208
Takehara, Hisako, 155
Takei, George, 263
Taketa, Alice, 154, 155
Takeuchi, Kono, "Kono-san," 16
Takiguchi, Jeff, 247
Takii, Dorothy, 129, 287
Takimoto, Michi, 246
Tamaki, Ben, 145, 146, 285
Tamanaha, Larry, 206, 284
Tamaru, Tug, II, 131, 132, 133, 229, 285
Tana, Akira, 19
Tana, Taisho, 19
Tanaka, Alfred, 159, 284
Tanaka, Chester, 237
Tanaka, Henry "Pete," II, 27, 29, 174, 286

Tanaka, Kazuo, 86
Tanaka, Kiyo Nishi, 165, 285
Tanaka, Mary, 223
Tanaka, Mickey, 174, 287
Tanforan "Assembly" Center, 180-183
Tanforan Tooters, 180-183
Tani, Hisashi, 180, 287
Tani, Nobuye, 20, 286
Tani, Tadashi, 20
Tani, Yasuko, 14, 24, 25
Taniguchi, Henry, 285
Tashima, Frank, 129, 149, 284
Tatum, Art, 256
Tawa, Chiye, 34, 37, 38, 101, 287
Tawara, Kazue, 39
Tea House of the August Moon, 260
Teal Joy, see Itashiki, Elsie
Teikoku Band, 15
tekisei ongaku (music of enemy origin), 50-52, 59
Teranishi, Roy, 143, 287
Teraoka, Joy Takéshita, 153, 157, 158, 162, 248, 284
Terazawa, Isaye, 163
Thomas, Joe, 245
Thornhill, Claude, 125, 126
Todd, John, 249
Togawa, Paul, 238, 241
Tokuda, Marilyn, 248
Tokyo Boogie-Woogie, 44
Tokyo Seisen Ongaku Gakko (Seisen Music School), 111
Tominaga, Osamu, 74
Tomita, Amy, 32
Tomita, Kiyoshi, 7, 82, 285
Tomita, Masao, 11, 13, 284, 285
Tomita, Virginia Kashino, 81, 184
Tomita, Yoshio, 11, 13, 142, 223-225, **284,** 285
Tonai, Rosalyn, VI, VIII
Toono, Masaki, 18, 284
Topaz Detention Center, 182-188, 280
Topaz Tooters, 183, 227
Torigoe, Kenji, 137, 287
Tormé, Mel, 249
Tough, Dave, 269

Townsend, Chitosé, 32
Toy and Wing, 109
Toyama, James, 153, 284
Tsuboi, Suma, 174
Tsuboi, Tomiko, 286
Tsubota, Minoru, 9
Tsuchida, H., 180
Tsuchiyama, Grace, 286
Tsuchiyama, Joe, 286
Tsuchiya, George, 261
Tsuda, Mas, 230, 232, 285
Tsuda, Matataro, 48
Tsuda, Taihei, 18, 20, 284
Tsuji, Tom, 39, 99, 180, 181, 183, 287
Tsujino, Ryoichi, 65
Tsukahara, Yosh, 144, 285
Tsuruta, Fujio, 63, 86
Tsuyuki, Mari, 154
Tucker, Ben, 240
Tucker, Orrin, 126
Tucker, Sophie, 17
Tule Lake Detention Camp, 174-179
Uchida, Koichi, 53, 78
Uchida, Yosh, 246
Uchiyama, Goro, 86
Ujiiye, Isamu, 155
Umeki, Nancy, 256
Umemoto, David, 278, 285
University of Washington, University Club, 9
Uno, Roy, II, 200, 203, 229, 230
Uramachi no Kokyogaku, Kawabata film, 40, 64, 65
Utsumi, Etsuji, 23, 24, 286
Utsumi, Mary Ann, 23
Uyemura, Lillian, 164, 285
Uyeno, David, 278, 285
Vallee, Rudy, 72
Vaughan, Sarah, X, 195
Vella, Tony, 278, 285
Ventura, Charlie, 231
Voorhees, John, 260
Wada, Bob, 132
Wada, Henry, 287
Wada, Jack, 131, 132, 285
Wada, Maye, 155

Wada, Richard, 257
Waka Fufu Shiken Bekkyo, Kawabata film, 65
Wakai, Charley, 148
Wakatsuki, Bill, 163, 164, 165, 166, 285
Wakatsuki, Lillian, 285
Waki, Terry, 287
Walker, Johnny, 9
Wallace, Wayne, 281
Walnut Grove, Calif., 30
Washington Wailers, a.k.a. New Deal Society Orchestra, 274
Washioka, Masao, 20
Watanabe, Eiko, 158, 284, 286
Watanabe, Mary, 152, 286
Watanabe, Ryo, 86
Watanabe, Sadao, 207
Watanuki, Frank, 47
Watsonville YBA Orchestra, 137
Weatherford, Teddy, 87
Webster, Ben, 71, 245, 288
White River Valley Buddhist Church, 9
White River Valley, Wash., 9
White, Florence "Chickie" Ishihara, 12, 245, 285
White, Josh, 248
White, Tazuko Usuki, 52
Whiteman, Paul, 24, 29, 71
Whittington, Dick, 274
Williams, Midge, 46, 104
Willy's Sweet Shop, 17, 21, 54
Wilson, Teddy, 46, 104, 108
Wing, Tony, 109
Witherspoon, Jimmy, 280
Wizard of Oz, Pat Suzuki, 264
Women's Army Corps, WACS, 141
Wong, Dr. Herb, 274, 275
Woods, Phil, 274
Yama, Frank, 287
Yamada, Kelly, 5, 8, 10, 81, 285
Yamada, Ken, X, XI
Yamaguchi, Jim, 155
Yamaguchi, Mitsuya, 30, 31, 285
Yamaguchi, Shiro, 261
Yamaki, Shig, 206

Yamamoto, George, 174, 287
Yamamoto, Jan, 278
Yamamoto, Katsuro, 11, 285
Yamamoto, Tadashi, Todd, II, 144, 147, 199, 229, 285
Yamamoto, Yutaka, 153, 284
Yamanaka, Dave, 6
Yamane, 102
Yamasaki, George "Yami," 269, 286
Yamasaki, George, 278, 285
Yamashita, Sak, 143, 287
Yamato Hall, Los Angeles, 37
Yasaki, Stuart, 285
Yasuda, Harry, 20, 22, 286
Yasukawa, Ted, 20, 21, 22, 286
Yasunaka, Kitch, 155
Year of the Dragon, Pat Suzuki, 263
Yokomizo, Tony, 19, 20, 284
Yonago, Tad, 5
Yonemoto, Jan, 285
Yonemura, Melba, 31
Yonemura, Paul, 278, 285
Yoshida, Clay, VI, 279, 285
Yoshida, Etsuzo, 114
Yoshida, George, II, VI, VII, VIII, IX, XI, 122, 131, 133, 165, 192, 206, 229, 236, 243, 268, 278, 279, 284, 285
Yoshida, Helen, VI
Yoshida, Yutaka, 120, 182, 183, 285
Yoshikawa, Bob, 149, 284
Yoshimoto, Junko, 165, 284, 285
Yoshimura, Mackay, 149, 150, 284
Yoshino, John, 19, 99
Yoshino, June, 152, 284, 286
Yoshino, Ruby, 39
Yoshioka, Giichi, 120
Yoshitomi, Roy, 11, 13, 284, 285
Yoshizaki, Harry, 32
Yoshizawa, Kathy, 47
Young, Leland, see Takao, Susumu
Young, Lester, 224
Yuasa, Hachiro, 23, 24, 286
Yui, Soichi, 114

SPONSORS

The National Japanese American Historical Society is grateful to the following sponsors for making the publication and exhibition *Reminiscing in Swingtime, Japanese Americans in American Popular Music: 1925-1960* possible.

Anonymous
R. Abe
Christine Iwanaga Aihara
Jun & Bessie Akagi
Jimmie Akiya
Wallace S. Amioka
Janet Y. Araki
Mr. & Mrs. Hiroshi Arisumi
Roy Y. & Fumi Ashizawa
E. Taylor & Zabrina Atkins
Anthony & Martha Brown
Sidney Devere Brown
Victor & Adrea Carter
Ben & Kiyo Chikaraishi
Ann Cook
S. Daniel Date
Gish & Takako Endo
Herbert Y. Endo
Jerry Enomoto
Frank K. Eto
Marjorie Imaizumi Fletcher
Mary K. Fong
Yukiye Fong
Moss & Ann Fujii
Sam & Teri Fujikawa
Haruo & Misa Fujisawa
Sam Fujita
Budd Fukei
Minoru Fukuda
Toshiko & Richard M. Fukuda
Harry & Teruko Fukuhara
Harry H. & Teruko Fukutome
Andrew Z. Fukutome
Steve & Naomi Furogawa
Charles Furuyama
Mr. & Mrs. Al Geron
Arthur Gorai
Dr. John J. & Mitzi Hada
Carolyn Hammerberg

George Hara
Leslie Hata, D.D.S.
Arthur Hayashi—Mikados of Swing
Haruo & Rose Hayashi
Carole Hayashino & Kyle Tatsumoto
Yaye Herman
Nobu & Yoshi Hibino
George & Janice Higashi
George Hinoki
PJ & Roy Hirabayashi
John & Ruby Hiramoto
Jordan F. Hiratzka
David T. & Yo Hironaka
Takashi & Lilly Hirota
Noboru & Pat Honda
Iris Ogawa Horner
Stephen K & Katsuko T. Ichiki
George J. Ichiyasu
David Iino
William T. Iino
Ernest & Chizu Iiyama
Maggie Ikeda
Mamoru & Yasuko Inouye
Mr. & Mrs. Ari Inouye
Sachi Y. Ishida
Edward K. Ishii
Tom T. Ishii
Tom & Mami Ito
Mr. & Mrs. Michio M. Iwahashi
Helen Chizu Iwanaga
Shig & Kazuko Iwasaki
Daniel Iwasaki
Nami Iwataki
Tatsumi Iwate
Jon Jang, Joyce Nakamura & Mika
Japanese Community & Cultural
    Center of Northern California
J-Town Jazz Ensemble
Jim & Nobu Kajiwara

Elisa Kamimoto & John Hayashi
Robert K. Kanagawa
Yutaka Kanemoto
Mary & Babe Karasawa
Hiroshi Kashiwagi
Tom T. Kataoka
Jiro & Kiyo Kato
Tom & Sudi Kawaguchi
Edward E. Kawahara
George Kawakami
Karen Nunotani Kern
Shigeya Kihara
In Memory of Koko Kinoshita
Hachiro & Kyoko Kita
Harry H. Kitano
Tamio Kitano
Dean N. Koba
Mrs. T. Kobayashi
Michi Kobi
Eugene Kodani
Joseph Koga
Hiroshi Kohagura
Jimmy & Mariko Koide
Kazumi & Florence M. Kondo
Dr. Gary Kono
E.H. Kudo
Jack Kusaba
Linda N. Kuwatani
Nobuo Kuwatani
Yutaka Kuwatani
Nori Lafferty
Kazu Maruoka
Joe & Takako Masuda
William H. & Rainbow Matsumoto
Joe Matsuo
Bryan & May Mayeda
Claude A. Mimaki
Mrs. Toshi Minamoto
Dale Minkoff & Greg Murai

Masako Kusayanagi Miura M.D.
Earl M. & Sue T. Miyagi
Ray & Suzie Miyamoto
Jack Mizuhara
Kit Y. Mizukami
Shoichi Morita
Patricia E. Mullan
Harold T. Murai
Nobu Murai
Tom T. Murakami
Kenji Murase
Art & Ann Muto
Betty F. Nakahara
Jiei Nakama
Noboru & Masaye Nakamura
Yoshimi K. Nakamura
Jack H. Nakashima
Steve Namba
Joe & Theresa Narasaki
Teruo Nishijima
Gayle Nishikawa
Henry H. Nishizu
George Nobori
George Nobori, Jr.
Hank Nogawa
Eiko Watanabe Nomura
Andy & Dorothy Nozaka
Wallace & Katherine Nunotani
Mary Hironaka Obayashi
Craney Ogata
George Ogata
Tami T. Ogata
Willie A. Ogino
Alexander J. & Jean A. Oka
Sue Okabe
Kazumi Okamoto
Yuji & Eimi Okano
Alice Okazaki
Michael Omi
Berdi Oshidari
H. Oshima
Frank M. Otsuka
Misao Otsuki
Kai, KG & Neal Ouye
M.T. Oyama
Paul & Mariam Oyama
Augustine Perez, Jr.
Mimi Sasaki Prather

Katherine Morooka Reyes
Barry & Yuriko Saiki
Margaret Saito
Lawson I. Sakai
Yozo & Yukiko Sakai
Cherry I. Sakakida
Col (RET) Thomas T. & Sadie Sakamoto
Mae Sakasegawa
Karen D. Sakuma, D.D.S.
Ko S. Sameshima
Dr. Yasuo & Lili Sasaki
Herbert H. Sasaki
Hiroaki Sasamoto
Helen & Hiro Sato
Yoshimi & Grace Shibata
Matao Matt Shigio
Stan Shikuma & Tracy Lai
Harry & Dorothy Shirachi
Tak & Maye Shirasawa
Ted K. Soyeshima
John Stephan
Henry I. Sugiyama, M.D.
Mabel Sugiyama—Tule Lake Downbeats
Ed Suguro
Clarence T. Taba
Henri & Tomoye Takahashi Charitable Foundation
Eugene, Tomine & Russell Takei
Roy & Mary Takai
Teri Takamoto
Fred M. Takashiba
George & Jo Takata
Tetsuo & May Takayanagi
Russell Takei
Mr. & Mrs. Taketsugu Takei
Hiroshi & Emiko Takusagawa
Terri Takusagawa
Minoru & Iyo Tamaki
Akira Tana
Isao Tanaka
Cecil Tange
Akira & Betty Taniguchi
Takeko & Seichi Tanisawa
Henry M. Tao
Mikiye Tashima
Joy K.T. Teraoka

Lorraine T. Tokimoto
Toshio & Mae Tokiwa
Eugene Tomine
Yoshio Tomita
Rosalyn Tonai, Grant Din & Kiyoshi
Yo & Ben Tonooka
Toyoko Toppata
Min Tsubota
Mas & Ann Tsuda
Ted Tsukiyama
Its & Marian Uenaka
Fumiko Ukai
Marvin T. & Miyo M. Uratsu
Takeo Babe Utsumi
Catherine Uyeda
Clifford I. & Betty T. Uyeda
Roy T. Uyehata
Theodore T. Uyemoto, D.D.S.
Kenji Ken Uyesugi
Richard Wada & Rita Yee
Takeko Wakiji
Sonoko Walter
Tom & Tazuko White
Dick & Jan Yamagami
Aiko M. Yamamoto
Kiyo Kay Yamamoto
George & Anne Yamasaki
Mrs. Tosuke Yamasaki
Alvin Isao Yamashiro
Karie H. Yamashita
Skip & Terry Yamashita
Sumika Yamashita
Mot & Mitsie Yatabe
Feb & Amy Yokoi
George Yokoyama
Mr. & Mrs. Mas Yonemura
Paul A. Yonemura
Cole K. Yoshida
Masako Yoshida
Sho Ruby Yoshida
Kiyoshi & Midori Yoshii
Noby & Tami Yoshimura
Fred Yoshino

* * *

National Japanese American Historical Society